Jean Baptiste de Saint Jure

The Spiritual Man

The Spiritual Life reduced to its first Principles

Jean Baptiste de Saint Jure

The Spiritual Man
The Spiritual Life reduced to its first Principles

ISBN/EAN: 9783337340612

Printed in Europe, USA, Canada, Australia, Japan

Cover: Foto ©Lupo / pixelio.de

More available books at **www.hansebooks.com**

THE SPIRITUAL MAN;

OR,

THE SPIRITUAL LIFE

REDUCED TO ITS FIRST PRINCIPLES.

TRANSLATED FROM THE FRENCH OF

REV. J. B. SAINT-JURE, S. J.,

AUTHOR OF "KNOWLEDGE AND LOVE OF JESUS CHRIST," ETC.

BY

A MEMBER OF THE ORDER OF MERCY,

AUTHORESS OF "THE LIFE OF MOTHER M'CAULEY," "LIFE OF ST. ALPHONSUS LIGUORI," "HAPPY HOURS OF CHILDHOOD," "ANGEL-DREAMS," "BY THE SEA SIDE," "GLIMPSES OF PLEASANT HOMES," "LIFE OF VEN. C. M. HOFBAUER," ETC., ETC.

"My heart hath uttered a good word: I dedicate my works to the king, Christ Jesus."
—*Ps.* xliv, 1.

NEW YORK:
P. O'SHEA, PUBLISHER, 37 BARCLAY STREET.

1878.

APPROBATION

OF

MONSEIGNEUR PERCHÉ.

As the writings of Reverend J. B. Saint-Jure, S. J., rank high among the best spiritual works, we joyfully authorize the publication, in English, of his book entitled, *L'Homme Spirituel*. The translation, by a religious of our diocese, is not only faultless, but elegant; and we rejoice in the hope that this excellent work, which we cordially recommend both to clergy and laity, will be useful to a vast number of souls.

Given at New Orleans, on the Feast of St. Gregory the Great, March 12th, 1878.

✠ NAPOLEON JOSEPH,

ARCHBISHOP OF NEW ORLEANS.

TRANSLATOR'S PREFACE.

THE following translation of *L'Homme Spirituel* was made some years ago, and collated with the original, at the time, by the Very Rev. Ferdinand Coosemans, S. J.

To place so useful a work within the reach of a greater number, I have reduced its size about one-fourth, by omitting the Latin text of quotations and Scripture references, avoiding the frequent repetitions common with the writers of Father Saint-Jure's time, and, in general, adopting a concise style in rendering into English the quaint, verbose French of the original, written in the earlier half of the seventeenth century.

Should any of my readers wish to verify quotations, etc., this may be done by procuring the French work in two volumes, which is by no means rare. The edition published by *Perisse Frères* (Paris, 1851) is, perhaps, the best.

ST. ALPHONSUS' CONVENT OF MERCY,
Feast of the Assumption of Our Lady of Mercy, 1877.
New Orleans, Louisiana.

CONTENTS.

	PAGE.
PREFACE.	iii
APPROBATION.	v

VOLUME I.

CHAPTER I.

WHAT IS MAN? - - - - - - - - - - 1
   Section 1. Conclusion. - - - - - - - 6

CHAPTER II.

WHAT IS A CHRISTIAN? - - - - - - - 11
   Section 1. The Christian is a new creature. - - - 14
   Section 2. The Christian is holy in his dignity, and he ought to be holy in reality. - - - - - 19
   Section 3. In what consists a Christian manner of life. - 24
   Section 4. Same subject. - - - - - - - 29
   Section 5. The example of our Lord Jesus Christ. - - 33
   Section 6. Our imitation. - - - - - - - 37
   Section 7. Of the indifference and obedience with which we ought to receive the movements of our Lord. - 41
   Section 8. Reasons to induce us to act as Christians, and to perform all our works in the spirit of Jesus Christ. - - - - - - - - 44
   Section 9. Practice. - - - - - - - - 50

CHAPTER III.

WHAT IS A SPIRITUAL MAN? - - - - - - 54
   Section 1. Continuation. - - - - - - - 57
   Section 2. What are the actions of a spiritual man? - - 59

Section 3. The truly spiritual man distinguished from the man who is spiritual only in appearance. - - 63
Section 4. The spiritual man leads a life above the senses. - 68
Section 5. Other proofs of the same truth. - - - - 72
Section 6. Of the discernment of spirits. - - - - 77
Section 7. Particular marks to discern spirits. - - - 81
Section 8. Danger of extraordinary ways.—Means of distinguishing the good from the bad. - - 87
Section 9. This truth confirmed by examples. - - - 93
Section 10. Marks to distinguish visions and revelations. - 97
Section 11. Other marks. - - - - - - - 102
Section 12. Four important admonitions concerning visions and revelations. - - - - - - 106
Section 13. Discernment between the movements of nature and grace. - - - - - - - 109
Section 14. More particular discernment. - - - - 113
Section 15. Conclusion. - - - - - - - 119

CHAPTER IV.

OF THE GIFTS OF THE HOLY GHOST IN GENERAL. - - - 126
Section 1. The effects of these gifts. - - - - 130
Section 2. Means of acquiring these gifts. - - - - 135
Section 3. Of the gift of fear. - - - - - - 137
Section 4. Of the gift of fortitude. - - - - - 144
Section 5. Of the gift of piety. - - - - - - 153
Section 6. Of the gift of counsel. - - - - - 156
Section 7. Of the gift of knowledge. - - - - 160
Section 8. Of the gift of understanding. - - - - 165
Section 9. Of the gift of wisdom. - - - - - 170

VOLUME II.

CHAPTER I.

FIRST GENERAL PRINCIPLE OF THE SPIRITUAL LIFE. - - - 181

CHAPTER II.

SECOND GENERAL PRINCIPLE OF THE SPIRITUAL LIFE. - - 185

CHAPTER III.

THIRD GENERAL PRINCIPLE OF THE SPIRITUAL LIFE.—THE
END OF MAN. - - - - - - - - - 195
Section 1. Signification of the word *end*. - - - - 197
Section 2. God being our end must necessarily be our perfection and beatitude. - - - - - 198
Section 3. Another reason for this truth. - - - - 202
Section 4. Conclusion of this subject. - - - - - 203
Section 5. Means to arrive at this end. - - - - 204
Section 6. Signification of the word *means*. - - -. - 206
Section 7. All creatures are to us means of salvation. - 207
Section 8. Discernment is essential in the choice of means. 209
Section 9. Good use is necessary to means. - - - - 211
Section 10. Effects of the acquisition of this end.—First effect:
The perfection of the soul. - - - - 213
Section 11. Second effect: Light of the understanding. - 216
Section 12. Third effect: Peace of the will. - - - 219
Section 13. Fourth effect: A just contempt of things here below. - - - - - - - - 221
Section 14. Fifth effect: A well regulated exterior.—Remarkable example of this truth. - - - - 224

CHAPTER IV.

FOURTH GENERAL PRINCIPLE.—UNION WITH JESUS CHRIST. - 227
Section 1. Means to acquire union with our Lord. - - 229
Section 2. In what consists this union, and the manner in which it ought to operate. - - - - - 235
Section 3. Conclusion of this subject. - - - - 239

CHAPTER V.

FIFTH GENERAL PRINCIPLE OF THE SPIRITUAL LIFE.—PURITY
OF INTENTION. - - - - - - - - 244

CHAPTER VI.

SIXTH GENERAL PRINCIPLE.—EXERCISE OF FAITH IN ALL
THINGS. - - - - - - - - - 249
Section 1. Qualities of faith. - - - - - - 254
Section 2. Why God obliges us to believe. - - - 258

		PAGE.
Section 3.	Another prerogative of faith.	261
Section 4.	Practice of faith.	267
Section 5.	Practice of faith more in detail.	270
Section 6.	Practice of faith still more in detail.	273
Section 7.	Conclusion of all that has been previously said in this chapter.	277

CHAPTER VII.

SEVENTH GENERAL PRINCIPLE.—CONTINUAL PRAYER. - 280

Section 1.	Necessity of prayer.	283
Section 2.	Conclusion to be drawn from its necessity.	286
Section 3.	Force of prayer.	291
Section 4.	Conditions necessary to render prayer efficacious.	293
Section 5.	Another condition.	295
Section 6.	Affection and fervor in prayer.	300

CHAPTER VIII.

EIGHTH GENERAL PRINCIPLE OF THE SPIRITUAL LIFE—PEACE OF THE SOUL. - 308

Section 1.	In what we ought to practise peace.—In our particular actions with our neighbor.—In our desires, even those which are good.—In our losses.—In our imperfections and sins.—Of scruples.—Conclusion.	314
Section 2.	Means for preserving peace of soul.	327
Section 3.	Of the ways of God with men.	332
Section 4.	The ways of God with souls are hidden.	335
Section 5.	Why the ways of God are so hidden.	340
Section 6.	The ways of God often seem contrary to their ends.	342
Section 7.	The ways of God are often contrary to our desires.	348
Section 8.	Why the ways of God are contrary to our wishes.	350
Section 9.	Conclusion.	351
Section 10.	Practice of peace.	358

THE SPIRITUAL LIFE

REDUCED TO ITS

FIRST PRINCIPLES.

Vol. I.

THE SPIRITUAL LIFE

REDUCED TO ITS

FIRST PRINCIPLES.

CHAPTER I.

WHAT IS MAN?

DESIGNING, as I do, to treat fully of the spiritual man, it will be necessary, in order to give full scope to so important and rich a subject, first, to consider man as man; second, as a Christian; and, third, as a spiritual man. The third includes the second, inasmuch as a spiritual man is only an excellent Christian; and the second includes the first, for a Christian is a perfect man, and something more. Therefore, before speaking of the nature and qualities of a spiritual man, we shall consider him as a man and as a Christian.

"Man is a great work," cries out Solomon, with admiration. The celebrated inscription engraven over the temple at Delphi, "KNOW THYSELF," ought not to be understood solely of the knowledge we should have of our inherent baseness and misery, to inspire us with sentiments of modesty and humility; but also the knowledge of our greatness and excellence, to inspire us with noble and generous sentiments, that we may never degrade ourselves.

St. Ambrose says: "It is a great gift, and a source of many advantages to a man, to know what he is;" and, indeed, as St. Augustine remarks, if the creation of each animal is capable of procuring God ineffable praises from pious minds, with how much greater reason should man, the noblest of all animals, inspire similar sentiments!

"Man is great," says Solomon; and his father had said before him: "What is man that Thou art mindful of him? With glory and honor hast Thou crowned him." "Man," says St. Ambrose, "is a magnificent work, a masterpiece." And elsewhere the same saint exclaims: "O man, excellent creature of God! how great are the graces He confers on thee!"

1. God created man on the sixth day, after He had produced all other creatures. He did not make him on the first day, with light; nor on the second, with the heavens; nor on the third, when He separated the dry land from the waters; nor on the fourth, with the sun and moon; nor on the fifth, with the fishes and birds; but on the sixth and last day, after the creation of all other living creatures, to teach him that, though he resembled them in having a body, yet he was raised far above all corporal creatures by his soul and by grace, to the end that the knowledge of his animal propensities might quench the fires of vanity which the remembrance of his glorious qualities might excite, and that he might thus preserve the necessary moderation and reserve.

Yet more: He would teach him that as, in the production of things, He had commenced by the most imperfect, and advanced gradually to the most perfect, making, first, plants, then fishes, then birds, then terrestrial animals, and, finally, man,—so man ought, in the matter of his perfection, to make daily new and greater progress, because God finished by him all His works, and collected together in him, as in a little world, all that He had spread abroad in the great world He had previously created for His own glory.

2. God did not use the same language when about to create man, as He had used with regard to His other works; He did not say : "*Let man be made,*" but, "*Let us make man.*" On which text St. John Chrysostom exclaims : "What novelty, what wonder, is this ! Who is he for whose production God takes counsel, the Sovereign Wisdom enters into deliberation ? But be not astonished," he continues, "whoever thou art, because man is the masterpiece of His works, the paragon and the miracle of all visible things, the most exquisite portrait of the increated world, namely, the holy and august Trinity ; and is, in short, the bond of creation, because he unites in himself all degrees of existence, spiritual and corporal. Plato elegantly calls him the *Horizon of the Universe*, because we find united in his person the superior hemisphere, namely, the angels ; and the inferior, that is to say, animal and material things ; inasmuch as he evidently resembles the former in his soul, and the latter in his body."

Certainly it was not without reason that God deliberated on the creation of man, foreseeing that, after He should have drawn him out of nothing, and enriched him with immense gifts of nature and grace, this glorious creature would be so ungrateful as to take arms against his Creator, to make war on Him by a thousand outrages, and that, moreover, reparation for these sins of His creature would cost Him very dear. Yet He showed His excessive love when, notwithstanding all these considerations, which might reasonably have deterred Him, and withal being happy in Himself, He created man.

3. When He created man, He put His own hands to the work, from which circumstance it derived no small portion of its dignity ; whence St. Ambrose, reflecting on this mystery, exclaims : "Thy hands have not formed the beasts ; Thou didst

but open Thy mouth, and they were made. The waters generated fishes and birds, and the earth sent forth beasts from its bosom; but Thy hands have made me, and given me the form and figure which I possess."

And for this purpose He used not merely one hand, but two: "Thy *hands* have made me and fashioned me," says David; and before him Job had said: "I am the work of Thy hands." With one hand, as St. Ambrose remarks, He made the solid heavens, and rendered them incorruptible. What was sufficient to give being to the great universe was not enough to give being to man. *One* of God's hands had established the heavens, and it takes both His hands to form and fashion man. The heavens are not made in His image, as man is. I say more: even the angels have been created to execute His orders, while man is His portrait. Though the angels, being pure spirits, are, by consequence, images of God, yet the Scripture accords this privilege only to man. And we possess, in the adorable Person of our Lord, and in ourselves, by alliance with Him, something which elevates us far above them, as the same holy doctor observes.

To this I add, that the *hands* of God, the *three divine fingers* with which, as Isaias says, He holds the earth poised, signify the three principal attributes which He employs in the production of creatures, namely, goodness, wisdom, and power: goodness in communicating to them His being, and sharing with them His treasures; power and wisdom in executing His good-will toward them; and as these were to appear with more magnificence in the constitution of man than in any other creature, He used His two hands in the creation of man: "Thy *hands* have formed me."

4. It is for love of man, and for his benefit, that God created this great universe. It is clear that it could not be for Himself, for He had lived a whole eternity without having need of anything outside Himself; nor for the angels, who, being

pure spirits, are independent of corporeal things, and derive from God alone all their felicity; nor for the things themselves, which do not even realize that they belong to the world. "Thou hast subjected all things under his feet," says David. It is for him Thou hast created this visible world, and dost preserve it, and people it with other creatures. For his health, for his happiness, and to be otherwise useful to him, the heavens have received perpetual motion, and the sun and moon their light, the stars shed their influence on earth, the winds blow, the rains fall, the rivers flow, the earth produces plants, animals exist, and all nature labors. Man is the end of all these operations.

5. God has given His angels to guide and assist man; and this, without doubt, is a very great grace, and a singular favor. These excellent creatures, these pure spirits, these admirable intelligences, these noble princes of the celestial court, are a perpetual escort for man, inseparably attached to him day and night, within and without, on land and on sea, sleeping and waking, in youth, in manhood, in old age: "He hath given His angels charge over thee," says David, "that they may keep thee in all thy ways; in their hands shall they bear thee up, lest, perhaps, thou dash thy foot against a stone."

Finally, He has given man reason, and made him capable of knowing things; He has also given him free will. By reason man has become God's image, which is the highest point of his excellence. Reason, as St. Gregory of Nyssa remarks, is a precious treasure, a sacred and divine possession. St. Gregory Nazianzen teaches that there are three species of spiritual light. The first is God, who is light inaccessible, and can neither be conceived nor explained, and who communicates Himself a little outside, when He illumines intelligent natures. The second is the angelic nature, which is a participation of the first light and its first ray. The third is the brightness of reason with which the soul of man is endowed, and which is called *light*, particularly in those who approach God most nearly by personal sanctity; hence the Hebrews, according to the remark of Eusebius, called man by a name which, in their language, signifies fire, whence this line of the Latin poet:

"Igneus est ollis vigor, et cœlestis origo." *

As regards the image of God engraven on the soul of man with such glorious majesty, David says: "Lord, the rays of Thy countenance enlighten us, and carry to us Thy divine lineaments." Hence St. Ambrose exclaims: "See, O man' what thou art. O human soul! enter into the knowledge of thyself, and learn that thou are not made of dust like thy body, but of the breath of God, which created thee a living spirit. How rich and magnificent must thy soul be which is formed by the breath of God! Learn hence, O man! wherein thy nobility consists. If the clay of which thou art framed renders thee vile, the image of the Divinity impressed on thy soul makes thee truly great. What can be more rich and precious than the living image of God?" St. Theresa well says that, to understand the singular beauty of a human soul, we need only consider that it is the image of God, because the portrait of sovereign and infinite beauty must necessarily be extremely beautiful.

§ 1.—*Conclusion of the subject.*

1. Since then, O man! thou art endowed with so many and such rare prerogatives, remember thy dignity, and bear always in thy heart and in thy deportment the celebrated inscription

---

* The above line of Virgil (Æneid, lib. vi, v. 730), Anthon translates, or rather paraphrases, as follows: "In these seeds (thus implanted within us) there is fiery energy and a heavenly origin, so far forth as our corrupt corporeal natures do not retard them, and our earth-born limbs and perishable members dull not (their keen edge)."— Anthon's *Virgil*, p. 656.

of the Delphic temple, which will assuredly open to thee the gate of wisdom : "KNOW THYSELF."

Know that thou art the most perfect of God's works, the masterpiece of His creation. The most beautiful painting of Apelles, the most finished statue from the chisel of Phidias, have undeniably procured these incomparable artists imperishable renown. As, then, thou art the most accomplished work of God, in which His wisdom and other perfections shine forth with most lustre, thou art the more strictly obliged to honor and glorify Him unceasingly. Know that God has created for thee the whole visible world; that He has commanded all other creatures to serve thee, and His angels to assist and defend thee; whence thou shouldst deduce this consequence: that thou art bound to serve, love, and obey Him diligently. Certainly, if all creatures are, by His orders, employed in thy service, and still more, if God Himself, as the first cause, is the source whence blessings flow to thee by these channels, thou oughtest to be employed incessantly in His service, nor is there any sacrifice which thou canst justly refuse Him.

Since God has given thee reason, thou must not live like an irrational animal. There are two distinctions between man and beasts: the first is reason, which ought to regulate all the actions of man, while passion governs all the actions of beasts. Man, if he be not guided by reason, acts wrong, because he acts against his rational nature, and destroys the order marked out for him by his Creator, in which consists, according to the Angelic Doctor, the sin of a free creature.

2. Man degenerates when he acts in an irrational manner; whence the Scriptures designate sinners by the names of divers animals, according to the passions and vices to which they abandon themselves. The Royal Prophet says: "Man, when he was in honor, did not understand; he is compared to senseless beasts, and is become like to them." Truly, as

reason distinguishes the being of man, and passion that of the beast, a man possesses his glorious prerogative only inasmuch as he suffers himself to be guided by it; and he becomes a beast, inasmuch as he permits himself to be carried away by passion, the guide of irrational creatures.

3. He is even worse than a beast, as Aristotle remarks, since he subjects his noble and glorious reason to that infamous slave, concupiscence, and this injustice subjects him to punishment here and hereafter; for, as the best and most useful of all animals is a reasonable man, so the worst and most pernicious of all animals is a passionate man,—a man who allows his passions to enslave him. The second distinction between rational and irrational beings is that God has made the former capable of knowing and loving eternal and future goods, while the latter care only for such as are present and temporal: whence may be gathered the greatness and excellence of man, and the baseness of all inferior creatures. "It is the property of man," says Aristotle, "to elevate the eyes of his soul to things immortal, for which reason he alone of all animals stands erect, and naturally turns his eyes to heaven." These illustrious qualities make us surpass in dignity all other animals; let us, then, show that we appreciate our dignity, by living like true men. Let reason, not passion or humor, be the guide of our actions in all circumstances. Diogenes, taking a lighted lantern, sought a man in the midst of men, because he knew that the greater number have only the appearance of men, and are little better than beasts, disguised under a human appearance. The Holy Ghost says, by Solomon: "The number of fools is infinite;" that is, of vicious men, whose actions are the result of passion, not of reason.

Verily, if we observe closely the conduct of the majority of human beings, we shall find that, in their aversions and friendships, their praises and censures, their fears and desires, they are often guided rather by passion than by reason. Among many beautiful things which the wisest of the pagan philosophers said for our instruction, is the following : "Eat like a man, drink like a man, act in all things like a man, not like a beast, so that your eating, drinking, love, hatred, thoughts, and all your actions, may be done with the light and moderation of reason, not with the blindness and impetuosity of passion." Socrates used to affirm that he loved nothing on earth more dearly than his reason. "I take more care of my reason," said he, "than of anything else I possess, having an extreme desire to be very rational in all my thoughts, words and works." These words may serve us as an example. But to take a far higher model, let us represent God residing continually within us, as the first cause and essential reason, who bestows on us, as a ray of His infinite light, the reason which we possess, and which, by His inspiration, and on His model, excites us to govern our eyes, our tongue, our hands, our feet, our whole interior and exterior, by the light of this torch. Let us become reasonable, after the example of God, since we have the honor to be His images. Let us direct our aspirations to eternal things, and not seek with avidity those which are base and perishable, like the blind animals that always burrow in the mire ; but, alas ! how few really despise these temporal things ! How much reason had the poet to exclaim, in reference to the greater number : "Vile and despicable souls ! empty of heavenly things, who have heart, and eyes and hands, only for what is mortal and corruptible" !

Let us, on the contrary, entertain ourselves with invisible and eternal goods, and be guided in all things by the truths which regard the life to come. Such was the practice of St. Louis Gonzaga, of our Society ; and hence he is often painted with an angel before him, who holds an unequally poised balance, in one scale of which is the world, with its honors, riches and pleasures, and in the other and the heavier, a crown, a flame

of fire, and a branch of palm, twined in a circle ; the crown
to represent paradise, the fire hell, and the palm eternity, under
which are written these words, which he so often repeated :
"Thou shalt become more holy the more thou shalt regulate
thy actions according to the maxims of eternity, and the less
thou shalt notice those of time." Finally, let us take all possible care to preserve in its lustre and beauty the image of
God with which our soul is ornamented. "O image of God !
O man!" cries out St. Bernard, "what care dost thou take to
preserve this imprint of the august Trinity, this mark of glory,
this inestimable treasure ? Thou art the image of God, wherefore never forget the supereminent dignity to which He has
elevated thee, and beware of doing anything to debase
thyself. God has given thee an upright body, that thou
mightest learn, by the rectitude of the inferior part, how
diligently thou shouldst preserve that of the interior, which
is formed in the likeness of God, and that the beauty of this
clay, which composes part of thee, may condemn thy soul,
should it become deformed or crooked : for, what can be
more shameful than a handsome, erect body, which contains
a hideous, curved soul ? It is truly absurd that the body of
man, which is made of dust, has eyes in its highest part, with
which it may freely gaze on the heavens, and the soul, which
is spiritual and divine, abases its eyes to grovelling, sensual
things. The eyes of the soul are will, understanding, thoughts
and affections ; and these, which ought, by the excellence of
its condition, to cover the whole man with the royal purple
of his dignity and origin, lower their gaze on smoke and
ordure ! O my soul ! be confounded for having sullied this
glorious image of God engraven on thee, and changed it into
that of animals ! Be ashamed that, having come from
heaven, thou shouldst permit thyself to revel in the vanities
of earth !

CHAPTER II.

WHAT IS A CHRISTIAN?

HAVING declared amply enough for our present purpose the nature and excellence of man, we shall now pass to something more important and elevated, which is, to give a clear definition of a Christian.

St. Macarius, of Egypt, considering the dignity of Christianity, and dazzled by the rays of its glory, says : "Christianity is no ordinary thing; it is a profound mystery, a great wonder. Christians are the most noble of all men, the flower and ornament of the human race ; and we may apply to them what an ancient poet said of the Romans : 'There is no person on earth who lives with more probity than a true Roman citizen. Such a man is preferable to one Cato, to three hundred Socrates, and to a thousand Alexanders ; yea, to all the orators and philosophers of antiquity.'" But let us consider what a true Christian is :—

1. A Christian derives his name from our Lord Jesus Christ. Our good and amiable Jesus, as St. Gregory remarks, makes us participators in His adorable name. We do not take our name from our riches or our poverty, our learning or our ignorance, our high rank or our mean condition, but, treading all earthly considerations under our feet, we style ourselves Christians. St. Paul writes to the Romans: *Estis et vos vocatis Jesu Christi,* that is to say : "You are called *by* Christ to em-

brace His law, but still more *from* Christ, bearing the very name of Christians, a name derived from His."

Let us be Christians not merely in name, but in effect. Our Lord is called by two names: the first is Christ, the second Jesus, though we commonly place Jesus first. The first, nevertheless, is Christ, which He received in the moment of His incarnation, when His humanity was hypostatically united to His divinity. That of Jesus was added in His circumcision; He is truly *Christ*, that is to say, *Anointed*, because His humanity is anointed with the balm of His divinity, as the fathers express it; and He is truly *Jesus*, that is to say, *Saviour*, because, as the archangel predicted to Joseph, *He shall save the people from their sins*. St. Bernard, speaking of the name of Jesus, says: "My Jesus has not vainly borne this name; it was not for Him, as for His predecessors, an empty title; He was not the shadow of a Saviour, but the reality." In like manner *Christian* ought to be in every case an active name, passing from the signification to the works of Christ.

2. We do not become real Christians by assuming the mere name, nor even by our faith, our Lord having said: "Not every one that saith to me, Lord, Lord, shall enter the kingdom of heaven;" nor yet by exterior works alone, as appears by the parable of the foolish virgins who went before the spouse, lamp in hand, and who, notwithstanding their vigils and their virginity, found the door of the heavenly Bridegroom shut. But we are Christians by the participation of the spirit of Jesus Christ. As that which specially constitutes man is the rational soul which animates his body, so that which constitutes the Christian is the spirit of Jesus, which animates his soul and body with the life of Jesus; so that, as the reasonable soul is absolutely necessary to vivify man, the spirit of Jesus is equally necessary to confer the life of a Christian. *God has sent His only Son into the world, that we may live by Him*, and that He may become in us the principle of the new life which He

wishes us to lead: "*In this we know that we abide in Him, and He in us, because He hath given us of His spirit.*" And St. Paul says in clear and formal terms : "'If any one have not the Spirit of Jesus Christ *he is none of His,*" and therefore he cannot justly style himself a Christian, a follower of Christ. We bear this glorious name legitimately, as St. Gregory remarks, when we are enlivened by the Spirit of Jesus Christ. St. Macarius illustrates this by two beautiful comparisons : "A piece of gold," says he, "is not placed in the coffers of the king if it be not stamped with his image ; in like manner a soul on which Jesus Christ is not engraved has no place in heaven. And as from a single flame we can ignite many lamps, so Christians, animated with one divine spirit, ought to shine as bright lights in the midst of the world, attracting others to Jesus, communicating to them His holy instructions and divine ardors, to enlighten their minds and inflame their wills.

But what is this Spirit of Jesus, which alone can entitle us to be called true Christians? I answer that this Spirit must be considered as twofold : 1. In Himself, and secondly in us. If we consider it in Himself, it is His divinity, because God is a spirit. 2. We may also consider it as the Holy Ghost, the Third Person of the august and adorable Trinity, who proceeds from the Father and the Son. 3. All the operations of the divinity of Jesus toward His humanity, and of His humanity toward His divinity ; the divine and ineffable life of the man-God ; the manner in which He loved and honored God, in which He thought, prayed, acted, walked, ate, and used all His spiritual and corporal faculties, illustrate for us His spirit. This spirit in us is the Holy Ghost, who is called the Spirit of Jesus, because Jesus merited that He should come and dwell in us, and that, living in us continually, He should animate us to imitate His virtues, and give us grace and strength to do so. It is, secondly, our participation with Jesus Christ, and the resemblance we bear Him who is our model,—this is what in reality constitutes the Christian. In this consists the true difference between the Christian and the heathen, whence it would appear that there are but few true Christians in the world, because there are not many really animated with the Spirit of Jesus. This made St. Macarius remark that, among such multitudes called by the name, there are but few real Christians, few truly agreeable to God. Many profess Christianity, and call themselves by the name of Christian; but this is not enough, unless they be also animated by a Christian spirit. St. Gregory of Nyssa elegantly observes that things do not derive their nature from their names, but their names from their nature. Give the name of man to a tree or to a statue, and still you cannot make a man of one or the other: we style men only such as are previously men in reality. Things even that refer directly to man can only usurp his name, as we see in the case of statues and pictures. Hence those who attribute to themselves the name and dignity of Christians ought to exemplify in their lives the signification of that illustrious name, otherwise they would bear it falsely, and resemble centaurs and other monsters, which the poets describe as having the head of a man, and the body of a horse, an ox, a dragon, or some other beast. Now as such monsters, having only something of men, cannot be truly styled men, so Christians who possess only the name or exterior of Christianity cannot be properly called Christians, since the spirit which makes the true Christian is wanting to them. Thus speaks St. Gregory.

§ 1.—*The Christian is a new creature.*

The Spirit of Jesus Christ is the essence of true Christianity; it works certain and admirable changes, and causes these strange revolutions by which the Christian becomes a new creature.

St. Paul, writing to the Corinthians, says: "Christ has abolished the ancient things, and given place to the new; he who is baptized, and receives His Spirit, becomes in Him and by Him a new creature." And to the Galatians: "In Christ Jesus neither circumcision availeth anything, nor uncircumcision, but a new creature in God," that is to say, a Christian.

The same apostle teaches that all who have been baptized have, in the salutary waters of baptism, put off the old man, Adam, and clothed themselves with the new man, Jesus Christ. St. Bernard remarks that these two men are very different: Adam is terrestrial, and Jesus celestial; the first is old, the second is new. Jesus Christ, then, being the new man, those who unite themselves to Him become by this union new creatures in Him.

St. Paul wrote thus to the Ephesians: "When in times past you walked according to the course of this world, by nature children of wrath, God, who is rich in mercy, for His exceeding charity wherewith He loved us, even when we were dead in sins, hath quickened us together in Christ, by whose grace you are saved." The Jews and the Gentiles mutually lived in mortal hatred; circumcision was a wall of separation between them, but Christ, who is our peace, broke down the middle wall of the partition, that He might make the two in *Himself into one new man*, and reconcile both to God in one body by the cross."

Now in what consists the renovation? Not in the natural soul or body, certainly, because the Christian cannot change his countenance, his hands, his feet, his understanding, his other physical or mental faculties, which remain the same whether he is united to Christ or separated from Him; but in the soul, taken morally, and in the actions of his life, "that we may walk in the newness of life, and serve in the newness of spirit," according to the explanation of St. Paul, who wrote to his disciple, Titus: "The grace of the Lord Jesus hath appeared to all men, instructing us that, denying ungodliness and worldly desires, we should live soberly, and justly, and godly in this world, looking for the blessed hope and coming of the glory of the great God and our Saviour." And St. Macarius says, in the same thought: "Our Lord Jesus has come on earth to change our nature, to make a metamorphose of our body, and to renew our soul, cleansing it with His divine spirit from the disorderly passions which are a consequence of the sin of our first father, bestowing on us a new spirit, new senses, a new tongue, that we may be thoroughly renovated, becoming spiritual and holy, new vessels fitted for receiving the wine of His Spirit, which the world cannot give, for new wine must be put in new vessels."

St. Paul, speaking of the old man, describes him as being "corrupted according to the desire of error," and says of the new: "God created him in justice and holiness of truth." He is divinely regenerated to live with innocence and true sanctity. The old man has a body of sin, of which the members are particular vices. "Our old man," writes the same Apostle to the Romans, "is crucified with Christ, that the body of sin may be destroyed, to the end that we may serve sin no longer." This head, filled with ambition and pride, this heart a prey to anger, revenge, and irregular attachments, these eyes curious and unrestrained, this tongue given to slander and blasphemy, these ears open to detraction and ordures, these hands which seized the forbidden fruit, and our other corrupt members, shall be destroyed, and the body of vice changed into a virtuous body. He says to the Corinthians: "Behold the old things have passed away, and all things are made new." What composed the old man is demolished by Christianity, all things are made new in it: new thoughts, new sentiments, new desires, are the portion of the true Christian. For this reason Isaias calls our Lord "Father of the world to come," because He is the Author and Founder of a new world, and in Him and by Him men are actuated by new hopes, new affections, new desires. St. Paul calls baptism the laver of regeneration, in which the Holy Spirit, by the infusion of His graces and the communication of His essence, renews us in Christ Jesus, our Lord.

The ceremonies practised in the administration of baptism in the early Church clearly demonstrate this. The priest demanded of the catechumen, when he arrived at the church, the reason of his coming; who replied that he came to accuse himself of his impiety and ignorance of the true God, and to beg to be admitted to a participation of divine things. The priest signified that his conversion must be entire; that he must not give himself to virtue by halves, as it regarded a God who is absolutely perfect, explaining the life which he must lead as a Christian, and, in conclusion, asking if he were firmly resolved to accomplish the obligations he desired to contract; to which the catechumen having replied affirmatively, the priest laid his hand on his head, and signed him with the sign of the cross. Then the deacons having disrobed him, he stood with his face turned toward the setting sun, and publicly abjured Satan; after which, with eyes and hands raised toward heaven, he thrice promised to observe his baptismal engagements, and having been three times immersed in the sacred font, he was clothed with the white robes of baptism.

All these mysterious symbols represent the truth of which we have spoken. The disrobing of the catechumen signifies that he must despoil himself of the old man. The standing with his face toward the setting sun, and the solemn renunciation of Satan, signify that he rejects all commerce with sin, which once filled his soul with darkness. He breaks entirely with the devil, and destroys all that can impede his progress to God; hence he turns to the east, toward the light, to show that he desires that the light of the Divinity may shed its pure and brilliant beams plentifully on his soul.

The Christian becomes a new creature by despoiling himself of the vices of the old man, and clothing himself with the virtues of the new. To this St. Paul continually exhorts his followers: "Those," says he to the Ephesians, "who enter into the service of our Lord should change their modes of life, *and put off the old man, who is corrupted according to the desire of error, and be renewed in the spirit of their mind, and put on the new man who, according to God, is created in justice and holiness of truth.*" To the Colossians he says that, "stripping themselves of the old man, with his deeds, and putting on the new, who is renewed unto knowledge, according to the image of Him that created him," they must, by loving and serving God, reëngrave the divine image which sin had nearly effaced in their souls.

In this manner we must divest ourselves of the old man, and clothe ourselves with the new man, else we cannot be styled true Christians. To typify the change to be wrought in his disciples, our Lord at His birth operated wonders in heaven and on earth, as ecclesiastical history relates, and as Isaias had foretold, saying: "Behold I create a new heaven and a new earth, and the former things shall not be in remembrance, and they shall not come upon the heart." St. Macarius says that whoever approaches God, and unites himself to our Saviour, must, of necessity, change his life, and completely destroying the old man, must clothe himself with the new man, Christ Jesus. I shall conclude this section with the following remarkable words of St. Augustine: "Whoever desires the baptism of Christ desires a new life: he must exchange the old for the new. For there were already an Old Testament, an old canticle, an old man, but now all these are abolished, and we speak henceforth of a New Testament, a new canticle, and a new man. 'The former things have passed away, says the apostle. What are the old things which have passed, and what the new ones which have come? The first man was earthly, the second is heavenly. The earthly man has departed, and the heavenly man, Christ Jesus, has replaced him. Old hearts are changed into new ones. The sensual life gives place to the spiritual life. Having been children of Adam, and stained with sin like your father, you have now become children of God, and must, therefore, imitate the virtues of His adorable Son, our Lord Jesus Christ."

§ 2.—*The Christian, being holy in his name and dignity, ought to be holy in reality.*

The Christian, being holy in his name and dignity, must also be holy in his works. St. Paul generally addresses all Christians as *saints*. Thus: "Paul, an apostle of Jesus Christ, to all the *saints* that are at Ephesus." "Paul, apostle of Jesus Christ, to the Church of God which is at Corinth, and to all the *saints* who are dispersed through Achaia." Now, why does he call Christians saints? Firstly, because all persons have been in a certain manner sanctified by the incarnation, for, as in that adorable mystery the Word became man, so man became the Word; and in this man-God, and by His means, all men participate in the divine nature; all have become gods, and consequently saints.

Secondly, because Christians have been cleansed from their sins, and sanctified by the waters of baptism. St. Paul writes to the Ephesians: "Christ loved the Church, and delivered Himself up for it, that He might sanctify it, cleansing it by the laver of water in the word of life." As a figure of this, according to the interpretation of the Fathers, Moses relates that in the beginning *the Spirit of God moved upon the face of the waters;* the Holy Ghost who, by His personal prerogative, is the principle and the author of the sanctification of souls, *moves upon the waters*, to give them seminal virtue, power to produce fishes and birds, as the hen communicates to the eggs which she hatches a vital heat which vivifies them, to show us that the same divine Spirit, under the law of grace, would veil Himself in the waters of baptism, to sanctify them, and render them capable of purifying and sanctifying souls.

Thirdly, the Christian, by baptism, is dedicated to the holy and august Trinity, who, in this mystery, imprints on his soul a peculiar and indelible character by these words : "I baptize thee in the name of the Father, and of the Son, and of the Holy Ghost;" he becomes the special property of the blessed Trinity, he is separated from a profane world, and consecrated solemnly to the worship of God. The three divine Persons, by this dedication, dwell in him in a new and perfect manner, and form a most intimate union with him, "that our fellowship may be with the Father, and with Christ Jesus, His Son," as the beloved disciple says, and by this happy society, by these divine bonds, to make him feel the effects of His love, and shower upon him benefits and graces.

Truly, if certain unctions are sufficient to render a place holy, and consecrate it to God, with how much greater reason should the Christian be holy who is interiorly sanctified by grace, and consecrated to God by the Holy Ghost Himself! Certainly the baptismal consecration is, after the hypostatic union, the most noble and divine consecration possible on earth, because it confers grace, it gives sanctity, it makes us children of God, which is the highest honor we can attain in this world or the next.

The Angelic Doctor teaches that the mystery of the Eucharist is an extension of the incarnation ; because, as in it the Divinity is united to a particular human nature, so in the holy communion the Divinity is united to all who approach the holy table. We may say, in like manner, that the sacrament of baptism is a participation in the hypostatic union ; because, as this union has consecrated forever this sacred humanity of our Lord to the Holy Trinity, and made it the first and greatest instrument of His glory, so baptism consecrates us to God, making us His inalienable property, giving Him a new right to employ us as instruments of His glory in whatever manner He pleases.

But Christians must also be holy by their works, for this is that second kind of sanctity which the first supposes. Hence St. Paul, writing to the Corinthians, does not simply say they are saints, but they are *called to be saints*. "The life of those who embrace the faith of Jesus Christ," says St. Cyril, "is a life of virtue. Christianity is a profession of sanctity, innocence, purity, and all good works." Jesus Christ, as St. Paul tells the Ephesians, "has loved the Church, and delivered up Himself to death for her, that He might present her to Himself a glorious Church, without spot or wrinkle, or any such thing; that she should be holy, without blemish." We are the work of God by creation, but we are also His work in a new fashion by redemption. He did not create and redeem us in order that we might lead a life simply natural, but that we should become holy, and exercise ourselves continually in good works. To the Colossians St. Paul writes: "My desire is that you may walk worthy of God in all things pleasing, being fruitful in every good work," carefully striving to please Him in every possible manner, and to regard yourself as His property and possession. St. James, in his canonical epistle, tells the faithful that the proof of their faith is the practice of patience, and that patience will render them perfect: "Patience hath a perfect work, that you may be perfect and entire, failing in nothing, replenished with everything essential to the sanctity of your calling to Christianity. To explain the obligation under which the Christian lies of living holily, the newly-baptized, on coming out of the font, was clothed with a white robe, and a wax light placed in his hand, the celebrant the while repeating these words:

"Receive this white robe, pure and holy, and live in such a manner that you may carry it unstained before the tribunal of the Sovereign Judge, that He may bestow on you eternal life."

By these ceremonies the Church would explain to the new Christian, first, the holy and exemplary life he ought to lead ; secondly, his deliverance from the captivity of sin and the power of the devil ; and, thirdly, his victory over the powers of darkness. The Romans always presented their slaves with white garments when they set them free. Conquerors were accustomed to make their triumphal entry into Rome clothed in white. "You wear the white robe," says St. Ambrose to a neophyte, "to show that you have put off the old vesture of sin, and that you are now robed in the beautiful garb of innocence and sanctity."

The Saturday and Sunday following Easter are, to this day, called the Saturday and Sunday *in albis*, in white, because the neophytes then laid aside their white garments, and received, instead, *Agnus Deis*, made of the wax of the Paschal candle, and blessed by the Pope, which they wore suspended from their necks, that they might have constantly before their eyes a lively symbol of the holiness of the faith they had embraced, and learn from the spotless Lamb of God to be humble, meek and innocent, in thought, word and deed. On the day of their baptism they partook of milk and honey, to remind them of their spiritual infancy and new life in Jesus Christ, and to assimilate them in some manner to our Lord, of whom Isaias said that He should eat butter, which is made of milk and honey, and to signify thereby the infantile meekness and suavity which should adorn a Christian. Since a Christian is obliged to join holy works to the holy name he bears, he should perform virtuous actions with all possible earnestness. He promises in baptism, before heaven and earth, to renounce the world and the devil, and he makes this promise, not to a man, who might easily be deceived, but to God, who is infinitely powerful to exact the performance of the promise. Churches, sacred vessels, and sacerdotal vestments are, in virtue of their consecration to God, employed only in His service. The greatest monarch on earth must not presume to drink from a consecrated chalice ; a priest can use it only at the altar, and a laic must not dare to touch it ! What reverence and respect ! Now how much greater reverence should we entertain for ourselves, who belong far more strictly than any sacred vessel to the Divine Majesty ! And ought we not, as a necessary consequence of our consecration to Him, to avoid all profane employments, and occupy ourselves only with what regards the worship and interests of our God ? "Know you not," asks St. Paul, "that your members are the temple of the Holy Ghost, who is in you by the gift of God ? Are you ignorant that you belong to God, not to yourselves ? Shall I then profane the members of Jesus Christ ? God forbid !" St. Ignatius of Antioch wrote to the Romans entreating them to pray that he might bear worthily the glorious name of Christian, and perform works suitable to his vocation and his name.

The Christian, therefore, ought to be holy, and to employ himself in the service of God, as a thing that belongs to the Divine Majesty by many titles ; but alas ! how few are worthy of their high prerogatives ! How many are satisfied with the mere name, and are careless of practising the virtue which that glorious name implies ! How many are mere phantoms of Christianity ! How many resemble the sponge, which has so little appearance of life that one can scarcely determine whether it is an animal or a vegetable ! There is so little sanctity in the life, the conversation, and the affections of the multitude, that one may reasonably ask whether they are Christians or infidels.

He only is a Christian who leads the life of a Christian. "My dear children," says the holy Bishop of Hippo, "do not deceive yourselves with vain hopes; it is not the dignity of the name which makes the Christian. Nothing will produce greater confusion before God and man, or deserve more dreadful punishment, than to bear this glorious title without the virtues which correspond to it." In fact how can he be called a Christian who, despising the promises he has made in baptism, the sanctity of his religion, the blood which Christ has shed for him, and the commandments and instructions divinely given him, abandons himself to sin, and lives a slave to vice?

St. Tiburtius, a young nobleman, son to St. Chromatius, governor of Rome, whom St. Sebastian had converted to the faith, being brought before the judge, Fabian, by a certain Torquatus, who had perfidiously abandoned his faith and betrayed his brethren, said to the judge: "For a time Torquatus, whom you see here, appeared to be a Christian, but he was only a liar and a hypocrite, because he did not perform the works of a Christian. For, truly, most illustrious lord, the name of Christian is a name full of divine virtue, which belongs only to the disciples and imitators of Christ, who resist their passions and practise sublime virtue." Esteem yourself, then, anything but a Christian if, like Torquatus, you abandon yourself to your passions, and lead an effeminate, licentious life. Persons of this description are never acknowledged by Jesus Christ as His friends and servants; He would not admit such renegades among His disciples.

§ 3.—*How to act in a Christian manner.*

The actions of a Christian should not only be holy, as becomes his name; they must, morever, be holy with the sanctity of Jesus Christ. All must be "holy in Christ," says St. Paul. This must be explained at some length, for in it consists chiefly the essence of Christianity. Human actions are universally referred to three sources : passion, reason, and the Spirit of Jesus Christ. As passion is the nature of irrational animals, so the actions it produces are the actions of beasts. As reason distinguishes man, so reasonable actions are human actions. As the Spirit of Jesus is the essence of Christianity, so the actions which flow from this noble source are properly the actions of a Christian. But to develop this truth more fully, we shall exhibit it in a clearer light. St. Paul teaches, as a fundamental doctrine of Christianity, that the Church is a body, of which Christ is the head, and we are the members ; he tells this thrice to the Ephesians ; he declares it emphatically to the Colossians and Corinthians. It is unnecessary to transcribe all his words, but we will quote some, as the knowledge of the truth is very important. In the first chapter of his Epistle to the Ephesians, he says : "God has subjected all things under the feet of His Son, Jesus, and established Him head of all the Church," that is to say, of the Church militant, which is on earth, and is composed of those who combat continually against the enemies of God ; the Church suffering, which is under the earth, and composed of holy souls, who satisfy the divine justice for their debts in the flames of purgatory ; and the Church triumphant in heaven, composed, as St. Thomas teaches, of angels and human beings. It will be good to remark here, with the Doctor : 1. That our Lord is the head and chief of the blessed, who are actually united to Him in glory ; of the just, who are united to Him by grace ; of those who are His by faith, and of those who are not united to Him now, but who will one day become so ; and, in short, of all who are capable of receiving His grace. But He is not the head of the damned, nor of those who die without baptism, for they are incapable of being the recipients of His graces, or sharing in the fruit of His labors, which is communicated only by faith.

2. St. Augustine, St. Hilary, St. Thomas, and other theolo-

gians, teach that our Lord is the head of the angels. In effect, since St. Paul affirms that He is the head of all the Church, He must be their head, for the Church is a spiritual republic, consisting of men and angels, who share, or hope to share, the same eternal dwelling, the same glory, the same felicity, and who are united by the bonds of the same charity. A body must necessarily have one head, and only one: and who is better suited by nature to fill such an office than our adorable Saviour, the man-God? He is, then, the head of the angels, and merited for them the grace they received in their time of trial, and the glory they now enjoy. St. Thomas, explaining these words of the apostle St. John, "Of His plenitude we have all received," says that they ought to be understood not only of apostles, patriarchs, prophets, and all the just who have ever existed, exist, or shall exist, but also of the angels, because the plenitude of the grace which our Lord possesses is the source whence flow all the graces communicated to all intelligent creatures, whether angels or men.

Our Lord is not only the head, but also the redeemer of the angels, as Theodoret and St. Bernard call Him, who understand of these spirits, as well as of men, what St. Paul said to the Hebrews, that our Lord died for all. Yet He has been their Saviour, as He has been the Saviour of His holy Mother, by *preventing* their fall, which is, without doubt, a more excellent sort of redemption than ours. In the forty-third psalm David tells us that God *redeemed* him from the furious sword of the giant, Goliath, because He did not *permit* him to be struck by it. St. Fulgentius beautifully remarks that the grace of Jesus Christ worked in man, to redeem him, and in the angels, to prevent their fall; the latter were not wounded at all, and the wounds of the former were healed. He has, therefore, preserved the health of one, and restored that of the other; to the angels He has been a preservation, and to man a remedy.

1. Finally, our Lord is the chief or head of all created things. And this is the interpretation given to these words of the Sage : "The Lord possessed me in the beginning of His ways," or according to the Hebrew : "The Lord constituted me prince of His ways and His creatures." Our Lord has dominion over all things by the irrevocable appointment of His Father, as David and St. Paul teach. 2. Terrestrial things are ennobled, and, as it were, deified in Him by the mystery of the Incarnation. 3. He can employ them for the salvation, perfection, and beatitude of His elect ; and, 4, after the day of judgment He will endow them with a new glory, and the purity of incorruption, similar to that of the children of God, to which they now so ardently aspire, as St. Paul observes, in this verse : "The expectation of the creatures waiteth for the revelation of the children of God."

But He is peculiarly the head of Christians, with whom He forms the body of the Church, they being His members, and called by His name. "Let us testify our gratitude to God," exclaims St. Augustine, "let us thank Him with jubilee, that we are not only Christians, but Christ's. Can you comprehend, my children, this immense condescension? Jesus is our head, and we are His members ; we compose the same body with Him." He is our chief, because He has really assumed our nature, and become one of us, and because, as head, He is raised above all the other members, surpassing them immeasurably in excellence and dignity : whence St. Paul styles Him "the first born of all creatures," because He is incomparably superior to all created things.

The head is the most important part of the body, the seat of the interior and exterior senses, where the eyes see, the ears hear, the tongue tastes, and whence the sense of touch extends itself to the whole body. Here the soul discerns and judges of things, here she decides and announces what is to be executed by the other faculties. On medals, pictures and coins, the head alone suffices to represent the whole man. The ancients esteemed the head so highly that they swore by it, as though it were something divine. The Egyptians reverenced even the heads of animals, which they would never eat. Aristotle said that the head was godlike, because in it reason had established her throne, and was accustomed to hold her councils. And the beloved disciple says of the divine face of our Lord: "We have seen His glory, the glory as it were of the only begotten of the Father, full of grace and truth." St. Paul tells the Ephesians that "in Christ are all things, whether of heaven or earth, so that He is the abyss of the treasures of God. All the divinity that is in human nature, whether by essence or by participation, is in Him, and comes to us from Him and through Him.

The head naturally rules and governs all the other members. Our Lord properly exercises these functions in our regard, since we are the members of His mystic body. St. Leo admonishes us not to be unmindful of our immense dignity, in being members of such a head. We ought certainly to conceive high ideas of our nobility, and never degenerate from our greatness, or tarnish in the least the lustre of our glory. The hand of a king never performs the office of a cook or valet; it will not touch lowly things, because it is the hand of a sovereign. We are all members of the infinite majesty of the Son of God: ought we not, then, to strive to acquire and preserve a becoming purity, which we will not suffer the least unseemly thought to sully?

Members naturally love and reverence their head, and have a great inclination to preserve it. When the head is in peril, the feet run to save it, the hands are raised to protect it, and willingly receive the blow for it. We ought, likewise, to despise our own interests, and forward those of our head. O hand, sacred member of a divine head! when thou seest this head in danger, defend it bravely, at any risk, since it was crowned with thorns to crown thee with glory. "I would rather," says St. Bernard, "that men should murmur against me than against God. To me it is a great honor to serve as a shield to cover Him. I willingly endure the bitter scorn of slanderous tongues, provided they spare Him, and I refuse not to be accounted a wretch, that I may save His honor. O who will grant me this favor that, like David, I may suffer opprobrium, and have my face covered with confusion, in the cause of my God?"

§ 4.—*Same subject continued.*

The proper and principal office of the head is to act on the body, communicating to it salutary interior and exterior influences: interiorly, distributing the animal spirits produced in the cells of the brain, which give feeling and motion to the members, whence Varro is of opinion that the word *caput* is made to signify the head (*quod ab eo capiant initium sensus et nervi*), because the senses and the nerves, by which the vital spirits are distributed, have their origin in the head; exteriorly, inasmuch as the head, by the conduct of the understanding and the will, and by using the eyes and other senses, directs all the members and their operations, so that the foot may not slip over a precipice, but take a safe road, nor the hand touch ordures, but what is neat and decent. This office our Lord exercises toward the Church, which is His body, and the faithful, who are His members, influencing them continually, and shedding upon them all virtues and graces. The Council of Trent says: "Jesus Christ perpetually communicates His virtue to the just, as the head distributes its spirits to the members, and the vine its sap to the branches. This virtue precedes, accompanies, and follows their good works, and without it good works could neither be agreeable to God, nor meritorious of eternal life." The apostle had previously said to the

Ephesians: "To every one of us is given grace according to the measure of the giving of Christ;" and to the Colossians: "He is the head of the body of the Church, because in Him it hath pleased the Father that all fulness should dwell." And again: "In Him dwelleth the plenitude of the Godhead, corporally. And you are filled in Him, who is the head." St. Thomas teaches that all the graces in the sacred humanity were in Him, not only as a particular man, but also as chief or head of the Church, to whom all the faithful are united as members to the head, whence these graces naturally flow out upon all, as the natural head sends its senses and nerves abroad upon the whole body, interiorly and exteriorly.

In this consists that amiable and august quality which theologians attribute to our Lord, and which they call *gratia capitis*, the grace of the chief. This merits for others the graces which personally reside in Him: the grace of the head flows out upon the members, and is sufficient for the justification of all men. Suarez remarks that the grace of the head is not, strictly speaking, the sanctifying grace which our Lord possessed, but the grace of the hypostatic union, inasmuch as sanctifying grace does not, of its own nature, merit for others, but only for its possessor, as appears evidently in the grace bestowed on the saints. If sanctifying grace had this particular efficacy in our Lord, this was owing to its reference to the hypostatic union which communicated to it this quality, and which peculiarly confers on our Lord the dignity of head of the Church, and sheds upon His actions an infinite value, both for Himself and for His members.

Thus our Lord, as head of the faithful, distributes to them all their graces, gifts, good thoughts, and movements of piety; it is from Him, and of His plenitude, they receive their humility, their patience, their sweetness, their charity, and all their virtues. All possible graces and perfections are contained in Him. The sanctifying grace and infused habits they find in themselves, are His virtues in reality, not mere copies or imitations of them. As He is verily present wherever a consecrated host is preserved, so His grace and virtue are truly present wherever there are just and holy souls.

The second function of the head is to guide the operations of the members. St. Paul, having exhorted the Colossians to put off the old man, and assume the new, adds: "Jesus Christ is all to all the faithful," that is to say, as Cardinal Cajetan explains, the cause and origin of all the actions, movements and graces of the new man, as being his head. And he says to the Ephesians: "The man is the head of the woman, as Christ is the head of the Church, His body, of which He is also the Saviour, by the life He gives it." He is to the faithful what the sap is to the tree, the root to the branches, the stem to the flower. By the communication of His spirit He enables them to produce, like trees planted near running waters, which never lose their verdure, flowers of holy thoughts, leaves of good words, and fruits of virtuous actions. He is the soul of the body of the Church, which, being a living body, must have a soul to vivify it, Jesus Christ. "The body of Jesus Christ," says St. Austin, "can live only in the Spirit of Jesus Christ. As the soul endows the body with life, beauty, movement and feeling, so all the interior and exterior graces of the just come from Jesus Christ, and are but emanations of His perfections, so that each may say of himself these celebrated words of the apostle: '*I live now, yet not I, but Christ liveth in me.*'"

"All my vital actions, as thinking, loving, acting," etc., says Cajetan, explaining this text, "proceed not from myself, but from Jesus Christ living in me, for whoever is crucified in Him (that is to say, all the faithful), has Him for the principle of all his works, governing him interiorly and exteriorly, whence he may truly say that his actions necessarily resemble their origin; and as Jesus is the origin of the Christian life, so all its works must necessarily be conformable to His works. While an animal is but an animal, it eats, drinks, and lives like an animal ; and when it is killed and eaten by man, who converts it into his own substance, it is ennobled by its union with him. Man, if enslaved to sin, leads a life of sin ; but when he is dead to vice, by the hatred he bears it, and united to Christ by true conversion, he no longer lives the life of a sinner, nor even of a man, but the life of a Christian and of Christ." "Being dead to sin," wrote St. Paul, in this thought, to the Romans, "you must now live to God, in Christ Jesus, our Lord," according to the Spirit of Jesus, after His model.

Thus our Lord, as the soul of the body of the Church, the sap of her mysterious trees, which are the just, and the head of these sacred members, operates in them, and guides all their actions. But we must not neglect to consider the ends for which He guides them. He has His own designs regarding the thoughts, affections, words, actions, souls and bodies of all men. This is His right, first, as their head ; second, because He purchased it with His blood. Now He invariably proposed to Himself, as the end of all His actions and sufferings, the glory of His Father and our salvation. Hence the angels sang at His birth : "Glory be to God in the highest, and peace on earth to men of good will." As He has dedicated us by His blood and His death to the honor of His Father, He sanctifies all our actions, even the most lowly, such as eating, drinking and sleeping, rendering them in Himself glorious to God, and teaching us interiorly and exteriorly how to refer everything to that divine end. Thus, as our head, He acts in and by us, provided we are docile to His inspirations, and offer no opposition to His divine influences. "Jesus Christ," says St. Paul, "is our chief corner-stone, in whom all the building, being framed together, groweth up into a holy temple in the Lord, in whom you also are built together into a habitation of God, in the Spirit. As, therefore, ye have received Jesus Christ, walk ye in Him, rooted and built up in Him." Let us, then, permit ourselves to be guided and regulated in all things by Him who is our head; let us enter into all the designs and intentions of Jesus Christ; let us attach ourselves inviolably to the honor of God, and, like our Lord, breathe only for His glory.

§ 5.—*The example of Jesus Christ.*

To excite in ourselves the perfect obedience we owe our Lord, as members to their head, and subjects to their chief, we cannot propose to ourselves a better example than Jesus Christ Himself, in the submission which His humanity rendered to His divinity. We must here consider, first, the mutual union of the humanity and the divinity; second, the humanity as the instrument of the divinity; and, third, the obedience the humanity in this capacity rendered to the divinity.

In our Lord, then, are four kinds of union between His divinity and humanity. The first is the union of dependence, which is common to all creatures, for all depend continually on their Creator, and but for Him would fall back into their original nothingness, just as a ray of light cannot be produced or preserved independently of the sun: if separated for a moment from its source, it immediately flickers and dies out.

The second is the union of local presence, by which the divinity, in virtue of its immensity, extends to all places, and even beyond all places, filling all things, and consequently His humanity. This union is, of course, common to all creatures, in every one of whom God is present by His essence and His power. The third is the hypostatic union, by which the humanity is personally united to the divinity of the Word, and forms with Him one person, who is the God-man and man-God, Christ Jesus, our Lord and Saviour.

These three species of union are substantial, but the fourth is only accidental, by the thoughts, words and affections, by all the interior and exterior virtues, which the sacred humanity exercised toward the divinity. In fact, all the acts of love which a friend exercises toward his friend, are but bonds which unite both more closely in perfect friendship.

The divinity, residing in our Lord's humanity, is the prime mover of all His actions, and gives them an infinite excellence and value. "The Father, who dwelleth in me, doeth the works," says He; and again, "My Father worketh always, and I work with Him." Hence He calls His works the works of His Father: "If I do not the works of my Father, believe me not." Now, if they are *His* works, how can they be the *works of His Father?* And if they are the works of His Father, how can they be His? "Because," says He, "the Father is in me, and I in Him." And when the apostles, after He had spoken to the Samaritan woman, pressed Him to eat, He replied: "My food is to do the will of Him who sent me, that I may perfect His work." Our Lord being God, His will was essentially the will of His Father; but, as man, He united His will to the divine will by a distinct act, emanating from His soul, of which the divinity was always the rule and the model. Hence St. Paul calls the divinity of Jesus Christ *His head.* He says to the Corinthians: "All things are yours, and you are Christ's, and Christ is God's." "You belong to Jesus Christ," explains Cajetan, "as to your Lord and head, and He belongs in the same manner to God, because the divinity deifies the humanity, not only in substance, in the body and the soul, but also in His operations; so that our Lord spoke no word, performed no action, not even the movement of a finger, entertained no thought or affection, without the direction and inspiration of His divinity: for which reason it will be appropriate to speak at some length of His actions. I remark in our Lord four species of action.

The first are to produce, with the Father, the Holy Spirit, coeval with Himself, to conserve the world, to destroy, each moment, millions of things, and create new ones ; the second, the conversion of sinners, the sanctification of the just, the healing of the sick, the resuscitation of the dead ; the third include acts of humility, love, patience, and other virtues ; and the fourth, eating, drinking, and other functions of His senses and faculties. The first action is purely divine, performed by the Word, inasmuch as "the Word was God." The second actions are *theandric*, divinely human, because the divinity inspired them, and the humanity has served merely as an instrument to produce them. The third are divinely human and humanly divine, because the humanity entered more largely into them : the two natures were, so to say, equally united to produce them ; and because the fourth are the peculiar effects of human nature, we call them humanly divine. They are, nevertheless, theandric, being the actions of a man-God, and the divinity applied and conducted the humanity in their performance for divine intention.

St. John Damascene, speaking on this subject, remarks that "our Lord did nothing of human things in a purely human manner, because He was not only man, but God : therefore His sufferings were fraught with benedictions, and His death with life. Neither did He do divine things in a manner solely divine, for He was also man. Hence He employed His humanity, the touch of His hand, the word of His mouth, to work miracles and operate divine things. I add that, as the actions and sufferings of our Lord were of infinite value and merit, they necessarily included something divine, because man, with all his strength, could neither do nor suffer anything of infinite value. And moreover, because these actions and sufferings are walking, eating, being scourged, crowned with thorns, and dying on the cross, they are peculiar to man, since God, who is a pure spirit, cannot do or suffer these things."

Moreover, the same doctor teaches that the *theandric* action of our Lord always included two actions : one of the divine nature, the other of the human nature; just as, says he, using an apt comparison, a red-hot sword will cut and burn at the same stroke. It was the work of the human nature of our Lord, for example, to touch the deceased daughter of Jairus, and the work of the divine nature to restore her to life.

St. Cyril of Alexandria had said, before St. John Damascene, that our Lord, being God and man, always acted according to these combined natures, divinely and humanly. An artist designs with his soul what he chisels with his hand; and his soul, as well as his body, will share in the glory with which the world receives his statue, since it has been done, not solely by his body, but by body and soul conjointly, and chiefly by the soul. Our Lord, before His incarnation, wrought works purely divine, but after He had clothed himself with our nature, He operated His miracles by the medium of His humanity: touching the blind, to give them sight, and the dead, to resuscitate them.

St. Thomas, treating this beautiful and important truth, remarks that when two causes, one of which depends on the other, combine to produce an effect, the lesser receives its movement from the greater, as the pen is guided by the hand, and the hand by the brain. Hence, as in our Lord the human nature has its own virtue and its peculiar manner of acting, and the divine nature its own, it follows that there are two different operations : one referring to the human nature, the other to the divine, in such a fashion, however, that the divine nature employs the human nature as its instrument, and the human nature takes part in the operation of the divine nature, as an instrument does in the operation of the principal cause.

3. The obedience which the human nature rendered to the divine was so perfect that it invariably accomplished all the designs of God. "Amen, amen, I say to you, the Son doeth

nothing of Himself but what He seeth the Father doing; for what things soever He doeth, these the Son doeth also. The works which the Father hath given me to do give testimony of me, that the Father hath sent me. I cannot do anything of myself. I seek not my own will, but the will of Him that sent me, for I always do the things that please Him. I say nothing of myself, but as the Father hath taught me, so do I speak." Hence our Saviour assures us that His most delicious food was to do the will of His Father, and that He always hungered after this aliment. In the womb of His mother He thus addressed His Father : " Sacrifice and oblations Thou wouldst not, but Thou hast pierced the ears of Thy servant; Holocausts and sin offerings did not please Thee. Then said I, Behold I come. In the head of the book it is written of me that I should do Thy will. I have desired it, my God, and Thy law is in the midst of my heart."

Never, during His earthly career, did He depart from this manner of acting. Never did He seek the riches, honor, or pleasures of this world. So little did He notice passing events that, when shown a piece of current money, He asked whose image and inscription were on it. When a certain man desired that He would induce his brother to divide his inheritance with him, He answered : " Man, who constituted me judge over you ?" All His care and His whole study consisted in subjecting Himself totally to His Father, with perfect indifference as to application, and entire obedience as to execution. Behold our model. Let us now see how we ought to imitate Him in this perfect obedience to His Eternal Father.

§ 6.—*Our Imitation.*

We have already remarked three things in our Lord : the union of His humanity with His divinity, the operation of the divinity in the humanity, and the obedience of the humanity to all the orders and movements of the divinity. Let us now consider how we ought to imitate Him in these things, since He is our head, and since we are so happy as to be His members. The first of these unions is substantial dependence; the second is local presence. These are also ours, because we have only the bodies and souls He has given us, and we depend perpetually on Him for our conservation. By reason of the divine immensity, we are present to God in all places, and, as St. Paul told the Areopagites, " In Him we live and move, and have our being." The third, which is the hypostatic union, casts over all human beings the rays of its glory, because God is united to man, and all men, by our Lord, and in Him, are united to God. Christians are more particularly united to Him by faith, baptism, grace, and the Holy Eucharist, and also because they are His mystic members, His disciples, His brothers, His spouses. To us all, as well as to the apostles, He says : " I in the Father, and you in me, and I in you." " He is in His Father," says St. Hilary, " by His essence, by His eternal generation : and we are in Him by the union of our substance with His, in the mystery of the incarnation, and by the sacrament of his body and blood, because He says : 'He that eateth my flesh and drinketh my blood abides in me, and I in Him.'" " I am in my Father," says the Gloss, "as a ray is in the sun, and you are in me as the branch is in the vine ; and I am in you as the sap is in the branch, to make it live and bear fruit." We practise the fourth union, which is accidental, by acts of faith, hope and charity, earnestly petitioning our Lord for this union, of which we shall speak more amply in another place.

2. Our Lord, who is our head, works in us who are His members, as the divinity operates in His humanity, that we may be entirely under His guidance. It is not the hand or the foot that directs the other members, but the head, which alone is capable of conducting each to its destined end.

Hence our Lord promised to remain with us to the consummation of the world, to protect and defend us exteriorly, and to illuminate us interiorly, inflaming the will, enlightening the understanding ; fortifying our courage, that He may be truly our *Emanuel, God with us*, to dwell in us, to sanctify us, and to deify us. Thus He is with the true Christian, as a head with its members, to direct their movements; as a king with his subjects, to govern them according to his laws; as a general with his army, to lead his soldiers to victory ; as a father in his family, which he governs, defends and enriches; as a pilot in his vessel, which he steers through tempestuous seas; as the sun in the world, giving light and beauty to all nature ; as the soul in the body, to enable him to live, not a mere human or rational life, but a divine life, that his thoughts may be not merely natural, but supernatural, glorious to God, and meritorious of eternal life.

Hence St. Paul says : "It is God who worketh in you, and moveth you to do good and to receive his faith." And he notices that there is a variety of graces, ministrations and operations in the body of the Church, but that only one God, one Lord and one Spirit, animate this body, and produce these effects. Hence he said that he himself lived, spoke and acted in and by Christ. And Jesus Christ Himself says : "It is not you who speak, but the spirit of your Father speaketh in you." St. Paul says to the Romans : "You know now what you ought to ask, but the Spirit Himself asketh for you with ineffable groanings. I give thanks to my God for you all, through Jesus Christ ; that is, by the inspiration and instruction of Christ Jesus."

These lights and motions of Christ in us ought to be consecrated by us to His Father, and acted on for His glory. St. Catherine of Sienna relates that our Lord one day took away her heart, and put His own in its place, that thenceforth she might always think, act, love and desire only in the heart of

Jesus. And not long since something similar happened to another young virgin of great holiness, to whom He said, after communion: "I take thy mind and thy heart to give thee mine." And He took such complete and intimate possession of her members that they seemed no longer hers, but His. This was very evident, for, if you said to her, "My dear sister, show me your hand," she did not show it; but if you said, "Show me the hand that belongs to Jesus," she immediately extended her hand, with amiable sweetness and angelic purity. Thus must we regard our members, since they are united to Jesus, and dedicated to the honor of God by so many titles. We should, as Christians, be able to say with St. Paul : "I live, yet not I, but Christ liveth in me ;" and with our Lord himself : "I do nothing of myself. The Father who abideth in me doth the works. I say nothing of myself; it is the Father who speaketh in me." We ought to think, speak and act toward our Lord as His humanity acted toward His divinity, and thereby render our actions *theandric*, at least in their principle and in their end. Their source must be Jesus Christ, that He may animate them with His spirit, and use us as His instruments. The member participates in the excellence of the head, and the member of such a head as Jesus Christ must necessarily be extremely honorable. If we fail to act by His Spirit, by what do we act—by corrupt nature, or by the devil ? What a horrible and infamous difference !

If the pen which writes were a rational being, would it not rather be used by a king than by a peasant, by an excellent writer than by a child, who only soils the paper ? Would not a chisel, in similar circumstances, choose to be handled by a Phidias or a Michael Angelo, rather than by an ignorant apprentice ? And the paint-brush by a Raphael, rather than by an unskilful hand, able to produce only imperfect figures ? We are used by the hand of God ; we are His instruments. The hand writes and the foot walks only by the direction of the head; the instrument works only at the will of its master. So we, who are members and instruments of Jesus Christ, ought, in imitation of Him, to work for the glory of God, for which we and all creatures have been created, as St. Paul tells us.

Verily, if the hand writes correctly, or embroiders neatly; if the feet dance gracefully, or walk steadily, the honor is due chiefly to the head. Not the hand of a writer, or the foot of a dancer, the brush of a painter, or the chisel of a sculptor, is praised, but the brain that directed all these to their respective perfections. We ought, in like manner, attribute to our Lord, our head and chief, the glory of all the good we do, and the praise of all our victories. Thus the four and twenty ancients whom St. John mentions in the Apocalypse, "cast their crowns at His feet," to show that it is He who combated and vanquished in them. We, as His members, must prepare ourselves for his movements, and follow his guidance, and He, as the source, deserves the honor of all our good works.

§ 7.—*Of the indifference with which we ought to receive the movements and inspirations of our Lord, and the obedience we should pay them.*

To dispose ourselves to be conducted by our head, to bear worthily the glorious title of His members, and to lead a life according to His Spirit, we must be indifferent as to the use to which He applies us, and obedient to execute all that He requires of us. We must be indifferent to riches and poverty, honor and contempt, health or sickness, life or death, time or eternity, and generally to all things, that there may be no resistance on our side, and that He may be perfectly free to use us as He pleases, to dispose of our soul and body, our privations and possessions, our affections and imaginations, as He shall judge most proper for His own glory and our salvation.

We are members of a divine head. In our body the foot is indifferent as to the road to be passed over, the hand when it writes cares not whether it forms an *A* or a *B;* it is the head that settles all these matters. The musical instrument is indifferent as to the tunes played upon it; the performer may select whatever he pleases. These are our models. We must hold ourselves in readiness to be disposed of as our head pleases, used where, when, and how He judges most suitable. The sacred humanity abandoned itself unreservedly to the guidance of the divinity, obeying all His orders without ever offering the slightest resistance. In the Garden of Olives, though overwhelmed at the prospect of His terrific sufferings, He drank His bitter chalice to the dregs, exclaiming: "Not my will, but thine be done." He heeds not His natural repugnances, but is obedient unto death, even to the death of the cross.

Behold what the Spirit of Jesus desires to accomplish in souls, which, on this account, is compared to living waters; for our Lord, speaking to the Samaritan woman, said: "If thou didst but know the gift of God, and who He is that saith to thee, Give me to drink, thou wouldst have asked Him for the living waters," that is to say, for the Holy Spirit, who cleanses all corporal things of their uncleanness, renders them fruitful in good works, extinguishes the fire of concupiscence, and, like liquids, has no essential form, but is adapted to the shape of whatever vessel He enters. Thus the Spouse says: "My soul melted away at the voice of my Beloved," to take whatever shape He pleases to give me. "Saul, Saul," said our Lord to His adversary, "why dost thou persecute me?" Truly we persecute Him when we resist His will, when we close our hearts to His inspirations, when we reverse His order, which tends only to the glory of God and our salvation. He cannot act in and by us if we will not permit Him, if we are determined not to yield to His movements, if we are not plastic in His divine hands. Let us then cry out, with St. Paul: "Lord, what wilt Thou have me to do?" Behold I am ready for whatever Thou shalt ordain; and with Samuel: "Speak, Lord, for Thy servant heareth." Command me; I am ready to execute Thy will. As our members obey the head, so must we obey Jesus Christ. And the better to do so, let us look at Him who was obedient, even to the death of the cross. Let us hear how He speaks by Isaias: "The Lord hath opened my ear, and I do not resist; I have not gone back. I have given my body to the strikers, and my cheeks to the pluckers; I have not turned away from the revilers or the spitters." Let us strive to imitate this accomplished model. "As you have learned of Jesus Christ, so walk in His footsteps." Isaias says of true Christians: "They shall be docile to the movements of God;" and Ezekiel says of mysterious animals which draw the chariot of the glory of God, and are types of His true children: "Every one of them went straight forward; whither the impulse of the spirit was to go, thither they went, and they looked not back. And they ran and returned, like flashes of lightning."

"Those who are led by the Spirit of God," says St. Paul, "they are the sons of God:" on which text the Angelic Doctor remarks, that as beasts are entirely ruled by their nature, so the true children of God are governed by the Spirit of God. Not that the Holy Spirit acts in and by them to the fullest extent, but that He concurs with them, and, according to St. Paul, "worketh in them to will and to accomplish what is good." Cajetan, explaining the above text, says: "By the word led, *aguntur*, which the apostle uses, it plainly appears that we are not forced or constrained by the Spirit of God, but that we choose to be perfectly submissive to Him; for we do not apply the word led to the result of force or coercion. The saints, animated and transported with the Spirit of God, are His legitimate children, because it is peculiar to true children to be docile and pliable to their father, to follow his will, not their own, and to obey the least sign he gives them. Let us consider the prompt obedience which the stars render to their Creator, since Christians ought " to shine as stars in a perverse world: " He sent forth light, and it obeyed Him with trembling. And the stars have given light in their watches, and rejoiced. They were called, and they said : Here we are ; and with cheerfulness they shined forth to Him that made them."

§ 8.—*Reasons to induce us to act as becometh Christians, and perform all our works in the Spirit of Jesus.*

Since we have the honor to be Christians, and consequently members of Jesus Christ, we ought to permit ourselves to be guided by His spirit. We should regulate our thoughts, words, actions and affections by His movements, and practise humility, obedience, meekness, gentleness, and all other virtues, in Him. " Be holy in Christ," says the apostle : which means, do all according to the example He has given you. Consider how His humanity loved, honored, adored and praised His divinity, and in like manner love, honor, praise and thank God, in Him and by Him.

The will and the heart are the most important parts of man, because the will is the organ of action, and the heart the seat of love ; yet the hands and other members in a certain manner act and love in the will and heart, inasmuch as the whole man is composed not merely by the will and heart, but also by all the other members. In the same way we who are members of Jesus Christ, love and act toward God, not solely in Him who is our head, but also in ourselves, on His model, and by His Spirit. Let us see the reasons which should persuade us to this. The Christian life being necessarily founded on Christ, and flowing from Him as from its source, there can be no true Christianity without His spirit : "If any one have not the Spirit of Christ," says St. Paul, "he is none of His." This spirit necessarily constitutes the Christian, as the soul constitutes the peculiarity of man among other animals. Adam is our first father; from him we derive our origin : we should not be human beings if we had not a body and soul substantially and organically like his. Jesus Christ is our head and origin by grace: we cannot be His children if we do not possess His spirit; without it, we should be mere ghosts or skeletons of Christians. As reasonable action must emanate from a reasonable soul, so Christian action must emanate from the spirit of Christ, and be marked by His seal. No action, however great or illustrious, which does not originate and terminate in Him, can glorify God, or be meritorious to its agent.

As Christians, reason is not the sole rule of our actions ; as men, we are not guided by passion. As Christians, Jesus Christ is our legislator. When He established the law of charity, He called it a new commandment, yet it was as ancient as the world; for the law of nature had inscribed it on the heart of the first man, and Moses had given it to the children of Israel. He called it new, because He willed that it should be fulfilled in a new manner, since the Christian ought to love his neighbor in the Spirit of Christ, and as Jesus Christ loves him : "Love one another as I have loved you." Behold our Model. The same should be understood, also, of all the commandments and virtues which are common to the Jews and to Christians. In this sense St. Paul says : "Gladly will I glory in my infirmities, that the power of Christ may be manifest in me." He calls the humility, meekness, gentleness, and other virtues which he practises on this divine Model, the *power of Christ*. All the holy actions ever performed before Christ's coming were the fruit of grace given in consideration of Him, whether they were performed under the law of nature or under that of Moses. But they were not performed *in* Jesus Christ, that is, after His example ; because, not having yet assumed our nature, He had not yet practised them.

Let us, then, with St. Gregory, regard Jesus Christ as the rule and model of our actions, and remember that saying of the apostle : "All that is not of faith is sin," which means, as the Greek fathers explain, all that is not conformed to conscience; or, as St. Austin and St. Bernard say, all that is born of infidelity, being contrary to faith, is sin. If we are not interiorly and exteriorly conformed to Jesus Christ, we cannot be Christians. A portrait which does not resemble the original cannot be called a true likeness.

Alas! if this be true, as it undoubtedly is, where are the Christians ? If, in order to be truly Christian, our actions must be done by the Spirit of Christ, how few of our nearly infinite actions possess that excellence ! The greater number of men lead the life of beasts, because they are ruled solely by passion. A few lead the lives of men permitting themselves to be guided by reason. But few, very few indeed, lead the life of true Christians, because they will not be governed by the spirit of Jesus. And yet they are obliged to do this. This is their greatest, their only real glory. All truly Christian action is noble and honorable ; it is agreeable and glorious to God. Vile though we be in our fallen nature, He sees His Son in each one of us; and because of this beloved Son, our actions please Him when done in His Spirit. Jesus Christ has destroyed the empire of sin, and repaired the injured honor of His Father. His Spirit alone is a spirit of glory to God ; and our actions are glorious to Him and meritorious to ourselves only as far as they are animated by this Spirit. All that is not consecrated to God is vile and infamous, while all that is dedicated to Him becomes glorious and illustrious by this dedication.

Trees, under the law of Moses, were regarded as unclean during the first three years of their growth, and the Jews were forbidden to eat of their fruits; but the offering made of them to God in the fourth year purified the trees and the fruits, and the fruits of the fifth year the Israelites were at liberty to use. All Christian action is holy, because it is directly or indirectly consecrated to God by Jesus Christ, His Son, who, by His blood and His death, has purchased all men, and all their good works, which He continually presents to the Father as the works of His members. For this end He clothed Himself with our nature, that He might render to God, outside of God, by and in His sacred humanity, in all men whom He deified by His incarnation, an honor worthy of His infinite majesty. All Christian action is operated by a grace more noble than that conferred on our first parents and on the angels, for they received grace in view of the merits of Christ, while the works of Christians are performed in and by Christ.

It is true, as the learned Suarez remarks, that though the grace given by God, in consideration of Jesus Christ, can receive no increase of perfection as regards its nature and principal effects, which are to destroy sin, and infuse virtue into the soul, yet it is infinitely ennobled as being bestowed on us in acknowledgment of His merits. Grace, as detached from our Lord, cannot be considered in this manner. A man is equally a man whether he be the son of a king or the son of a peasant, yet the latter is, by his condition, incomparably below the former. The grace which God gives us is gratuitous, so far as we are concerned; but if considered with reference to Jesus Christ, it is justly ours, because He died to purchase it for us. It is a singular and unspeakable honor to man to be redeemed, sanctified and justified by the merits of a man-God: whence we may deduce this probable consequence, that the grace which is found in Him, and flows from His merits, is to the just man a principle more powerful to merit before God, to satisfy for sins, to pray with greater success, and in general to obtain all virtues, than if it had not this reference to Him. Without Him it would be the *gratuitous* gift of God, while with Him and in Him it seems due to His merits and a consequence of the love the Father bears Him, and the honor He designs to procure Him.

The dignity and excellence of the least actions of the sacred humanity are absolutely infinite, because of the hypostatic union. The value of these actions is perfectly incomprehensible. As the accidents of bread and wine in the Holy Eucharist are worthy of reverence and adoration, because they are the sacramental veils of Jesus Christ, so the Christian action is truly sublime, because it is united to Jesus, and inspired by Him. When we labor in a Christian manner, our Lord Himself works in and by us. Whatever emanates from Him is truly great and excellent; whatever emanates solely from us is but human, or animal. When we yield ourselves unreservedly to our head, He guides us securely to the noblest of ends,—the glory of God and eternal salvation; whereas, when we guide ourselves, no matter how wise and learned we may be, we fall over the precipice. "The thoughts of mortal men," says the sage, "are deceitful, and their providences uncertain." The wisdom of a man resides in the head, not in the hand or in the foot. Jesus is our head and our wisdom. Our highest prudence is to abandon ourselves entirely to His guidance, and to follow His orders as subjects obey the orders of their chief or head.

As the actions of Christ have been most profitable for the glory of His name, the beatitude of His person, and for our salvation, so all Christian action participates in these advantages, as flowing from this divine source. The more abundantly we possess the Spirit of Jesus, the more surely and perfectly shall we operate our own salvation, and contribute to that of our neighbor; because, as the Spirit of

Jesus is the Spirit of our Saviour, it is also the spirit of salvation. Our Lady, being possessed of this spirit in a higher degree than all creatures together, did more for men than did all other beings. The same may be said in proportion of the apostles, and, after them, of the other saints, according to the measure in which they possessed this salutary spirit, without which men cannot serve their fellow-creatures, being destitute of the principle from which true benevolence should flow.

Great is the joy, and profound the repose, of a soul submissive to the movements of Jesus. He can freely dispose of her, because she offers no resistance to His Spirit. Let us, then, abandon ourselves confidingly to His wise guidance. He will conduct us to sanctity, to happiness, to paradise. "*I know a man in Christ,*" says St. Paul; that is to say, a man united to Christ by faith and charity, animated by His Spirit, acting only by His movement. Such a man is the picture of a true Christian. But what happened to this *man in Christ?* "He was ravished to the third heavens; He heard secret words which it is not given to man to utter." Behold the felicity of a true Christian. The Spirit of Jesus already introduces him to heaven. St. Macarius well remarks that when a soul has bid adieu to earthly things, and is united to Jesus, she becomes all light, all eyes, all mind, all joy, all goodness, all mercy, all compassion: as a stone in the sea is surrounded with water on all sides, so those who are intimately united to Christ become like to Him, and live in Him and by Him. All that has been said, considered attentively by the wise and judicious soul, ought surely to inspire a great desire and a firm resolution to live and act by the Spirit of Jesus, our Lord and Saviour. Let us now see the order which should be observed in the practice of this.

§ 9.—*Practice.*

Four things are necessary to dispose us to practise the important truth of which we have been speaking, and which is the essence of true Christianity. 1. The first is great moderation and tranquillity in our actions, words, gestures, and all our interior and exterior movements, that the Spirit of Jesus, which is a sweet and peaceable spirit, may inspire and conduct us. To this, impetuosity and precipitation oppose a great obstacle, because, as Elias says, our Lord does not come in a hurricane, but as the breathing of the gentlest zephyr; and David says: "His place is in peace, and His habitation in Sion," that is, in tranquil souls. Verily, His movements are secret, and His inspirations delicate; like the waters of Siloe, they move in silence, and, therefore, the agitated soul cannot distinguish them. Solomon says: "Let the words of the wise be heard in silence." In this manner we should hear the words which the Eternal Wisdom speaks within us. His voice cannot be distinguished in turbulent souls; it is heard only by the gentle and peaceable. 2. The second is indifference, by which the soul is freed from all disorderly affections and desires, that our Lord may dispose of her as He pleases, without experiencing the slightest resistance on her part. The more disengaged she is, the more capable she is of being guided by Him, and, consequently, of happiness and perfection. To see if we possess this disengagement, it would be well to enter often into ourselves, and examine whether anything holds us captive, or disturbs our repose; and if we find anything of this nature, we must gently, but firmly, uproot it as an enemy to our happiness and perfection. We should produce interior acts of disengagement, saying, with David: "I am thine, Lord: dispose of me as Thou pleasest. O Lord! I am Thy servant, and the son of

Thy handmaid. Thou hast broken my bonds, I will sacrifice to Thee a host of praise. Shall not my soul be subject to God, since from Him is my salvation?" And with St. Paul : "Lord, what wilt Thou have me to do? Behold, I am ready to obey Thee in everything." We must frequently, during the day, renounce our own judgment, inclinations and sentiments, to enter into those of Jesus Christ, saying, for this purpose : "My Lord, I renounce entirely my memory, my understanding, my will, my desires, my affections, my imaginations, my passions, and all interior and exterior movements of soul and body, subjecting myself entirely to Thee, to be ruled and governed by Thy Spirit, and to adopt Thy thoughts, judgments and affections, in place of my own." To animate ourselves to this renunciation, let us remember the peace and joy which it will produce in our souls. Instruments in the hands of Jesus, we shall accomplish works worthy of Him who guides us. The pencil, in the hands of a Zeuxis or a Michael Angelo, produces wonders ; guided by a mediocre artist, it can do nothing deserving of fame. Under the guidance of our Lord, we can work wonders ; when we govern ourselves, our efforts accomplish but little. Let us not lose sight of our great model and head. In the first moment of the incarnation, His humanity was perfectly subordinate to His divinity. When we shall have been despoiled of our own will and inclinations, the Word Incarnate will come to dwell in us and govern us, directing all our movements, mental and physical, to the glory of God and our eternal salvation.

A pious lady whom I knew, made the following resolutions on this subject : "I shall begin every morning by making an interior act of honor and adoration to Jesus Christ, God and man. Then, with profound respect, I will view Him as my Sovereign Lord, my Saviour, and the only source of my happiness, humbling myself before Him, because of my nothingness and sin; after which I shall abandon myself absolutely to His love, His wisdom and His power, that He may do with me as he pleases, freely following His inspirations, and subjecting myself to Him alone. I shall receive indifferently from His hands joy or sorrow, light or darkness, riches or poverty, honor or contempt, ceding to Him all the rights He has given me over my own life and liberty. I shall protest that I belong to Him alone; that all my actions have Him for their origin and their end, and that I shall never have any will but His. Finally, I must beseech Him to communicate to me His Spirit, and give me the necessary dispositions to accomplish perfectly, in and by me, whatever He desires."

The resolutions of this holy woman are well worthy of imitation, and may serve as a model for us. Many, even among spiritual persons, are deceived by secret desires of liberty; they do not like constraint or subjection; they avoid it when they can, and hence they are under our Lord's guidance only in appearance and by words. They cherish their own desires and opinions, they will not renounce their own sentiments, and their actions are guided by hidden and subtle self-love, though they do not always think so. 3. The third is an interior attention to the divine inspirations. Our Lord, being physically and morally in us, is not inactive. He enlightens our mind with His lights, and excites our will to desire and accomplish what is good. The eyes of the soul must be open to receive these lights, and the ears eager to hear His divine whispers. David beautifully says: "As the eyes of the handmaid are on the hands of her mistress, so are our eyes on the Lord God until He have mercy on us." A negligent or turbulent soul cannot hear the gentle whisperings of the meek Lamb of God. "I will hear," that is to say, "I desire to hear, what the Lord God shall speak in me," said the same prophet. And it is good, often during the day, to listen to Him speaking within us, and to say to Him, with St. Paul:

"Lord, what wilt Thou have me to do?" We read that Blessed Mary of the Incarnation was so attentive to these divine breathings that she sometimes hesitated in the middle of a discourse or an action, to take the side to which Jesus attracted her by some inspiration. 4. The fourth is to beg continually and earnestly of God that He would animate us with His divine Spirit, and to ask the Father for grace to obey the command He gave on Mount Thabor: "This is My Beloved Son, in whom I am well pleased: *hear ye Him.*" "Lord," says David, "lead me in Thy paths, and conduct me in Thy truth;" that is, conduct me in Thy Divine Son, who is the way, the truth and the life. "Send forth Thy light and Thy truth; they have conducted me to Thy holy mount and to Thy tabernacle. Make the light of Thy countenance, which is Thy Divine Son, shine upon Thy servant, and by Him teach me Thy justifications." Let us, then, address our head and chief: "Lord, teach me Thy paths, and conduct me in Thy truth. Thou art my God and my Saviour, and I have waited for Thee the whole day. Thou art my lamp to illuminate me: my God, enlighten my darkness! Let the splendor of our Lord Jesus be upon us. O Lord! order Thou the works of our hands, and conduct all our actions! O Lord! lead me in Thy justice, direct my ways in Thy truth, for fear of my enemies. Perfect Thou my coming in and my going out, that I may not wander from Thee. Deal with me according to Thy mercy, and teach me Thy justifications. I am Thy servant, give me understanding, that I may know Thy testimonies. Direct me according to Thy word, that I may never offend Thee. Make my heart keep Thy justifications without blame, that I may not be confounded before Thee. Thou art my head and my chief: govern Thy member and Thy slave. Thou art my First Cause: use and direct Thy instrument."

CHAPTER III.

WHAT IS A SPIRITUAL MAN?

A SPIRITUAL man is nothing more than an excellent Christian, for the excellence of a Christian consists in possessing more perfectly and abundantly than ordinary men that which constitutes the Christian, namely: the Spirit of Jesus Christ, our Lord and Saviour. We may discourse of the spiritual life in three ways: First, as the principle of corporal life, since the soul is the source of all the functions which the living body can exercise. Secondly, as the soul united to the body, which it animates and vivifies. And, thirdly, with reference to the vital actions which the body thus vivified produces. The life of our body, which is our soul, communicates to the body all its beauty and perfection; life is, in fact, but the presence of the soul in the body, which it animates, by which this body walks, sees, desires, imagines and performs all its other functions. When our body is dead, we no longer see, or walk, or exercise any vital function, because the soul has left its earthly tenement. Life, under the first and second aspects, is called, by philosophers, life in its root or source; and under the third, life in its exercise and use.

If you ask me what is the principle of the spiritual life, I answer in the words of St. Bernard: "God is the true life of the soul;" and with St. Austin: "As the soul is the life of the body, so God is the life of the soul; and as the body dies when the soul leaves it, so the soul would die if God should abandon it. Whence has your body its life? From your soul. Whence does your soul derive its life? From God. Your body cannot animate itself. It is the soul that animates the body: so, the soul does not communicate life to itself; it is God who vivifies it."

2. The life of the soul is peculiarly attributed to the Holy Ghost, whose special office it is to sanctify souls, and distribute to them the divine gifts, of which He Himself is the chief. Hence He is called, by excellence, *the gift of God*, and consequently the source of all other gifts. It is He who properly vivifies the soul, because He is God; and the Church, in the Creed recited at Mass, calls Him *the Lord and Life-giver*. He is communicated to holy souls, for, as our Lord says, *"that which is born of flesh is flesh, and what is born of spirit is spirit."* But there is also a bad spiritual life, which the wicked spirits inspire, and which is known by its fruits. The divine Spirit confers sanctity, purity and innocence. He is the personal love of the Father and the Son—the bond which unites them; therefore, He changes souls into sacred salamanders, capable of living in the intense flames of divine love. Moses, treating of the creation of man, says that God, having formed him from the slime of the earth, breathed upon his face the breath of life, and man became a living soul; that is to say, according to the explanation of St. Basil, that He filled his soul, figured by the *face* as the most beautiful part of the body, with His divine Spirit, who is equal to Himself.

The Holy Ghost, then, is the principle of life. His presence in the soul is the presence of grace and charity; the actions of the spiritual life are performed by His grace and inspiration. As the soul communicates its life to the body, as it looks through our eyes, hears with our ears, touches with our hands, and loves with our hearts, so the divine Spirit confers His life on the soul, raises it above itself, and renders it capable of grace and glory. He loves God in our will, thinks of Him in our understanding, and, according to St. Paul, inspires our prayers, for He Himself *asketh for us with unspeakable groanings*.

3. The Holy Ghost is the life of our souls, because He is the Spirit of Jesus. "He shall receive of me," says our Lord, "the truths He will announce to you. When the Holy Ghost cometh, whom I will send from the Father, He will teach you all truth." "He calls him *the Spirit of Truth*," says St. Cyril, "because he is the Spirit of Christ, and Christ is Truth, since He has said: 'I am the way, the truth and the life.'" He has merited, by His sufferings and death, that the Holy Ghost should imprint His virtues and engrave His image on our souls. Whence the Fathers, especially the Greeks, in choice, appropriate language, style Him "the image, the Face, the Word, and the Seal of the Son." They designate Him, too, the Breath of the Son, His Exhalation, His Balm, His Perfume, His Strength, His Energy.

As the Holy Ghost is the Spirit of Jesus, He communicates to souls the life of Jesus, for which reason St. Paul tells the Colossians that, "when Christ shall appear, who is their life," they will produce the actions of this life by practising meekness, gentleness, charity, and other virtues on the model He has left them. "The law of the spiritual life in Christ Jesus," says he, "has delivered me from the law of sin and death." Cajetan remarks that the apostle, in the chapter from which these words are taken, mentions six different laws, namely: the law of our mind, the law of our members, the law of sin, the law of death, the law of God, and the law of the spiritual life in Christ. The law of our mind is reason, which inclines us to act in a rational manner. The law of our members is concupiscence, which impels us to gratify our passions, careless whether we resist reason or follow its guidance; whether we please God, or displease Him. The law of sin plunges us into all sorts of vice. The law of death condemns us inevitably to lose our lives. The law of God is contained in His precepts, which teach us His will, and exhort us to accomplish it perfectly. Finally, the law of the spiritual life in Christ is the law of a virtuous life, on the model of Jesus Christ. The Old Law, given by Moses to the Jews, and the New Law, given by our Lord to Christians, are both good, inasmuch as they have emanated from the Holy Ghost. But the latter has this advantage over the former, that it models us on Christ, to the end that our words, works and affections may be conformable to His. "The Spirit of the Lord," says St. Paul, "engraves on our souls and bodies the resemblance of Christ." By it we are assimilated to Him.

In effect, Jesus Christ is the work of the Holy Spirit, who formed Him in the chaste womb of Mary, according to the words of the Angel Gabriel to our Lady: "The Holy Ghost shall come upon thee, and the power of the Most High shall overshadow thee. Therefore the Holy One who will be born of thee shall be called the Son of God." He, too, forms this Holy One in our souls, for "no one can name the Lord Jesus but by the Holy Ghost," as the apostle assures us.

Whoever, then, who is truly spiritual has the spirit of Jesus ever present in his soul, by grace and charity. This spirit animates and assists Him to lead a holy and divine life, producing all his mental and physical acts on the model of those of Jesus Christ.

§ 1.—*Continuation of the same subject.*

St. Lawrence Justinian, treating this subject, says: "I esteem those persons truly spiritual who subdue the appetites and passions of the flesh; who subject the body to the spirit, the soul to reason, affection to devotion, and all their designs to the guidance of the Eternal Wisdom." Behold the scope of this celestial science, wherein consists true spirituality.

Behold how nature is elevated above itself, and makes every day new progress in virtue. Another wise and learned author observes that we may judge of what the spiritual man is by contrasting him with the carnal man. The one thinks only of the base pleasures of sense, desiring and eagerly seeking terrestrial and sensual things; the other is emulous of adorning his noblest part, his soul, with every virtue, and thus uniting himself to God. The one leads the life of a soulless animal, incapable of seeing or knowing its great Creator; the other, as far as is possible here below, lives as if he had no body, because the Spirit of Jesus governs him in all things.

St. Bernard, or the author of the Epistle to the Carthusians of Mont-Dieu, says well on this subject: "The animal life desires only to satisfy its own sensuality; when the soul departs, as it were, through the senses, the body seeks only its own gratification. But the spiritual life desires only what is spiritual, spiritualizing even the body and other corporal things by tending to God in them, as the carnal man in all his thoughts, words, actions, imaginations and affections, tends only to sensual things." "Carnal men have only carnal thoughts," says the apostle; they are capable of valuing and esteeming only what gratifies their passions; while spiritual men desire only spiritual things, and esteem and love only the pleasures of the soul. St. Paul describes natural and spiritual persons under the names of the interior and the exterior man; the old man and the new man; the earthly man and the heavenly man. The man who is natural, old and earthly, is the sinner, whose soul and body, with their members and faculties, receive their movements from pride, anger, avarice and other vices. The interior, new and celestial man is he whose soul is clothed with grace, ornamented by charity, and replenished by the Holy Spirit, the principle of all his works, who resides in his understanding, to direct his thoughts, and in his will, to produce its affections; who looks through his eyes, hears with his ears, touches with his hands, and models all his actions on those of our Lord Jesus Christ.

St. Macarius, illustrating this subject, says, that when the devil takes possession of a man, by means of sin, he puts manacles on his hands and fetters on his feet, reducing him to a vile, base slavery. He clothes him with the black robes of pride, blasphemy, infidelity and avarice. He leaves nothing in the human soul or body which he does not disfigure, reversing the whole order of God. It is the devil that guides all the members and faculties of the sinner, and corrupts the whole man by his contagious touch. We read that the tyrant Maxentius used to bind dead bodies on the bodies of the living whom he wished to slay, joining hand to hand, foot to foot, face to face, till the living wretch expired in intolerable tortures, and there were two dead instead of one. Behold a figure of how the sinner is clothed, and to what he is joined.

The Holy Ghost, on the contrary, wishes to make the natural man become spiritual, the sinner just, the wicked man good. He would despoil the sinner of his vesture of opprobrium, and cover him with the brilliant robes and precious jewels of grace, of charity, and of all the virtues peculiar to the new man. Instead of the body of sin, and the soul of iniquity, the Lord and Life-giver designs to bestow on him the immaculate body and soul of Jesus Christ, who will guide and direct him here, and sanctify him both in soul and body.

§ 2.—*Of the actions of a spiritual man.*

As, according to philosophers, effects are always in proportion to their cause, the actions of the spiritual man, being inspired by the Holy Spirit, and performed on the model of Christ, must, of necessity, be holy and excellent. The actions of the spiritual life are to love God for His own sake, to prefer interior to exterior goods, heaven to earth, eternity to time; to chastise the body, and keep it in subjection, as a rebellious servant, after the example of St. Paul; to refuse what it desires, and impose what it does not wish for; to look upon wealth as an obstacle to salvation; to despise the honor and esteem given by men, and to desire contempt and opprobrium. The actions peculiar to the sensual life are: to prefer self to God, to flatter the body, to love riches, to seek self-interest, to covet honorable offices, and to fly sufferings and contempt.

The actions of the spiritual life are produced by the inspirations of the Holy Spirit, and not according to the movements of passion. I love some one who loves me, and wishes me well: this is not properly an action of the spiritual life, for dogs and cats do the same. But I love a man who hates me, who defames and persecutes me: this is an action of the spiritual life, because it is inspired by the Holy Spirit, the personal love of God, who loved us and gave us His own Son when we were His enemies, and who, even after we had crucified this dear Son, gave us His Holy Spirit, who will abide with us forever. "He maketh His sun to shine on the bad as well as the good, and sendeth His rain upon the just and upon the unjust." I am sad, I wish to indulge my melancholy in silence; or, if I speak, my words are rude, bitter, or impatient. Magpies and parrots are silent in this fashion; they grow sulky when they do not want to be gay; and bad weather gives the swan periodical fits of ill-humor. But if, when tempted to indulge melancholy and weariness, I strive to overcome my imperfect inclinations, compose my countenance sweetly, speak with gentleness, kindness and politeness,—this is to act as a spiritual person. I grieve because I am despised and undervalued; well, so do Turks and pagans. But if I receive their attacks upon my honor with patience and humility, casting my eyes not on secondary causes, but on God, the First Cause, considering that this contempt is sent by Him for His glory and my perfection, it immediately becomes a fruitful source of merit to me, and I prove myself, on this occasion, a truly spiritual person.

The apostle expatiates diffusely on the characteristics of the two lives: "The flesh," says he, "wars against the spirit, and the spirit against the flesh." By the flesh is understood the sinner; by the spirit, he who leads a virtuous life. But let us ask him to specify the works of the flesh? He answers: idleness, idolatry, envies, jealousies, quarrels, dissensions, homicides, gluttony, and other monstrous vices which close forever the gates of paradise. But the fruits of the Holy Spirit are charity, joy, peace, patience, benignity, mildness, longanimity, modesty, faith, continence and chastity.

Since we have the honor to be Christians, and desire to live conformably to our profession, we must divest ourselves entirely of the vices of the old man, and clothe ourselves with the virtues of the new man, that is, with the likeness of God which sin had obscured in our souls. We must become merciful and compassionate to our neighbor; meek, humble, modest and patient, sweetly supporting the defects of others, and forgiving all injuries with a good heart, as God forgives us. Above all, we must preserve and increase charity, which is the bond of perfection, loving all men in Christ and for Him, and loving Him in all. We must endeavor to have Him in our hearts, our inclinations, our thoughts, our words and our works, that He may be in reality our Sovereign Lord. To be truly spiritual, it is not enough to perform one or two spiritual actions; nor are we purely sensual because we yield once or twice to our passions. These things, when *persevered* in for days, months, years, render us really spiritual or really sensual.

We should not describe a secular as a highly spiritual person, because he says his morning prayers, fasts when the Church obliges Him to fast, gives an alms sometimes, but spends the residue of his life in temporal occupations, performed in a worldly spirit. But we describe as spiritual a person who is *generally* employed in good works, and fulfils the duties of his state through a motive of virtue, and with the spirit of God. It is not necessary that the soldier should always have his sword in hand, or that the merchant should always be occupied in buying or selling; that the horsedealer should always be purchasing horses; but it is necessary that whoever makes open profession of warfare or traffic, should employ himself *chiefly* in what regards his calling, spending in these occupations a considerable portion of his time.

St. Eucherius says very well on this subject: "We do not account a person a sage for having some trait of wisdom, or a prophet because he sometimes happens to predict a future event with accuracy. You need not imagine yourself truly spiritual because you recite daily, but tepidly, the Divine Office, or make a little half-hour's meditation, with a distracted mind, and are, nevertheless, very careless of avoiding venial sin and moderating your impetuosity. Do you really regulate your affections, practise true virtue, seek purity of heart? Do you not, on the contrary, waste your time in useless employment, secular affairs, and superfluous discourses? You are deceived if you act thus, and yet imagine yourself a spiritual man. You are only like a rustic among a troop of prophets; and we say to you, not with real admiration, but in derision, what was said to the ancient ass-hunter: "What has happened to this son of Cis? Behold a wonder! What! is Saul among the prophets?"

2. To be spiritual, it is not necessary that we never experience any assaults of the passions, but only that we do not acquiesce in them. "Walk in the spirit," says St. Paul, "and

fulfil not the desires of the flesh." He does not affirm that you are *exempt* from these desires, as if you had no body, but only that you must not *yield* to them. One may be assailed for many days by bad thoughts and sensual emotions ; he may be tempted to vanity, envy, impatience; he may suffer from obscurities of the understanding, aridities of the will, sadness of the soul ; he may be distracted in his prayers, experience great difficulty in the practice of virtue, and, notwithstanding, become truly spiritual, because it is not these things, but the *consent* to these things, that can injure him. To be truly spiritual, we are not obliged to be free from these miseries and assaults, but only to vanquish them. Let us, then, embrace this excellent and divine life, and strive to become really spiritual. *Walk in the spirit*, says St. Paul, live like spiritual persons : "My brethren, we are not debtors to the flesh, that we should live according to the flesh, for, if you live in this manner, you shall die ; but if, by the spirit, you mortify the deeds of the flesh, you shall live. " Certainly, the life of a Christian ought to be a spiritual life, since it is a sketch of the life he is destined to lead in heaven. The life of grace is the commencement of the life of glory, and glory is only grace perfected. Our life in heaven will be perfectly spiritual, because not only will our soul be animated by the Divine Spirit, but our body, also, will have become, as St. Paul says, a spiritual body. Hence, as Christians, our profession is to live like spiritual persons, governed, not by the movements of the flesh, but by those of the Holy Ghost.

§ 3.—*How to discern between a man who is truly spiritual, and one who is spiritual only in appearance.*

We are liable to be deceived by the mere guise of virtue, for actions apparently good may be only phantoms of goodness. A man may wear the face of a spiritual man, and use the words of one, who, nevertheless, has neither the heart nor the works of one, so that we may say of him what Isaac said to his youngest son, when he disguised himself as the elder : "The voice, indeed, is the voice of Jacob, but the hands are the hands of Esau." There are certain animals in nature which, at a distance, shine like stars, but when you view them closely, you find they are only worms. All is not gold that glitters, nor is every brilliant that sparkles a diamond. When Pope Clement VIII was attacked by the malady of which he died, the physicians proclaimed that the sovereign remedy for his disease was contained in a very rare stone ; whereupon the servants of the Pontiff procured these stones in such abundance that the doctors had to prohibit the bringing of any more : yet in this great quantity they found only one little morsel, which was capable of easing the pains of the patient. In like manner, among men and women, religious and secular, several make professions of piety who are not really spiritual. "Oh, how few men are truly spiritual!" exclaims St. Lawrence Justinian ; "and of the many who bear the name, how few show the effects!" *I know thy works*, said the angel to the Bishop of Sardis ; I know thou seemest to be alive, but, nevertheless, thou art dead, for thou dost not lead a really holy life.

The prophet Ezekiel relates that God one day ordered him to make a hole in the wall of the temple, and, by looking through it, learn how the men and women consecrated to the divine service comported themselves. And having done so, he saw seventy old men with censers in their hands, incensing and adoring idols, and the images of serpents, lizards and other animals, which were frescoed on the walls ; and after that, "women bewailing their Adonis : " that is to say, men who adored their passions, and women who lamented the loss of their lights and consolations, when God, for their trial or purification, allowed them to experience darkness and aridities ; for women are somewhat subject to have their *Adonis*, to seek their pleasures even in the spiritual life. Behold how false spirituality masks itself! But there are certain and secure marks of true spirituality, infallible criteria, which enable us to distinguish the real diamond from the false gem.

1. It is well known and commonly remarked that a man does not become spiritual by his habit, or by exterior show, or by pious discourses, or by making profession of a holy life. Were this the case, all ecclesiastics and religious would be truly spiritual. Now, as all know, it may happen that while the body is clothed with a holy habit, the soul may wear the garb of sin and evil customs; that the profession of a heavenly life may be joined to the practices of an earthly life; that pious talk may originate in evil designs and infamous thoughts, and that a sanctified exterior may cover a corrupt and sensual heart. Do we not see in the theatres that the son of a peasant can assume the name and vesture of a prince, and feign the actions of an Alexander or a Cæsar? Do we not know that a hypocrite can assume the virtues of the greatest saints? Our Lord Himself said to His apostles: "One of you is a devil." Notwithstanding his fasts, and miracles, and exterior show, Judas was a devil, because he performed the works of one.

2. A person is not spiritual because he approaches the sacraments frequently, spends much time in prayer, is often seen in the church; otherwise, all who profess a devout life would be truly spiritual, which they are not. "Miserable man that thou art!" cries out St. Bernard, "thou takest great pains to polish thy exterior, and yet dost neglect thy interior; thou thinkest thyself to be something, whereas thou art nothing. Thou art deceived, and the word of the prophet Osee shall be executed in thee: "Strangers have devoured his strength, and he knew it not; yea, grey hairs are spread about him, and he is ignorant thereof." Thou bearest the tonsure, thou keepest the fasts of the order, thou art present at the singing of the Office, but thy heart is far from me, saith the Lord.

If thou desirest to know whether thou art truly spiritual, consider what thou lovest and what thou fearest; examine the source of thy joy and thy sadness. See if thou dost not love forbidden pleasures, or if thou dost not love even lawful pleasures with a disorderly affection. Art thou not afraid of poverty, injury and contempt? Dost thou not desire too ardently the affection, the esteem, the praises of creatures, and, when these fail thee, art thou not presently overwhelmed with sorrow?"

3. Jesus Christ is the great original and perfect exemplar of truly spiritual persons. No one can be spiritual who is not formed on this pattern, who does not bear His traits, and imitate His virtues. The whole secret of spirituality is contained in these words, *Verbum caro factum est;* the divinity is united to humanity, which, by this august union, becomes infinitely holy. Whoever desires to be spiritual must lead the life of the spirit—a life superior to the senses. The spiritual man, by his very name, is supposed to lead an interior life. "Be converted to me with your whole heart," says God, by the prophet Joel. He does not say, change your body, change your dress, change your condition, but change and convert your whole heart to me.

"Behold the hour cometh and now is!" said Jesus to the woman of Samaria, "when true adorers shall adore the Father in spirit and in truth, for the Father also seeketh such to adore Him. God is a spirit, and they that adore Him must adore Him in spirit and in truth." Behold the important instruction our Lord gave to this woman, to show the difference between Christianity and Judaism, between the New Law and the Old. In the Old Law more care was taken to strike the senses than to please God. Not only the common men, but those who were accounted the most pious, as the Pharisee, were accustomed to wash often, to take baths when they returned from any secular business, and to wash even the couches on which they reclined while they took their repasts. "The Pharisees and all the Jews," says St. Mark, "eat not without often washing their hands, holding the tradition of the ancients : 'And when they come from market, unless they be washed they eat not, and many other things there are that have been delivered to them to observe : the washing of cups and pots, and of brazen vessels and of beds.'" The Christian law has abolished these superstitious ablutions. It teaches us rather to purify the heart and soul by interior acts of faith, hope, charity, and other virtues ; and, retrenching the multitudes of Jewish ceremonies, it has established but few exterior symbols, and these are most significant ; it places its chief study in adoring and glorifying God in *spirit and in truth*. *In spirit*, because God is a spirit, and a spirit naturally demands spiritual worship. "*Shall I eat the flesh of bullocks?*" asks David, "*or drink the blood of goats?* Shall I not rather offer to God a sacrifice of praise ?" God being the Sovereign Lord of the universe, the best of everything should be offered to Him ; our soul is our most glorious possession, being immortal and divine, and, consequently, it is with it that we all must serve Him. Our worship, moreover, must be true, which it cannot be if the mind and the will do not produce it ; for it is possible that a man should show great exterior reverence, and kneel before God, yet rebel against Him in heart, and, consequently, not worship Him in truth. This is what God complains of by the prophet Isaias, when He says : *This people honor me with their lips*, they glorify me with their words, *but their heart is far from me ;* their affections are not placed on me.

St. Basil and St. Athanasius say, moreover, that to adore God *in spirit* is to adore Him by the movements of the Holy Spirit, not by those of nature or humor ; to adore Him with the acts and affections which the Holy Spirit suggests, for the intentions which He inspires, and for the ends for which He

communicates His graces ; and, as He is the personal love of
God, to adore and serve God in Him is to act always through
a motive of pure and perfect love. They add, that to adore
God *in truth* is to adore Him with sincere adoration in His
Son, who is the Truth, to love and serve Him on the model
this Divine Son has given us, to adopt His views, and in all
things to follow Him as closely as we are able.

These are the marks of true spirituality, which we must
strive earnestly to acquire. Remember the device of Am-
phiaraus, *Non videre, sed esse :* not the appearance, but the
reality. God rejected from among the victims He chose to be
offered to Him the swan and the ostrich—the swan because it
has white feathers and black flesh, and the ostrich because it
has wings, but cannot fly. The three children in the fiery
furnace did not invite the rainbow to praise God, with all the
other creatures, because, though it appears to be exceedingly
beautiful, yet its colors are not real colors, and its beauty is
an optical illusion. God is a Spirit, and hence He wishes to
be adored in spirit and in truth : *in truth*, not deceitfully ; *in
spirit*, not by mere exterior observances. We must not serve
God as did the Jews of the synagogue, but after the manner
of true Christians. Let us, then, imitate St. Paul, who says
of himself : God is my witness, *whom I serve in my spirit*, not
in the Ancient Law, but in the New Law ; in the Gospel of
His Son, Christ Jesus, and according to the example He has
given.

§ 4.—*The spiritual man leads a life above the senses.*

The spiritual man leads a life disengaged from the things
of the body ; he has the name and appearance of man, but he
is not inordinately attached to mere natural pleasures. Moses
relates that God made birds and fishes of the same element,
namely, water ; the fishes to live always in it, but the birds to

fly above it, and people the higher regions. This illustrates true and false spirituality : spiritual and sensual persons are made of the same material, but the sensual are content in their natural element, while the spiritual soar far above it.

Whoever is attached to sensual gratification, nay, whoever does not occasionally mortify his body even in lawful things, can never become truly spiritual ; he may, indeed, have the appearance of spirituality, but he cannot possess the reality. "My Spirit shall not remain forever in man, because he is flesh," said God, in the days of Noah. And, as St. Paul says : "Flesh and blood cannot possess the kingdom of God." The sensual man in incapable of discerning the things of God's Spirit. Isaias asks who are they to whom God will communicate His lights, and he answers : "Those who are weaned from milk, those who have left the breast;" and Job tells us that "wisdom is not found in the land of them that live in delights." Richard of St. Victor says : " Never shall the will of man be inflamed with the desire of eternal things, nor his understanding capable of contemplating them, if he have too much care of his body, even in things permitted and necessary." Remark these last words.

The spirit is diametrically opposed to the flesh, and the spiritual life to the sensual life. The heavens are not more elevated above the earth than is the spirit above the body. As the eye cannot distinguish sounds, nor the ear perceive colors, so man, of his own nature, cannot discern spiritual things, nor even desire them : this is the work of grace.

Moses, perceiving in the desert the burning bush, said : "I shall go and see this great wonder: a bush on fire, and yet not consumed." But immediately his progress was retarded, and he heard a voice saying to him: "Loose thy shoes from off thy feet, for the ground upon which thou standest is holy." St. Ambrose explains that the shoes, which were made of the skins of beasts, signify our body, our disorderly affections, which we must put off before we become capable of receiving the knowledge of divine things. The Book of Wisdom contains the following apposite passage: "This corruptible body weighs down the soul, and the earthly tabernacle presses upon the mind that muses on many things." The necessities of the body are a heavy burden to the soul; they render the exercises of piety difficult and even insipid, casting drops of gall upon our milk and honey, which drops, if they do not destroy the sweetness, at least embitter it to a greater or less extent.

Hence when sensual persons experience some touches of devotion, such feelings ought generally to be regarded as the productions of their soft, effeminate nature, rather than the movements of grace. Women, who are naturally tender and compassionate, weep when they read of the sufferings of our Lord, or when their faults are represented to them; but their tears are of little value before God unless they sincerely resolve to correct these faults, and take part in these sufferings.

2. The faculty of reasoning and judging with which we are endowed resides not in the body but in the soul, whence we must infer that the body of itself can be guided only by passion. It cannot discern whether its movements accord with the commandments of God or oppose them, whether they conduce to its salvation or its ruin. It desires to eat on a fast day as well as on any other day, without examining whether eating be prohibited or not. But the soul is ruled by reason and by grace; and consequently, whoever wishes to lead the life of the spirit must be detached from his body, and resist its unlawful desires.

3. The world, the flesh and the devil are our three capital enemies, but the flesh is the most dangerous of all, because the two others are outside of ourselves, but this is within us. Enemies who attack our houses from without are dangerous, but a domestic enemy is incomparably more so. The devil

addressed himself to Eve, who typifies the flesh, as St. Austin and St. Bernard remark, and through her he ruined Adam. As we know that the world and the devil are obstinately bent on accomplishing our ruin, it is easy for us to foresee and ward off their attacks, because we are prepared for them. If you wish to break all commerce with the world you can retire into solitude, where you will be far from its snares, and secure against its charms; and if the devil should follow you thither, his power will be greatly weakened by the dissolution of partnership between him and his great ally, the world. But from ourselves we cannot fly: the flesh is always with us and in us. Flee to the arid desert or to desolate isles, to the heights of the mountains or the depths of the mines; go even where the devil cannot follow you, if that be possible, and you still must carry with you your most dangerous adversary. We hate our other enemies; nobody loves the devil, and we all admit that the world is the arch deceiver; but naturally, according to St. Paul, no one hates his own flesh; on the contrary, every one loves and caresses it. Even when we love the world, we love it not for its own sake, but for sake of the flesh which it pampers.

From all this it is clear that we ourselves are our own worst enemies, and consequently that, in order to be truly spiritual, we must renounce ourselves. In fact our own experience shows us that our want of progress results from our want of mortification. Our flesh inclines us to seek sensual satisfaction, to provide for our wants with unnecessary solicitude, to fly hunger, cold, contempt, sickness and afflictions; to murmur and complain when any little convenience is wanting to us. To all these natural and sensual weaknesses we must die, for, if we would live according to the spirit, *we must mortify the deeds of the flesh.*

§ 5.—*Other proofs of the same truth.*

Plato elegantly says that God has attached two wings to our souls, which wings are two inclinations to celestial things : one enables our understanding to fly to the first truth, the other raises our will toward the Sovereign Goodness ; and he adds that these wings are fettered and broken by the inordinate affection we have to our flesh. The felicity of man consists in the sovereign good, that is, in true wisdom ; and the greatest obstacle to the attainment of this is the burden of the body, which is subject to the illusions of the senses, and has, besides, its own peculiar necessities and infirmities. Hence, whoever desires to be truly wise and happy, must daily die more and more to the inclinations of corrupt nature. Our soul, according to the old philosophers, is inflamed with two contrary affections : the one impels us upward, toward the sovereign beauty ; the other drags us downward to corporal things. These domestic loves bear us, the one on high, hence called *Calodaemon*, or the good demon ; the other to earth, and is hence called *Cacodaemon*, the bad demon. These are the Eros and the Anteros of the ancients.

We have an excellent figure of this in Isaac and Ismael. Abraham had two wives : Sarah and Agar. Sarah was the lady of the house, she was of the noble blood of Abraham ; Agar was a slave and an Egyptian. Sarah, who had no children, was despised by Agar as soon as she herself expected to become a mother ; and, being unable to endure this, she complained of it to her husband, and dealt so hardly with the servant that she fled from the house. But an angel of the Lord admonished Agar to return and humble herself to her mistress, telling her that she should have a son who would become a great chief. This son, being born soon after, was called Ismael, and in the course of time God gave Sarah also a son, who was called Isaac. One day Sarah, the mistress, saw Ismael playing with her son Isaac, and she complained to Abraham, saying: "Cast out this bondwoman and her son, for the son of a slave shall not be heir with my son Isaac." And Abraham took this grievously for his son. And God said to him: "Let it not seem grievous to thee for the boy and for the bondwoman; in all that Sarah hath said to thee hearken, for in Isaac shall thy seed be called." Abraham punctually obeyed the divine injunction, and, giving Agar some bread and a bottle of water, sent her and the boy away. Behold the figure! Let us now make the application of this figure to our subject.

According to Philo every man has two spouses: a Sarah and an Agar, the spirit and the flesh; the soul is the mistress, and the flesh the servant. These wives have each a progeny; Agar gives birth to Ismael, and Sarah to Isaac; the flesh has its sensual appetites, and the spirit its inclinations to virtue. Ismael plays with Isaac, and Sarah is offended, because, during the play, according to the opinion of the doctors, Ismael, who was twenty years old, taught Isaac, who was only five, to make little idols and adore them; or he beat him, and had secretly resolved to murder him, that himself might become the heir; or that he taught him some other wicked practices. The flesh acts in this manner toward the spirit, inducing it to play, to waste time, to worship honors and riches, and to desire wicked pleasures. Hence we must *cast out the bondwoman and her son;* we must drive this vile servant and her offspring far from us.

The ancient Fathers, with much vigor and wisdom, describe, under fictitious names, the qualities and effects of the flesh. St. Gregory of Nazianzen elegantly calls it the *Remora of the soul*, because this life is a tempestuous sea, on which our soul will sail to a happy eternity, if our flesh do not arrest its course, and give it over to pirates, or dash it against the rocks with which the ocean abounds. Synesius says that it is a thick cloud, which obscures the rays of the sun of justice, and engenders the thunders and lightnings of our misfortunes. St. Ambrose describes it as a house of corruption, which covers the soul with uncleanness. St. Basil affirms that it is a prison, in which the soul is held captive; and as a prison is a dismal, poor place, and the prisoner often badly treated, so the soul suffers in the body if the body be permitted to rule it. Plato, and, before him, Pythagoras, called it a tomb, because a tomb is a narrow, dismal and infected place, which abounds in worms, and the body is no better with regard to its divine guest. Others have called it a powerful sorcerer, a most dangerous magician, which, by charms and enchantments, metamorphoses man, like another Circe, and treats him as Delilah treated Sampson, or as Hercules was treated by Omphale.

Let us hear the angel who exhorts us, saying: "Cast out the bondwoman and her son," and let us obey, like Abraham. "The wise man," said St. Ambrose, "in order that he may be capable of flying to God, disengages himself from terrestrial things, for how could the soul be elevated to the throne of truth unless she be raised above the body?" This is why the apostle cries out: "Touch not, taste not, handle not" that which may corrupt you, that which is desired by the flesh and its unruly appetites. As the soul is by death delivered from the contagion of the body, and freed from the captivity of the flesh, we ought, even during life, to imitate this death, by dying to our corrupt inclinations. Let us rise out of the sepulchre, leave, inasmuch as we can, the things of the flesh, and, borne aloft by the wings of ardent charity, fly toward our Sovereign God and Eternal Lover. Let us arise and come out of this place, that our youth may be renewed like the eagle's. Then shall our soul, like a royal eagle, pierce the clouds, spreading its wings on high, taking its flight toward heaven, secure from all dangers, for the bird that flies above the clouds easily escapes the nets of the fowler. The Spouse in the Canticles withdrew to a beautiful garden : let us, too, enter that happy place which Plato called the garden of Jupiter, the garden of the spirit, the orchard of wisdom, where grow the sweet and delicious fruits most suitable for our nourishment.

"The flesh," says St. Basil, "must be kept in subjection, and punished when it rebels. We must renounce what is unlawful, and be reserved and moderate even in the use of lawful pleasures, if we desire to acquire true wisdom. Pythagoras, having learned that one of his disciples was very effeminate, reproached him, saying : "Why do you not cease to cherish your miserable person?" The mortification of the senses is the beginning of the spiritual life, the annihilation of vice, and the enemy of voluptuousness. Sensuality puts us in the net of the devil, because it inclines us to commit sin, which is our ruin.

But let us hear the advice a pagan gives to his son : "My son, if thou dost not hate thy body, thou canst never truly love it. Thou canst not, simultaneously, apply thyself to divine and human things. All things are either matter or spirit, mortal or divine. The remembrance of spiritual things is the forgetfulness of sensual things. To choose divine things is blessedness and glory ; to choose human things is wickedness and misery." (Trismegistus.) "Let thy first study be," continues the same wise pagan, "to divest thyself of inordinate affection to thy body, this foundation of wickedness, this source of wickedness, this band of corruption, this thick veil which blinds thee, this living death, this moving sepulchre, this domestic enemy, which hates thee in caressing thee, and loves thee in hating thee. It covers thee as a tent or pavilion, lest thou shouldst see the beauty of truth, the happiness which virtue would place within thy reach, and the snares which the passions continually lay for thy destruction.

Hence, *cast out the bondwoman and her son*, though they be dearer to thee than Agar and Ismael were to Abraham. No matter how much you love them, delay not to take leave of them. It seems strange that a man so rich, so liberal, so hospitable, so merciful to the poor, should send away his wife and son with only a bottle of water and a loaf of bread; and Tostal remarks that he did it, not through want of good-will, but by a mystery, to teach us how we ought to treat our flesh and its appetites. Verily, since our flesh is our most prejudicial enemy, and the cause of most of our falls, we shall, if we are wise, treat it in a similar manner. We must remember that, if we yield to its passions, we cannot receive the lights and sentiments of God, because, as St. Peter assures us, we must mortify the flesh if we would live in the spirit. The passions are like those importunate creditors who are always watching at the door of a poor debtor, to seize him the moment he makes his appearance. If the flesh be not ruled, it will rule; for, as it cannot be a companion, it must necessarily be either the master or the valet. Now, how shameful it would be if the soul, which is created to govern the body, were to become the slave instead of the ruler of the passions and appetites!

If a man espoused to a rich, noble, learned and beautiful princess, should prefer a hideous Moorish slave, a wretch, a sorceress; if he should order his royal and legitimate bride to serve such a person in the meanest capacity, to wait on her, to flatter her,—would he not be considered infamous or mad? Yet this is what those do who prefer their bodies to their souls. The soul is a princess, issued from heaven, daughter of God, the Creator of the universe, the lady and queen of the earthly habitation: to suffer it to be ruled by the body would be worse than to subject a princess to a slave, for, after all, the princess and the slave are both women, endowed equally with a reasonable soul; whereas the soul is intrinsically superior to the body, and has nothing in common with it. Let not the slave, then, usurp the authority of the mistress; give the bondwoman the rank she deserves.

Let us ever regard our body as our greatest impediment in the way of virtue; let us regard it as a traitor and our slave, and strive to weaken its powers, to conquer its passions, and to resist its appetites. A man whose enemy lives with him is always on the defensive; he remains in constant fear of being surprised. Let us always be thus upon our guard against our domestic enemy, who is ever ready to attack us. When the body demands eating, drinking, sleep, clothing, or any little comfort, supply its wants so long as they are reasonable; but supply them only so far as they are consistent with the glory of God and the salvation of your soul.

We should give the body requisite nourishment, because otherwise it would not have sufficient strength to be used as an instrument of the soul. But this *requisite* is a very delicate and difficult point to decide, for self-love can use a thousand artifices to get what it desires, and it is not always easy to know *precisely* what is necessary. And if sometimes the body is treated, as regards food or any other necessity, a little better than usual, we must practise mortification in this very circumstance, so as not to satisfy our appetite fully, but hold a tight rein lest the servant begin to domineer over the mistress.

§ 6.—*Of the discernment of spirits.*

We have now to treat of the discernment of spirits, that is to say, of being able to distinguish when our interior movements are inspired by God, when the devil is their source, and when they come from ourselves. This is a very difficult and important matter, because it is of great consequence to us, and the things that it regards are spiritual, and, consequently, not easily understood; besides, we are generally very ignorant and blind, because of the thick veil of sin which obscures our understanding, and the deceit of the devil, who is more than our match in cunning. Yet, notwithstanding its apparent difficulty, it is easy if we watch closely over ourselves, and are sincere in our desires of perfection. St. Paul tells us to beware of Satan, for he can transform himself into an angel of light; he cautions us thus that we may reflect on what we are about, and, having "proved all things, hold fast to what is good." The beloved disciple says: "Believe not every spirit, but prove if the spirits be of God." And our Lord: "See that you be not seduced, for many will come in my name saying, I am the Christ." He was even accustomed to frequently say to His followers, as the Fathers remark, *Estote probi trapezitæ*: Be good money-changers; do not take false coin for genuine.

Our capacities are so limited, our lights so poor and scanty, our providences so uncertain, that, in order to hinder us from being deceived, God has given to His Church, according to St. Paul, the gift of *discerning spirits:* but, to speak of this with accuracy, I will premise:—

1. That the word *spirit* in the Holy Scriptures signifies a great many different things; but we here understand it to be the interior movements by which our soul is excited by knowledge in the understanding, and inclination in the will, to do, or refrain from doing, some action.

2. That St. Thomas teaches that the discernment of spirits is a heavenly prudence, by the light of which he who possesses this gift has a clear perception as regards the things of salvation, which he could not have by mere human intelligence; that he penetrates the depth of consciences, and discovers the secrets of hearts, in order to judge rightly of them. St. Chrysostom says that this penetration is the true difference between one who is solidly spiritual, and one who has only the

kernel of spirituality; between a true prophet and a soothsayer. "It is," says another, "a supernatural light by which is distinguished good from bad, precious stones from false brilliants, and the inspirations of God from the illusions of the devil and the movements of nature."

3. St. Bernard mentions six different species of spirits for the discernment of which this gift is conferred. These are: the divine, the angelic, the diabolical, the human, the carnal and the worldly, which are all mentioned in various parts of the Holy Scriptures. Of these six spirits, three are evidently bad, namely, those of the world, the flesh and the devil; one is neither good nor bad, but indifferent, namely, the human spirit, which becomes virtuous or vicious according to the side it takes. And as the spirit of an angel acts only by the orders of God, and is the minister of the Spirit of God, it is necessarily good; hence five of our spirits are reduced to two: the good and the bad, the spirit of God and the spirit of the devil, while the human spirit hovers between these two, and is led sometimes directly by the Spirit of God, sometimes through the ministry of His angels, and again by the devil directly, or by him through the instrumentality of the world and the flesh; hence all species of spirits may be reduced to three, namely: the divine, the human and the diabolical.

By the gift of spiritual discernment, a person may distinguish these spirits, and thereby discover the source of our thoughts, words and affections; he can penetrate the sentiments of other men, and, by a ray of this light, perceive their origin, and the origin of his own, also, as St. Monica did, according to the relation of her son, St. Austin: "She told me," says he, "that she could discern between the revelations she received from God and the vagaries of her imagination, by a certain interior sweetness which her soul experienced, but which she could not explain." "She knew this," says Gerson, "by an inspiration which she felt in the depth of her heart, by a hidden manna which her soul tasted, or by rays of the sun of justice, shot forth from the eternal hills, which chased away all doubt and darkness." Let us now come to the marks by which we may distinguish what proceeds from the Spirit of God from that which proceeds from the devil.

There are two passages in the Bible which diffuse much light on this subject, by contrasting the qualities of the Spirit of God with those of the diabolical spirit. The first is from the Apostle St. James, who says, in his Canonical Epistle: "*The wisdom that is from above,*" that is to say, the Spirit of God, "*first, indeed, is chaste, then peaceable, modest, easy to be persuaded, consenting to the good, full of mercy and good fruits, without judging, without dissimulation.*" The spirit of the devil is directly contrary to all this. The other passage is taken from the Book of Wisdom, when the Sage gives to the Church of God these illustrious titles and magnificent eulogies: "In her is the spirit of understanding, holy, one, manifold, subtle, eloquent, active, modified, sure, sweet, loving what is good, beneficent, gentle, kind, merciful, having all virtues." The spirit is holy because it proceeds from sanctity itself, which is God. One, because it draws the soul from multiplicity to unity, and unites it to God, who is one and very simple. Diverse, because it leads to perfection by different paths. Subtle, because it enters the understanding and the will by unknown doors and by secret ways; causes that to promote our salvation which we think may injure us. It is persuasive, because it speaks to the soul words of life so sweet, so eloquent and so efficacious, that it produces whatever effect it pleases. It is active, because it gives the heart prompt and sudden movements, and works in it admirable changes. Pure, because it confers purity of soul and body, and inspires a horror of the least word or thought that could sully chastity. Certain, because it does not affirm anything but what is established on eternal truth. Sweet, humane, meek, because it inspires those qualities. It loves good, because it inclines to good, and turns away from evil. It is steady, because it fortifies the soul in her weakness, and gives her courage and resolution. It is omnipotent to touch the obstinate, to enlighten the blind, to inflame the cold and tepid, to regulate the passions, to root out vices the most inveterate, and to heal maladies the most desperate. These are the magnificent qualities that clearly distinguish the Spirit of God from the spirit of the devil, which is diametrically opposite.

§ 7.—*Particular marks to discern spirits in particular cases.*

The inspirations of God are invariably truth, sanctity, doctrine, and the imitation of Jesus Christ; while the suggestions of the devil are deceit, vice, and all that is contrary to our Lord. As it is impossible that the sun should produce darkness, or cease to shine where he is, so the Spirit of God cannot produce anything but what is true and holy, without any mixture of falsehood or sin. *All Thy ways are true,* says David, and *all Thy words are true,* because they flow from truth itself. As the Spirit of God is the Spirit of Jesus Christ, it insinuates into the soul the virtues which Jesus Christ has practised, and the truths which He has taught, giving light to know the truths, and power to practise His virtues, and working continually to perfect His image in our souls.

On the contrary, as the devil is the father of lies, all his suggestions tend to produce falsehood and sin, whence come heresies, novelties in religion, illusions in the spiritual life, false weights and measures for vice and virtues, holiness which is but the mere smattering of sanctity, false humility instead of true, deceitful patience, pretended obedience, spurious charity, modesty and devotion, instead of such virtues as are solid and sure. His suggestions teach us to make light of our defects, to value the honors and esteem of this world; they inspire a contempt for small faults, and innumerable errors concerning perfection. And because he nourishes a furious hatred against our Lord, who has conquered him, and destroyed his empire, he always and everywhere, to the utmost extent of his ability, thwarts His designs, and strives to rob Him of His glory; in short, the devil is the true Antichrist, of whom he that is to come will be only the minister. He strives to induce men to sin, and, if he cannot succeed, he makes the most strenuous efforts to hinder their progress in perfection, and tarnish their virtues. When he has unusual power over men, he makes them use language of hatred, contempt and blasphemy against God, as appears evidently in sorcerers, magicians, and those into whose bodies he enters by possession.

2. The suggestions of the Spirit of God always tend to the glory of God and our salvation, exciting us continually to desire and procure the honor of God, and extend His glory by all our thoughts, words and works, whether toward ourselves or our neighbors, to render our actions holy and perfect, according to our state in life, and the measure of grace conferred on us. On the contrary, as Satan is the irreconcilable enemy of God, who banished him from heaven, and condemned him to hell, this proud spirit unceasingly endeavors to dishonor God and hinder His glory. And since, with all his efforts, he cannot injure God, he discharges his fury against man, who is the divine image, whom he tempts to commit enormous sins, and, if resisted in this point, to venial sins and imperfections, gnawing and biting what he cannot entirely destroy; prowling about for this purpose like a roaring lion, as St. Peter remarks.

3. The Spirit of God animates the soul to virtue, and bestows on it peace and consolation. The soul in which He dwells has one evident sign of His indwelling, which is holi-

ness. He bestows humility in a special manner, and inspires humble thoughts and sentiments. St. Bernard, speaking from his own experience, says, at some length: "When the Divine Spirit enters a heart, it awakes from its slumbers; His touch sweetens and mollifies the heart that was bitter, and hard as a stone. He roots out and demolishes, He builds and He plants on the ruins; He waters the herb dying of thirst, He enlightens my darkness, opens that which was sealed, inflames that which was cold, rectifies crooked paths, and thus draws from my soul great sentiments of gratitude for His goodness, and from my mouth a thousand praises and benedictions. I recognize His presence, and the certainty of His visit, by the secret changes I feel in my heart, by the diminished heat of concupiscence, by the correction of my manners, and the reformation of my interior. If, after the fire of penance has purified the conscience, and consumed the rust of its vices, we feel the heart suddenly dilate with joy, and the understanding replenished with light, let us not doubt that these operations result from the divine glance of the Spouse."

The eyes of the Spouse are compared, in the Canticles, to the eyes of doves: "Thine eyes are as the eyes of doves." Why as the eyes of doves? It would seem a richer comparison to resemble them to the eyes of the eagle, or the eyes of the lynx, which are extremely piercing. But the Holy Ghost would teach us that the eyes of our Lord, like those of the dove, are pure and loving, and that His visits produce purity, horror of sin, and the love of God. "His eyes seemed a flame of fire," says St. John: now, fire purifies, warms, inflames and penetrates. "The eyes of Jesus," says Rupert, "are the windows of salvation, the gates of mercy, by which grace and virtue enter and come out." Some have aptly represented them as darting rays like the sun, one of which, falling on a dead body, resuscitates it; another, on a rock, breaks it to pieces, and a third, on a mountain, liquefies it like wax; with these words for a motto : *The eyes of God to us.* See, then, what the glances of our Saviour can work in us, when we oppose no obstacles to His merciful designs.

Thus our Lord, by casting His eyes on Magdalen, Matthew, and other sinners, dead and hardened to grace, bruised their hearts and gave them life; and one look from Him made Peter dissolve in tears of love and contrition for his crime. "Those on whom Jesus looks," says St. Ambrose, "bewail their sins; His glance moves them to tears. Peter did not weep at his first or second denial of his Master, but at the third, because then Jesus looked upon him, and henceforth his eyes became a fountain of tears." O! how we should cry out with David : "O Lord! look upon me, and have mercy on me. Regard me with those eyes that raise the dead, that break rocks, that melt mountains, that soften the hardest hearts, that enlighten the blind, that inflame the frozen. With these eyes Thou dost not look on the reprobates, nor on senseless animals, but only on Thy elect. With them Thou didst cause the tears of Peter to flow, and didst attract Matthew from his custom-house, and didst inflame the sinful heart of Magdalen. With the same eyes, O Jesus! look Thou on me, and have mercy on me!"

The inspirations of God confer peace and repose, working the effect of the words which Jesus said to the apostles, after His resurrection : *Peace be with you.* The Royal Prophet says : "I will hear what the Lord God will speak within me, for He will speak peace ; when He deigns to visit me, He will calm the agitation of my soul, and establish it in repose. He enters souls according to their dispositions, flowing on pure and holy souls like a gentle rain, which softens and moistens without noise ; but those in which vicious habits reign, He enters with force and terror, to the end that, after overcoming their resistance, and subjecting them to Himself, He may leave them in tranquillity and joy." "The look of Jesus," remarks

St. Bernard, "does not always produce the same effect; it diversifies itself according to the merit of him whom it regards, astonishing some and rejoicing others, intimidating these, and consoling those." In fine, God, as David says, *looks upon the earth ;* that is to say, upon the man that has an earthly heart, *and it trembles.* He terrifies sinners at first, and then consoles them. He must attack and destroy their sin, to render them capable of experiencing His peace and joy. "The voice of God," says the Saint of Clairvaux, "first terrifies the soul, but immediately after, if you be attentive, it vivifies, sweetens and melts it; it heats, enlightens and purifies it." And St. Augustine says very well, from his own experience: "What is this light which enters the eyes of my soul, and wounds my heart without hurting it? I am seized with fear, inasmuch as I am not like Him, and with desire, inasmuch as I resemble Him. It is wisdom and the Spirit of God which come to enlighten my soul, and with divine rays dissipate my darkness." It is necessary to remark that imperfection and vice are not the only source of the wonder and fear that the soul experiences in the visits of God. The brightness of the divine majesty, the beauty of His angelic messenger, the greatness of the wonders announced, or the extraordinary manner of the visit, is capable of producing this effect in pure and perfect souls, as happened to Daniel, when the angel announced to him the deliverance of the Jews from captivity; to Zachary, when the angel, on the part of God, promised him the birth of the Baptist; and even to our Lady herself, when the Archangel Gabriel treated with her concerning the mystery of the incarnation, and declared that God had chosen her to be His Mother, because this announcement seemed to touch her virginity, of which she was exceedingly jealous.

The devil operates in a manner utterly opposed to the acting of the Spirit of God. Darkness, indevotion, hardness of heart, inflexibility of will and trouble of mind, are the ordinary effects of his visits. If he should console, it is only in the beginning, and with deceit, for he always leaves the soul sad, discontented and dejected; he acts like the rose, which first enchants by its perfume, and then pierces with its thorns; for, as St. Chrysostom remarks, it is the property of the devil to disturb the soul, and fill it with doubt and trouble, as it is the property of God to calm and enlighten it. By these marks we can easily distinguish the Spirit of God from the diabolical spirit, in particular instances.

The spirit of the devil, the spirit of the flesh, and the spirit of the world, agree in one point, that they all oppose the will of God, and tend invariably to the destruction of our soul; they are poisons, each of which kills, but in a different manner. St. Bernard alludes to this difference in the following terms: "The world and the flesh are the agents and ministers of the prince of darkness, the executioners of the will of this cruel tyrant, the scouts of this infamous robber. There is, nevertheless, some distinction between them. The carnal spirit always inclines to sensuality, the mundane spirit to vanity, and the diabolical spirit to malice. When attacked by sensual thoughts of eating, drinking and other things which refer to bodily enjoyment, know that it is the spirit of the flesh which addresses you. When your temptations regard the pomps, the honors of the world and the esteem of men, be sure it is the spirit of the world which cajoles you. But if you experience sentiments of anger, bitterness and revenge, refer them to the infernal spirit. Thus may you discern between these three wicked spirits. Though they should artfully disguise themselves at first, the mask will soon fall off, because the spirit of the flesh always delights in sensuality, the spirit of the world in vanity, and the spirit of the devil in malice. But be on your guard against them all, for they all combine to destroy you. Listen not to the hissings of the infernal serpent; close your ears to the voice of the siren, that you may not hear the suggestions of the sensual spirit, which impel you to seek carnal pleasure; or of the spirit of the world, which incline you to vanity; or those of the devil, which tempt you to discord, bitterness and malice.

§ 8.—*Of the danger of extraordinary ways, and the manner of distinguishing the good from the bad, with regard to such ways.*

The Spirit of God conducts souls by divers paths, and visits them in various ways, hence the Sage avers that it is *one and many*, because, as Richard of St. Victor exclaims: "It is one, by being simple in its essence, and by tending always to one end,—the glory of God and our salvation; it is, nevertheless, many, because it leads souls by various roads, gives different kinds of light, inspires divers affections, erects multiplied batteries to destroy the enemies of salvation, and to perfect souls." God can use for this purpose poverty and riches, honor and contempt, joy and sadness, health and sickness; there is no good, no evil, which cannot contribute to His design when He pleases. Weak and powerless things become strong and potent in His hands, and are made capable of working prodigious changes. The Spirit of God comes sometimes on a sudden, as St. Bernard and St. Ignatius remark; He enters without knocking, because He is the master of the house; He holds the key of His creature's heart, to open it when He pleases. Sometimes He gives notice of His coming by certain presentiments and affections, particularly those of fear, respect, contrition and desire. Thus, He diversifies Himself as He pleases, but all His diversities are reduced to two species, namely, the ordinary and the extraordinary paths to salvation and perfection.

The ordinary paths are, first, the commandments of God and His church: *If thou wilt enter into life, keep the commandments,* says our Lord. Secondly, the graces, proportioned to the age, constitution and state of each, and to the period in which he lives. Every age has its peculiarity; what is good for the young, who have lively passions, and a high degree of concupiscence, would not be suitable for the more mature and moderate; and what is proper for middle life would be unfit for the old man, who is sometimes weak and imbecile. A beginner in the spiritual life requires certain things for his advancement, and a proficient requires other things. As dispositions are varied, the bilious, the sanguine, the melancholy, the phlegmatic, all must be variously treated; and what would be suitable for one would be injurious for another. Married persons have their peculiar obligations, priests and religious have theirs. The times, too, have their diversities What is practised with advantage in one age must be omitted in another. The spirit most approved in this age is to avoid extraordinary things, to practise solid virtue, to accomplish the Gospel law, that we may be fortified against Antichrist, whose days are always approaching, and who, by his illusions and false miracles, will seduce men from virtue, and lure them to his side. It is to receive often the sacraments of penance and the Eucharist, according to the judgment of the Church of to-day, which is as wise as the ancient Church, being invariably governed by the same Spirit. These and similar things constitute the ordinary ways of God, because they are His inspirations, and the movements by which He inclines men to live well, and gives them grace to do so, according to character, constitution, state of life, and the times in which they live.

Coming to extraordinary routes, I say that there are exceptional cases, by which God occasionally leads souls to perfection in an extraordinary manner. Among these are, first, heroic actions in the military warfare of the spiritual life, more worthy of admiration than imitation : as, for example, when Abraham was about to sacrifice his son Isaac ; when St. Bennet cast himself nude among thorns ; when St. Francis Xavier applied his mouth to an ulcer, to suck out the corruption ; when St. Simon Stylites chose to live on a pillar. Secondly, visions, revelations, extraordinary suspensions of the spirit, ecstacies, interior words, miracles and like things, to which God does not call all, but only a few, as He judges fit. The angel who announced the birth of Christ to the shepherds, the miraculous star which guided the Magi to Bethlehem to adore Him, belong to this class, of which I shall speak at greater length ; because it is one of the most important points in the discernment of spirits, and the elucidation of it is of great consequence. Previous to giving the marks and signs which distinguish true revelations from such as are false, it is necessary to make two important remarks on this subject.

1. These extraordinary gifts are conferred not only on those whose virtues seem in some manner to merit them, but also on persons whose vices and imperfections render them unworthy of such favors ; not only on the predestined, but also on the reprobate. The gift of prophecy, the power of healing the sick, of working miracles, of speaking divers languages, of explaining the Scriptures, were, in the time of the apostles, commonly granted to Christians who were not yet perfect in virtue. And we know that Judas, the most wicked of men, was gifted with the prerogatives of the predestinate, in his quality of apostle. Richard of St. Victor says on this subject : "The impious, over whose heads hangs the curse of eternal damnation, are sometimes, in this world, endowed with particular gifts, and fed with delicious food." Of such persons, David says : "The enemies of the Lord have lied to Him ;" yet, by a special bounty, "He fed them with the fat of wheat, and filled them with honey from the rock." And, on this point, it is necessary to bear in mind an im-

portant truth which theology teaches, namely: that all the gratuitous favors and prerogatives of which we have spoken, and even all the graces which sanctify the soul, as habitual grace, acts of contrition, and, according to some, the grace of the pure love of God, and the graces which dispose to it, as actual graces, good works and virtuous actions, are, absolutely speaking, compatible with reprobation; that is, we may receive them, and yet not persevere to the end.

There is only one grace which unfailingly opens the gate of heaven, the grace of graces, the benefit of benefits, namely, the grace to die well. All other favors, however numerous and excellent, may exist in the reprobate, to whom God often gives more succor than to the predestinate, as appears evidently in children who die after baptism; and in many men who, after receiving numberless graces during their long lives, come at length to die in mortal sin. It appears, also, in Judas and the good thief; in Lucifer and the angels of the last and lowest choir, who remained faithful.

2. Many go astray in these extraordinary paths, and are in danger of falling over precipices. Seeing themselves raised so high, they grow dizzy, their heads are turned, they cannot walk steadily, they fall into vanity and secret pride, become self-opinionated, refuse to listen to those who would undeceive them, and, finally, lose their souls.

St. Chrysostom observes that gifts of this nature were injurious to the Corinthians, and became an occasion of pride, divisions and breaches of charity—those who had more, contemning those who had less, and the latter envying the former; and he notices that the Christians at Rome were slightly affected in a similar manner. Hence the apostle, after making some efforts to undeceive the Corinthians, says: "But be ye zealous for the better gifts, and I show you a more excellent way to glorify God, and promote the salvation of your neighbor, which is charity." Verily, the high-roads are not always the most secure, though they may sometimes be the shortest. In spirituality, the common ways are by far the best and safest, while the high paths are always perilous, because—

1. Divine Providence has designated the ordinary paths as the paths by which all men are to arrive at salvation, and, consequently, they must be the most secure, because we ought to think that the infinite wisdom of God has established the best paths for all in general, since He wills the salvation of all; the path in which all can walk securely is better than that to which only few are called. In nature, we see that the best things are the common things : the sun, the stars, the elements; and in grace, what is equal in utility and goodness to the incarnation, the life, the passion of our Lord, and the sacraments, which belong equally to all? Moses, when leading the Israelites to the promised land, sent to the king of Edom for permission to pass through his territory, making his request in these words : "We beseech thee that we may have leave to pass through thy country. We will not go through the fields, nor through the vineyards, but we will go by the common highway, neither turning to the right nor the left." And to the king of the Amorrhites he sent a like message. It is in this manner that we ought to travel to our true promised land, the heavenly Jerusalem, toward which we journey.

2. The enemy does not dislike these rare things ; on the contrary, they please him, because they give him occasion to tempt the recipients to vanity, and persuade them to prefer themselves to others, and turn aside from the solid virtues. If permitted, he will often produce false raptures and revelations himself, to deceive souls, and inspire sentiments of pride and vanity in his deluded victims.

3. Nature loves these favors. She desires prerogatives. She covets something that will draw her out of the common, and raise her above others, that she may be able to say, with the proud Pharisee : *My God, I am not like the rest of men.*

4. Extraordinary ways, being unusual, are not so well known as ordinary ways, and, by consequence, are more dangerous and more subject to illusion. Hence the great roads of faith and the commandments are always better than any other. "Oh!" exclaimed St. Lawrence Justinian, "how much do we daily read and hear of men who became remiss, and even fell away from virtue, because they were not satisfied with the beaten path, but would rush into this ambush of the devil." The erudite and pious Gerson, Chancellor of Paris, wrote the following remarkable words: "It is impossible to say how immensely curiosity to have revelations, to predict the future, to see or work miracles, has deceived people, and even caused them to renounce the faith." Hence proceed many of the abuses and superstitions which sully Christianity. Foolish people desire, like the Jews, to see signs and wonders that make a noise, and they canonize men whom the Church has not declared holy, and pay more attention to the reveries of diseased minds than to the authenticated revelations of the saints, or even the Gospel itself. In this advanced age, this last hour before Antichrist, the world, like a poor old man in his dotage, allows itself to run after fancies and imaginations, and regards as realities the most grotesque dreams. Truly, many shall say, *Lo, I am the Christ;* and some, forsaking the truth, will embrace fables and seduce multitudes. If Gerson, who departed this life some centuries ago, had reason to speak in this manner, much more reason have we, since the world is now older, perhaps more foolish, and certainly very little wiser than in his day.

People are sometimes disposed to think too much of these extraordinary favors, to make a sort of traffic of them. The prophet Jeremias says: "The prophets have prophesied falsehood, and the priests clapped their hands, and my people have loved such things; what, then, shall be done in the end thereof?" Subtle imaginations and caprices, false lights and chimerical devotion, drive souls from God, instead of attracting them to Him. Of this there are but too many examples, a few of which we shall here set down.

§ 9.—*This truth confirmed by examples.*

The famous Magdalen of the Cross who, in the last century (the sixteenth), deceived all Spain, was born at Cordova, and from her earliest years seemed to be endowed with singular prudence and extraordinary sanctity. Her companions in religion esteemed her so highly that, while she was still young, they chose her abbess. She spoke like an angel, discovered the secrets of hearts, gave wise directions on things above her province, and foretold future events. She had visions, revelations and ecstasies; occasionally she was raised above the earth. Her hair sometimes extended itself to her feet, and entirely covered her, and the walls of her chamber not unfrequently divided of themselves, that others might see her in her raptures. Princes, lords and other great personages came from far and near to consult her; and ladies of the highest rank, when expecting to become mothers, sent their linen to be sanctified by her touch, and trusted to her prayers to procure them a happy delivery.

These and other wonders acquired her great fame and admiration; holy and learned men, even after mature examination, were deceived by them; yet they were all only pure illusions of the devil, as appeared after a long time, and as she herself acknowledged to the inquisitors of the holy faith, with great candor and contrition.

Father Ribadeneira, after having related this in the Life of St. Ignatius, adds these wise and sensible remarks: "We have seen in many places, especially in Lisbon, Seville, Saragossa, Valencia, Cordova, and even in the court of the king, several other examples of persons who were thus deluded, who had visions, stigmata, ecstasies, and the gift of prophecy, who counterfeited sanctity so well that not only the unlearned, but even wise and holy men, were deceived by them, and the evil had gone much further if the holy Inquisition had not arrested its course.

A young maiden of Rheims, called Nicole, who is mentioned by Dr. Du Val, a celebrated theologian, deceived all France not long since. She was so prodigiously deluded that I know not how to describe it. Great persons, religious and secular, examined, point by point, her life, her words and actions, but everything connected with her appeared so singularly virtuous that, humanly speaking, it was impossible to doubt that she was guided by the Divine Spirit. As she lived during the troubles which occurred under Henry III and Henry IV, she maintained that these public calamities were caused by the sins of the people, and would cease if atonement were made to God. On her recommendation, processions were formed in many cities, and people confessed and communicated with extraordinary fervor. In Paris, she one day threatened the bishop that he must die during that year if he neglected the advice she gave him on the part of God; in short, parliaments and inferior courts, with the whole people, set out in public procession at her bidding. She told various persons their secret sins, which they had never confessed; she foretold things, and they happened exactly as she predicted; she spoke divinely, and explained obscure passages of the Canticles, giving them meanings so sublime and appropriate that divines were amazed. Her revelations and ecstasies were wonderfully frequent. Great lords, within and without the kingdom, sent expressly to beg her prayers, and sought her advice in their difficulties, domestic and foreign.

One day she was so sick that she seemed dead, but, being wrapped in a winding-sheet, she revived, and, on recovering consciousness, said in a low, sweet voice: "Ah! my God, since Thou art pleased to restore me to life, I consecrate myself anew to Thy service." She desired to have for director a father of a very strict order, whom she named, and described so accurately (though she had never seen him), that it was thought God had shown him to her in a vision. Another day, she was indisposed, and several divines and ecclesiastics, coming to her chamber, saw a great light around her bed, and heard a voice say distinctly *Ave soror, salvete fratres: Hail, sister, good day, brothers;* and the light suddenly disappearing, she was instantaneously healed, which greatly astonished the holy visitors.

One day while assisting at Mass with Mary of the Incarnation (who was yet a secular), in a Capuchin church, near Paris, she was raised in ecstasy, and continued for an hour motionless, and when it was ended, she affirmed that she had been to Tours, to confer with some great personage on a subject important to religion. Notwithstanding all these prodigies, however, Mademoiselle Acarie* sustained that Nicole was led by the evil spirit, who could transform himself into an angel of light, to deceive souls. One day, wishing to try whether this person had any inordinate curiosity, she gave her a sealed letter, which contained several little bits of paper, so small as to be almost imperceptible, and which must fall out if the letter were opened. Our ecstatica failed not to open it, and sealed it up again very carefully; but, while reading it, the little papers fell out. Mademoiselle soon after asked her whether she had opened the letter, but Nicole protested that she had not.

This fault of curiosity and deceit, though it might be small in another, was very considerable in one raised to such sublime virtue, and who professed to practise such great perfection; but it confirmed Venerable Mary in the opinion she had

---

* Secular name of the Venerable Mary of the Incarnation.

already formed of her favored friend. Satan, angry to find that he was discovered, quitted this poor girl, who directly fell back to her natural state. There were no more raptures or beautiful discourses; she became rough and imperfect; she could not fast or remain long in the church; she even married, against the advice of her parents and friends, and would have become a Huguenot at last, if a father of our Society had not hindered her, and, with much ado, persuaded her to lead a good life in the world, in the state she had entered, and to think no more of her past imaginary perfection.

The quaint Cardinal of Vitry relates, in the Life of Blessed Marie D'Oignes, that a great friend of this saint, a religious by profession, was almost destroyed by the illusions of the devil, who, disguised as an angel of light, often appeared to him in visions, and, in order to deceive him with more facility, reprehended him for his faults, and excited him to good works. The impostor, however, soon began to insinuate some little lies among the truths he announced, to mingle bad with good, which his victim, not noticing, simply believed, and was thereby conducted to the brink of a precipice, over which he certainly had fallen, if the saint had not proved to him that these revelations were not from God, and prayed, with tears, that God would show him the *ruse*, and open his eyes to truth. One day the devil appeared to Blessed Mary, while she prayed, and when she asked him who he was, he replied, with a terrible look: "I am he whom thou hast robbed of a friend, and who have come here to curse thee. I am called *Sleep*, because I deceive many, particularly religious, while they sleep, with illusory visions and false lights, by which I enchant them, and make them believe what I say, and think themselves worthy to be visited and entertained by angels; and thou hast stolen from me a dupe whom I had drawn to the edge of the precipice."

The example of the unfortunate Heron is well known. After passing fifty years in solitude, in great fasts and austerities, he, at the suggestion of the devil, cast himself into a well, persuaded that, by reason of his virtues, no evil could happen to him; and, having been drawn out half dead, and horribly bruised, survived his leap for three days, in great agony, but so obstinate that he could not be convinced of his error. Cassian, having related this and other similar examples, adds: "We have now said enough to show that extraordinary things are always perilous; and that it is easy for men to be deceived in these matters, as well as women."

Truly, as on one side spiritual things are, of their own nature, difficult and obscure, not being cognizable by the senses; and as, on the other, the devil is a spirit incomparably more subtle than we, who has, moreover, the experience of six thousand years, it is, after all, no great wonder if he should deceive a girl, a woman, or even a learned man. Hence, to avoid his snares, we must watch carefully ourselves, fear him continually, and be well instructed in the marks which distinguish good visions and inspirations from bad ones. Of these marks we are about to speak, but, first, we must pause a while to take breath.

§ 10.—*Marks to discern divine illustrations from diabolical illusions.*

As there are false illustrations innumerable, with which the devil endeavors to seduce souls, and as there are true ones by which the Holy Spirit works His designs for the good of the elect by extraordinary ways, in elucidating this matter I must premise that there are certain things which God alone can give, as grace, virtue and salvation; and certain other things which bad spirits alone can produce, as vice and damnation; and a third species, which God or the devil can operate, as visions, revelations, ecstasies, and the like. Now, it is necessary to verify the doubtful by those which are certain, esteeming inspirations good when they have relation to those of which God alone is the author, and holding them as bad if they have reference to those of which the devil is the author.

Cardinal Torrecremata, writing in defence of the revelations of St. Bridget, is of the opinion that revelations are always good when they have the five following conditions: 1, when they are approved by the judgment of great persons, eminent for knowledge and piety; 2, when they produce good effects in the minds of those who receive them, increasing their charity, humility, and other virtues; 3, when nothing untrue is found in them; 4, when they are conformable to the doctrines of the Holy Scriptures; and, 5, when the receiver herself is virtuous, and elevated to high perfection. Should all these conditions combine with respect to any revelation, such a revelation is certainly good.

Gerson, who was well versed in the spiritual life, compares good revelations to genuine currency, and false revelations to counterfeit coin, and adds, moreover, that the good revelations ought to have the fine, essential qualities of sterling money, namely, weight, flexibility, solidity, form and color. To judge correctly of a revelation, we must consider whether it has the weight of humility, and is not light by vanity or curiosity; if discretion and docility render it flexible, and make it yield to counsel; if it shows patience and strength in adversity, not murmuring when blamed, and not concealing passion under the semblance of zeal; if truth, exempt from error, doubt and impertinence, gives it its shape, and charity, purified of all sensual love, gives it its color. The first thing to be looked for in these revelations is truth, because, if they come from God, who is truth itself, there cannot be any falsehood in them. This is the mark which God gave to Moses when he said : "If you ask, How shall I know when a prophet speaks to me on the part of God, that God speaks by his mouth? I answer, Thou shalt know if the thing he predicts happens or happens not; for, if it does not happen, then he is not a true prophet, and speaks only his own inventions." As all that God reveals is certainly true in all and each of its parts, so whatever comes from the devil is always false, partially or entirely; for, to deceive the more surely, he sometimes slips into a hundred truths one falsehood, and this alone is sufficient to stamp a vision as his work. As divine truths are expressed in the Holy Scriptures, we must diligently examine if the extraordinary lights we experience accord with the instructions contained therein. Hence our Lord, in His transfiguration, appeared, with Moses and Elias on either side, to teach us that to legitimatize these transfigurations, raptures and visions, we must always have, as Richard of St. Victor explains, the testimony of Moses and the prophets, and see if they accord with the doctrine of the same.

St. Gregory the Great says : "Preachers are accustomed, when they hear or learn anything by revelation, to have recourse to the Holy Scriptures, and examine if the thing come from God, by its accordance with them; otherwise they should be easily deceived, and deceive themselves, for Satan can transform himself into an angel of light. Samuel, when the Lord spoke to him, ran to Heli. Therefore, that preachers may not be deceived, they examine the supernatural by the light of the Holy Scriptures."

St. Augustine had said, before him : "On the subject of false visions, the Scriptures assure us that Satan can transform himself into a beautiful angel, hiding all his deformity under the most enchanting figure. Pagans attest that their gods often appeared in admirable guise, yet these gods were only devils. Many, and not only Catholics, but Jews, infidels and heretics, have heard demons in various ways, which God permitted for

His own designs, or have heard God Himself, either to punish their malice, or solace their sadness, or excite them to seek their eternal salvation. Our Lord Jesus, after His glorious resurrection, showed His sacred body to His disciples, to be seen with their eyes and touched with their hands, that they might entertain no doubt of this mystery, and believe all the words of Moses, David, and the prophets concerning it. We ought to believe God when He speaks, and because He speaks; yet not His naked words, but His words resting on those of the Scriptures."

Our Lord and His apostles did not work on the credulity of the people, or refrain from proving their mission by their holy lives, and by the glorious miracles which they wrought in sight of all. St. Peter, writing to the faithful, tells them that he heard a voice on Mount Thabor which assured him of the divinity of our Lord, and that, if he had any difficulty in believing, he had the guarantee of the prophets to assure him of its truth, which guarantee serves as a lamp to enlighten obscure places, and to dissipate the darkness of his doubts.

The second sign which necessarily accompanies good revelations is humility; and pride is inseparable from false revelations, because, in proportion as God elevates a soul to sublime favors, He humbles her by communicating His light more abundantly, to enable her clearly to see her sins, defects and nothingness; whereas, when the devil produces extraordinary things, he makes the soul imagine she has many virtues, and is worthy of heavenly visits. Not but a person on whom God confers some of these extraordinary graces may b ` tempted, *afterward*, to pride: this may occur, yet the favors themselves do not inspire pride, but humility. But many are deceived by the appearance of humility. They can confess themselves great sinners, unworthy of supernatural favors, and even of treading on the earth; they use many exterior ceremonies of humility, while, nevertheless, their hearts are corrupted with pride, which they themselves do not perceive, because, as the learned and enlightened Gerson says, "the proud man neither sees nor feels the pride which is hidden, as it were, in the marrow of his bones, no more than the haughty Pharisee could recognize his pride. What is more easy than to say, 'I am a vile, miserable sinner'? But to say this in the heart, and to *believe* it firmly, is not quite so easy, because for this our own efforts are not enough without a particular grace. Hence, some are offended if they be reprehended, if their visions be looked on as dreams and imaginations; while the truly humble suffer all things with patience and sweetness, and humble themselves when persecuted, calumniated or reproved, according to this saying of the sage, 'A man is known by his patience;' and by this means we discern that his revelations come from God."

Humility is a sure and infallible mark in these matters, because the devil hates this virtue, and, indeed, there is nothing to which he is more opposed. St. Catherine of Sienna, astonished at the wonderful caresses and frequent revelations she received from our Lord, was seized with fear lest the devil, by being their author, should deceive her. But our Lord, appearing to her, said that He approved of her fear, because no one, during this life, ought to be without a salutary fear in the things of salvation, adding that humility is the indubitable mark by which to distinguish His favors from the illusions of the devil. For, said He, *I am truth itself*, and, consequently, always produce in the soul, by my favors, a just knowledge of truth, of myself, which leads her to despise herself and honor me ; while the devil, who is the father of lies and the king of the proud, always inspires self-esteem and pride, and produces in the soul a certain audacity and self-confidence which clearly evince his presence.

The Holy Spirit bestowed admirable graces on the Blessed Angela of Foligno ; treating her as His spouse, His well-beloved child, He designed to execute great things in and by her, and through her to manifest His glory to the whole world. But the saint, casting her eyes on her defects, protested that she was not worthy of these favors, and would not believe that the Holy Spirit was the author of them. Our Lord told her that, even if she tried, she could not banish the remembrance of her sins, which actually happened. "No matter what I did," wrote she, "I had always before my eyes the images of my offences. I could see in myself only sins and imperfections, and this sight inspired the greatest humility I ever felt." The Holy Spirit gave her, as a certain index of His presence, an ardent desire to suffer; so that henceforth she endured contempt and outrage, not only with patience and humility, but even with joy, regarding them as great favors, of which she was utterly unworthy.

Gerson is of opinion that true humility alone is sufficient to prove that any given revelations have come from God. "It is," says he, "the first and principal mark by which to discern that our spiritual money is good and loyal. Hence, all the visions, interior words, ecstatic love, miracles, great movements of piety, that are preceded, accompanied and followed by humility, certainly come from God, and there is no danger of illusion in them. If preceded, accompanied or followed by pride, they are always to be suspected. Pride and humility are sufficient criteria to distinguish all spiritual operations, and most clearly discover the author of them in particular instances."

§ 11.—*Other marks by which to discern these things.*

The third point has reference to the preceding, and is: that the person divinely led by extraordinary paths ought not to speak of what passes within her, but rather to hide it, saying, with Isaias: "My secret to myself, my secret to myself.' I will keep these things hidden in my heart, lest, by speaking of them, I expose myself to the danger of vanity, or inadvertently mention them to such as, not being capable of understanding matters of this nature, might turn them into ridicule; or to others who, dazzled by their brightness, would desire to be led by the same paths. It is necessary that these favors be succinctly, but faithfully, declared to spiritual directors, and to such as ought to know them, in order to be able to guide the soul; for she should submit to their judgment, otherwise she would inevitably fall into the snares of the devil. *Diffide in thine own wisdom*, says the Holy Ghost, *and lean not upon thine own prudence*. Do nothing in this important matter without taking advice, else thou shalt have reason to repent.

Our Lord sent Saul to Ananias for instruction, and the angel sent Cornelius, for the same purpose, to St. Peter. The Magi learned from the priests of the law where they should seek the new-born King of the Jews. Joseph recounted his mysterious dreams to his father, Jacob. When little Samuel heard the voice of God, instead of answering, he ran to the high-priest, Heli, to learn of him how he should act in this conjuncture.

The Abbot Joseph, speaking of this, remarks, with St. Paul, that the devil often disguises himself as an angel of light, to deceive the soul with his false illuminations. Hence, he says: "If we do not expose our interior to the examination of wise and enlightened directors, and submit to their decisions, whether they condemn or approve of our lights, we shall receive immense damage, and fall into extreme misery." The Abbot Moses makes similar observations, when speaking of Heron, and other sad examples of persons who, in consequence of leaning on their own prudence, fell into lamentable errors.

The qualities and effects of these revelations must be carefully considered. Good ones are always serious, and accompanied with wisdom, not representing God as saying light and puerile things that a wise man would not say. God can say nothing frivolous or unworthy of His infinite majesty; all that comes from Him bears the seal of His perfections. Useless visions or indiscreet words cannot be referred to Him. Gerson admonishes us to consider if the truth that has been revealed is not such as could be humanly discovered. In such a case the vision is doubtful, because it is unnecessary that one should receive in an extraordinary manner information which could otherwise be conveyed. In order to be above the danger of deceit, it ought to be above the capacity of men and demons to discover it.

Good visions always produce salutary effects in soul and body; they teach profitable and important truths; they give excellent instruction for salvation and perfection; they excite great horror of sin, and even of the slightest defects, and inspire in the soul all sorts of virtue. They bring us to Jesus Christ, as the angel did the shepherds, and the star the Wise Men, to see Him, to imitate His virtues, His poverty, meekness and humility; they conduct souls to patience, to mortification, to the cross. Our Lord, on Mount Thabor, spoke with Moses and Elias of His approaching passion and death; the angel in the Garden of Olives exhorted and strengthened our Lord to suffer. These are the effects of divine revelations, while diabolical revelations have a contrary tendency, and always, either openly or covertly, inspire evil of some kind or other.

The last species of circumstances to be considered in these extraordinary matters regard, first, the body: they are the sex, the natural character, the age, the constitution. Secondly, with reference to the mind: we must consider whether the person is naturally credulous or incredulous, lettered or unlettered, strong-minded or weak-minded, etc. Generally speaking, a woman is more liable to be deceived than a man, because a woman is naturally weaker in body, and may have less strength of mind. St. Paul observes that Adam was not deceived by the devil, but by Eve; and it has been remarked that God has frequently inspired men, but rarely women, to announce His mysteries. In the Old Law there were but few prophetesses: Mary, the sister of Moses, Deborah, the two Annas, Olda, and a very few others, while there were a great many prophets. The devil uses women and young girls to publish his deceits, much more frequently than men. It is one of his *ruses* to address himself to those whom he judges more easy to be deluded, and by them to compass the ruin of the strong, as he did that of Adam by Eve. St. Jerome remarked that the devil and heresiarchs have used women, who they said were animated with the Holy Spirit, to establish and spread their errors. Thus, Simon Magus had his Helen, Apelles his Philomena, Montanus his famous prophetesses, Priscilla and Maximilla, who deceived Tertullian, the wisest and most learned man of his age, and extinguished his brilliant lights, even after he had defended the truth learnedly against them.

Not long since, Dr. Perou, an ecclesiastic of great piety, and famous for his skill in theology, which he publicly taught,— a person, in short, who was regarded as an oracle in these parts, became so fascinated by the communication he held with a certain woman, whom he often saw ravished in ecstasy, that he fell into an abyss of misfortunes, abandoned the faith, and finally advanced, as Acosta, an eye-witness, relates, over a hundred heretical propositions, which he obstinately defended before the Inquisition, and refused to retract. *Women have made wise men apostatize,* said the Sage; and that saying is as true to-day as when he wrote it thousands of years ago.

The age must be considered, because old people, in whom the organs are nearly used up, and the strength greatly diminished, are naturally somewhat visionary; and young people, in whom physical strength and the vivacity of the passions obscure a little the light of reason, easily deceive themselves. The sick, who are subject to low spirits, and whose brain becomes weak by suffering; the melancholy, who are naturally umbrageous and imaginative; the phlegmatic, whom the meekness of the phlegm renders credulous; and, in general, all who are transported by love or hatred or violent passions, often mistake their dreams for realities, and imagine they see and hear what they do not see or hear. A person of mature age, of cheerful disposition, blest with good sense and solid judgment, who is naturally moderate, and has a tranquil mind, is not so subject to be duped by these illusions as is one of a contrary temperament.

§ 12.—*Four important admonitions concerning visions and revelations.*

The first is, that we ought never desire or pray for them. If you tell me that a few of the saints, as St. Ephrem, St. Maurus, and St. Herebert, have asked and obtained them from God, I answer, that we read in the lives of the saints a great deal which is to be admired rather than imitated; because in them such things flow from pure sanctity, while in us they might proceed from pride or secret self-esteem, which believes itself worthy of such graces, or from some idle curiosity to experience what the saints experienced.

Neither virtue nor perfection consists in extraordinary things: they cannot of themselves render us more agreeable to God; on the contrary, they often imperil our salvation, by becoming an occasion of vanity. The higher one is raised, the greater danger there is that he will grow dizzy and stagger, and, perhaps, fall. Low ground is always the most secure.

St. Teresa, appearing to one of her religious, after death, desired her "to admonish the provincial not to make any account of visions or revelations, because it is very difficult in these matters to distinguish truth from falsehood. Faith is the secure and infallible virtue; and to hold a person for a saint because he has these visions, is to reverse the order which God has established for the justification of the soul, namely, the fulfilment of His laws. Some women are easily deceived, and, if they fail to have recourse to wise and learned persons for their spiritual guidance, many inconveniences may ensue. Besides, in heaven, it is virtues that are rewarded, not revelations."

St. Augustine, having remarked that the devil often strives to induce people to beg of God some extraordinary favor, miracle or illumination, adds that in such cases he is to be vigorously resisted, because curiosity of this nature has ruined many. Hence the saint advises us not to seek the kingdom of God, which is within us and invisible, in sensible and apparent things, whether natural or supernatural.

The second admonition is, that if a vision comes, even without being asked or desired, it is good to resist it with fear and humility, and this mode of proceeding will never offend the Holy Spirit. St. Diadocus illustrates this by saying that a faithful servant will not immediately open the door to his master who returns in the night from a long voyage, lest, being deceived by his voice, he should admit robbers, and put that master's goods in danger. So far from blaming him for this caution, his master, knowing his design, will praise him for it. Thus we read that the admirable virgin, St. Colette, said to our Lord, when He would declare to her His secrets: "My Jesus, it is enough for me that I know Thee and know my sins, and hope that Thou wilt have mercy on me." The devil appeared once to an anchorite, in the form of our Lord, and desired him to adore him. "And why," said he,

"Should I not adore Jesus Christ every day? Look well if I am the person to whom thou art sent, for I am not worthy to see Jesus Christ." The devil was thus put to flight. Another, in a similar conjuncture, placed his hands over his eyes, and exclaimed: "I do not wish to see Jesus Christ on earth; it will suffice that I shall see Him in heaven." Gerson says that it is a very salutary counsel to arm one's self with humility, and believe that we are unworthy of the particular visits of God. If anything of that kind should happen us, let us resist it with humble fear, attribute it to weakness of the brain, or to force of imagination, and let us fear that God, in punishment of our great sins, has permitted the devil to delude us. This humility will cause the visions to vanish, if they are satanic; or, at least, they cannot injure those who act thus.

If God be the author of them, He will Himself dispose the soul to receive them, and say to her: "Friend, come up higher." Moses, when God would send him to deliver the Israelites, begged of Him to send some one else, as he judged himself unworthy of so high a commission, and yet he executed it with wonderful success. Jeremias said to God: "Ah, ah, Lord! I am but a child; I cannot speak," and yet he became a wonderfully great prophet. St. Peter said to our Lord, "Retire from me, O Lord! I am a sinful creature;" and we all know how highly our Lord esteemed him, and the honorable rank to which he was appointed, as prince of the apostles.

The third admonition is, that if, after all possible resistance, a person cannot hinder these extraordinary things, he should receive them with fear, and examine them with great precaution, after the example of our Lady, who, having heard the salutation of the archangel, "was troubled," says the sacred text, "and began to consider within herself what manner of salutation this should be." When the violent wind, the great noise, the fire and the zephyr, passed before the prophet Elias, he prudently considered in which quarter God manifested Himself, and used the necessary discernment in this matter. When an angel appeared to Josue, under the form of an armed man, the wise captain, wishing to know who he was, said to him : *Art thou one of ours, or an adversary*—art thou come to aid us or to injure us? And when he learned that it was an angel, he fell prostrate and worshipped with reverence. To assure ourselves of the divine origin of these things, it is good to make the sign of the cross, or to pronounce the holy name of Jesus, because this will make the devil fly, if the revelations are satanic.

The fourth and last admonition is, that if, after all that has been said, a person led by these extraordinary ways cannot discern either by herself or by others the precise spirit by which she is conducted, she must not trouble herself, but take care to make a good use of them, by becoming more humble, more obedient, and more detached from creatures, and more charitable, like St. Aldegonda, of whom the author of her Life says : "This holy and prudent virgin leaned on her revelations only to become more humble, to advance in perfection, and to increase in love for her heavenly Spouse." The devil, by visions and other uncommon means, endeavors to make people become more proud, impatient and vicious. His visions are, sooner or later, known by their deleterious effects on those who suffer themselves to be deluded by him.

§ 13.—*Discernment between the movements of nature and grace.*

We understand, in this place, by *nature*, not that *nature* which God made right and innocent, but that which we have at present, which is corrupted by the sin of Adam, and by our own sins, and the human spirit which induces us to commit evil, according to what God said of the times of the deluge : "The thoughts and affections of man are prone to evil from his youth." Our nature, considered under this aspect, produces of itself only briers and thorns, becoming alternately the devil, the world and the flesh to itself, and gravitating by its own movement to sin. "It happens sometimes," says St. Bernard, "that, after having vanquished our other enemies, we take up arms against ourselves, and are, by our own spirit, impelled to pride, vanity, and impatience and other sins."

St. James says: "Every one is tempted by his own concupiscence, being allured and drawn aside, for concupiscence, when it is conceived, begetteth sin." St. Athanasius relates that the devil, under the figure of a man so immensely tall that his head touched the clouds, one day knocked at the door of St. Antony, who, on opening it, asked who he was. "I am Satan," said he, "and I have come to complain to you of religious, and Christians in general, who are continually abusing me." "They are right," replied the saint, "for you continually incite them to sin, and torment them." "You are deceived," said the devil, "for I can do nothing of the kind. Have you not read these words, *The swords of the enemy have failed unto the end, and their cities Thou hast destroyed?* I am now disarmed. I have no place, no city, of which I can dispose. Everywhere, even in solitude, the name of Christ is invoked; hence, Christians should not attribute to me the sins they commit. They themselves are the sole authors of their crimes, and they reproach me unjustly." Behold how our own spirit and our corrupt nature may lead us to evil, without temptation from any other source!

That golden book, the "Imitation of Christ," has an excellent chapter on this subject, which begins by remarking the cunning with which nature seeks her own ends. *The heart of man is perverse and unsearchable,* says Jeremias : *who can know it?* Neither the labyrinth of Crete, nor the river Meander had as many windings or turnings as the human heart, and an old hare has not so many tricks to escape the huntsman as nature has to elude grace, when pursued by it. *Behold*, says the same prophet, *every man follows the malice of his perverse heart.* Hence, we are often deceived, and mistake self-love for the love of God, cunning for prudence, effeminacy for meekness, and, in general, vice for virtue.

2. Our nature most cunningly refers its affections, works, and all that it thinks and does, not to the glory of God, but to its own gratification; while grace refers all to God and salvation. Nature would gladly live always in this miserable life, which is filled with troubles and bitterness, vice and defects, in darkness of the understanding, disorders of the will, extravagance of the imagination, the tyranny of the passions, and the bondage of the senses. But grace endeavors to die to nature, to destroy corruption, to lead a spiritual life, to be freed from her captivity and delivered from darkness, and to enjoy celestial repose, knowing that her death is absolutely necessary to her perfect happiness. Our Lord has declared this in the following words: *Amen, amen, I say to you, unless the grain of wheat die, it remaineth alone; but if it die, it will produce much fruit. Whoever loveth his soul shall lose it, and whoever hateth his soul in this world preserveth it to live everlasting.*

"Amen, amen, I say to you." These words show the necessity of this mystic death. To save our soul, we must hate it. "A great and wonderful saying," cries out St. Augustine. "A man can love his soul in such a manner that in loving it he really hates it, that in loving it he shall lose it; and can hate it in such a manner that in hating it he shall save it. Thou hatest it if thou dost love it with a disorderly love, and thou lovest it in bearing it a holy hatred. O, blessed are those who thus wisely hate their soul to save it; and wretched those who, by an inordinate love, ruin themselves!

The Angelic Doctor, explaining the above words of our Lord, says: "Every man values his soul and his life, because every one naturally has great love for himself; but some love themselves truly, while others bear themselves a sort of deceitful love. He loves his soul who wishes well to his soul, for to love is properly to esteem and value. Whoever, then, loves his soul with true love, seeks its true felicity, which is God and eternal goods; but he falsely loves his soul who seeks riches, pleasures, and the passing, and often hurtful, goods of this life, which may deprive it of the solid goods of grace and glory. One who loves his soul in this latter manner loves it to its destruction, and this made the Royal Prophet say: *Whoever loves iniquity, hates his own soul.* When we see two persons sick of a dangerous fever, one of whom will not take medicine, nor will suffer himself to be bled or dieted, but drinks wine and eats what he pleases, while the other follows all the prescriptions of the physicians, eating and drinking only as directed,—we say that the first hates his life and kills himself, and that the other, who is willing to suffer something for the restoration of his health, really loves himself and values his life.

3. Nature uses every artifice, and spares no pains, to preserve life, though it be a life of pain and misery. She would rather live in this manner than die, though death should secure her solid happiness. She desires and procures, diligently and eagerly, all that can preserve life. Grace ever seeks to die to nature; she rejoices in occasions of resisting it, like the bee, which sucks honey out of bitter flowers, while nature, like the wasp, extracts poison out of the sweetest.

Grace, whose end is the salvation of man, acts in this manner, because, when dead to self, we shall receive true life, and dispose ourselves for real happiness here and hereafter. "The diminution of concupiscence," says St. Augustine, "is the increase of charity, which shall be perfect when concupiscence is entirely destroyed." Gold is purified in proportion as it is freed from its alloys; and when all the substances foreign to it shall have been melted away, the residue will be perfectly pure.

§ 14.—*More particular discernment between the movements of nature and grace.*

As that which has just been said is merely general, we shall now speak in detail of what nature does for its conservation; and not to speak of that which is more evident,—such as not being contented with what is necessary, or even with mediocrity; coveting abundance; seeking all the pleasures of sense; pursuing passionately honors and preferments, ecclesiastical or secular; striving to procure a high reputation, and such like things,—let us consider its more delicate *ruses*, taking, first, those of the understanding, and then those of the will.

1. Nature loves to think of natural things, because corporal and sensible things are like itself; of sublime things, which nourish ambition and her secret desires of honor and esteem; of pleasant things, because they, in some manner, satisfy her inclination for self-gratification; of curious things, because they appease her hunger for news; but she does not so willingly consider things spiritual and divine, which grace loves to reflect upon.

2. If nature should be constrained to think of invisible things, to meditate on the mysteries of salvation, she cunningly diverts the mind to such as have more direct reference to natural objects, and which detach it less from creatures; she considers some mystery which will not wound her as much as another would, for, in the spiritual life, there are always certain things which are more capable of depressing nature than others are: and nature is adroit enough to avoid whatever she finds mortifying. Thus, she applies herself with

difficulty to the passion of our Lord, because she fears sufferings, which it inculcates, for there is no mystery that gives such mortal blows to self as the holy passion. She prefers high thoughts, sublime conceptions, which ordinarily come to nothing, or are merely as rays of the winter sun, which enlighten without warming. Grace takes an opposite course, because it proposes heavenly things which regard salvation, and retrenches the useless multitude of thoughts and objects, simplifying the operations of the soul as much as possible, thereby to render it more capable of being united to God, who is one and very simple. Grace loves to consider the passion of our Lord, His life and death, that she may strive to imitate Him, being the conquest of His blood. She loves the cross, because it is the mystery of perfection and salvation; and all other mysteries which help to conquer corrupt nature, are dear to her.

For want of this love of the cross, many deceive themselves in the pursuit of perfection. After having made some progress, and acquired some union with God, they, by an artifice of corrupt nature, which does not relish this advancement, relax in other things, and become merely human, when they were before spiritual. There are few who really wish to die entirely to self, to annihilate their own sentiments, and who sincerely desire that all their affections should be transformed into God. For, we reflect in a thousand ways on self, and loving it such as it is, we prefer to be with it rather than to pass to God, the Sovereign Good.

But the will is still more liable to be deluded. Self-love, the special venom of nature, resides peculiarly in the will, and, rushing in all directions from this source, it spoils everything; because nature does not wish to die to self, and, openly or secretly, seeks her own contentment in every possible way.

1. She is attached to her own views, and is pained if obliged to relinquish them. She easily yields to bad humor,

if she be interrupted in her actions; she is sad and impatient when deprived of what she loves, and cannot endure opposition in anything. Grace, on the contrary, is not attached to earthly things, no matter how good they may be, except for sake of grace and virtue, and not through passion or self-love. She takes all occurrences peaceably, as things which conduct to God, and instruments of her perfection. She does not desire to do her own will, because all sin is but the effect of self-will. She combats incessantly against the great enemy, and strives, on all occasions, to vanquish it, for the spiritual edifice is raised on the ruins of corrupt nature and self-will.

2. Nature wishes to live in perfect liberty; she does not willingly submit to the rule of another; she rebels not only against equals and inferiors, but also against legitimate superiors; she cannot bear to be conquered, and, should all resistance prove ineffectual, she lays down her arms with a very bad grace. On the contrary, a man is inclined by grace to live in an orderly manner and with discipline, to divest himself of his liberty, to avoid high posts, and to apply himself entirely to the love of God.

3. Nature dislikes contempt and confusion, and flies them as much possible. When corrected for her defects, she will not acknowledge them, but, should they be too evident to admit of denial, she excuses them adroitly, and attributes the reprehensions given her either to envy or unkindness; and through the double motive of avoiding blame and acquiring esteem, she often abstains from sins she would otherwise commit. But grace confers the desire to suffer contempt and opprobrium. St. Luke relates that the apostles left the council, rejoicing that they had been accounted worthy to suffer something for the name of Christ. Grace leads a man to discover his faults frankly, to acknowledge them, when corrected; not to excuse or diminish them, but rather to amplify them; to be satisfied that others should know them, that thereby he might

have more reason to humble himself, and even, for this purpose, to do certain things which will lessen the esteem in which he is held, if he can act thus without offending God.

4. Nature desires always to increase in possessions, and never has enough; she likes two things better than one, two habits, two houses, and so of other necessaries, because she always fears being in want of anything. She relies on creatures only, and, creatures being perishable, she fears that she may perish with them. Hence, she always likes to have two or three things, when one would suffice. But grace, being founded on God, the inexhaustible source of all good, is satisfied with a little. She confides in Him, and experiences the truth of these words: "Who has God has all. He is too avaricious for whom God is not sufficient." In place of multiplying conveniences, she diminishes them, divesting herself of creatures, to prepare for the divine union to which this nudity is essential. "*One to one, one to one,*" the Blessed Giles used often say, to signify that to unite the soul to God, who is one, we must go to Him divested of, or detached from, all created things.

Grace inclines us to desire less rather than more, as regards earthly things, striving to become like Jesus Christ, who despised worldly things; she esteems a single good thought, a single sentiment of piety, which God gives her, as more valuable than the kingdom of France or Spain, because this thought or sentiment is the effect of the grace of God, purchased with the blood of His Son, and can render her more holy in this life, and more elevated in the next. The goods of this world have powerful charms to captivate the human heart, and ultimately to corrupt it; grace, therefore, does not desire them, and holds it for a singular mercy not to have great riches or high dignities, which would give her occasion to indulge in good cheer, and enable her to take her ease. She knows that people who revel in abundance and pleasures rarely live long without committing mortal sin, and still more rarely without committing venial ; and she regards it as a particular bounty of God that she is not placed in such occasions of offending Him. Nature chooses things nice and curious, rejecting such as are simple and poor, while grace prefers what is ordinary and of little value to rare and precious commodities.

5. Nature, being light and giddy, loves to amuse herself with ridiculous nonsense and the foolish sports of children. Nero aped the comedian ; Domitian spent his time catching and killing flies ; Hartalic, King of the Hycausans, in snaring moles ; Erope, King of Macedon, in making lanterns and like plebeian occupations, little suiting the dignity of a monarch, and little conformable to the saying of Isaias : *The prince should have thoughts worthy of a prince*, and employ himself suitably to his august position. The cause of this weakness comes from corrupt nature, aided by passion, by which human affections and desires easily degenerate to the occupations of children, in whom reason does not yet hold full sway. "We are no longer infants in age," says Seneca ; "but, what is worse, we are infants in morals, and use the authority which age gives us to procure for ourselves the sports of children, and practise their vices." But grace is serious and wise, because it is enlightened and governed by the Holy Ghost, who is the Spirit of Wisdom.

6. Nature is prompt, rude, impetuous and ardent in her desires, because passion, which is her guide, and gives her movement, is not free, but necessarily precipitate : "All vice is precipitate," said the Chancellor of Paris, "even that of sloth, because all vice is an effect of an inconsiderate mind." On the contrary, grace is reserved and circumspect : "The desires of the just are all good," says Solomon, not only because of the rectitude of intention, but also because of the goodness of their matter. They are temperate, while the

desires of sinners are always burning, tempestuous or furious. "Everything has its time," says the same Solomon; be not, therefore, in too great a hurry; take your leisure, impetuosity would spoil all your business. The hands of a clock move in an orderly manner, without tripping each other, but posedly and gravely advancing in the proper way. We ought to follow this model in all the actions of the day and of our lives. And to take a more illustrious example: the decree by which God produced visible things was issued a whole eternity before its execution, God peaceably awaiting the hour in which He had resolved to accomplish this great work. Grace teaches us to act in a similar manner. A little delay to reflect on a thing is very useful, while precipitation may ruin all you undertake.

7. Nature is indiscreet, she advances in confusion and disorder, she upsets everything, she is always too fast or too slow, because her lights are clouded by the mists of passion. But grace is prudent; she applies to her business the rule and compass, and lets nothing out of her hands which is not weighed, measured and numbered. She arranges things in their own places; she chooses the right moment for doing and saying everything, exercising even virtue prudently and with order, advancing slowly, but surely, and going gradually from that which is less perfect to that which is more perfect in the spiritual life.

Passion rushes blindly on, without rule, or measure, or reflection. "God," says St. Bernard, "who is wisdom itself, wishes to be loved, not only with affection, but with wisdom; therefore the apostle admonishes us to pay Him a *reasonable service.*" If you despise this reason and order, you will easily fall into error and indiscretion in your zeal, and the devil will deceive you. *He led me into his cellar of wine,* says the Spouse, *and set in order charity in me.* He gave me leave to drink of His choice wines, but yet with sobriety; He wishes that I should love Him, but yet in an orderly manner. "The Holy Scripture does not permit anything to be done without counsel," says Cassian. Even the spiritual wine, which rejoices the heart of man, must be taken in moderation. Discretion must guide everything; hence, St. Antony placed it at the head of the virtues.

In fine, nature regards things present and temporal, and applies herself entirely to the concerns of this life. She rejoices in temporal prosperity, and grieves immoderately over temporal losses. She always inclines toward creatures, amusing herself with vain affections and intrigues. But grace loves things eternal, and teaches the soul to employ all possible care in acquiring the goods of a better life. As her heart is where her treasure is, namely, in heaven, the losses of this transitory life do not sadden her. She withdraws the soul from creatures as far as she can; she loves solitude and silence, and communicates with others only through duty and charity. She moves from multiplicity to unity, from the circumference to the centre, ever increasing in recollection and union with God; while nature tends to multiplicity, and continually strives to extend her sphere, and dissipate the mind upon many vain and superfluous things.

§ 15.—*Conclusion of this subject.*

We have given marks by which to distinguish good inspirations from diabolical suggestions, illumination from illusion; we have described the effects of grace, as distinguished from those of nature, and laid open some of the deceits of the human heart. There are many others which the Holy Spirit will teach us as circumstances may require: "You have no need to think of what you shall say," says the beloved disciple, for the unction of the Holy Spirit will instruct you.

But, to deserve this unction and this divine teaching, three things are requisite, with an explanation of which we shall finish this subject.

The first is to ask them of God. St. Bernard suggests this when he says: "Our poverty and misery undoubtedly show that we do not seriously wish to be delivered from them. For if, according to the counsel of the Sage, we had knocked early at the doors of God, and prayed Him to direct our steps, preparing the avenues of His entrance, according to the advice of Isaias, and fixing our eyes always on Him, according to the words of the Royal Prophet, we should certainly receive the benedictions of God, and experience the effects of His mercy. Assuredly God would often visit us, and give us light in our darkness, and grace to escape the snares of the enemy." As we are very blind in spiritual things, and as the ways of salvation are full of dangers, the devil, who is replete with cunning and malice, strives unceasingly to catch us in his nets. As our own nature adroitly deceives us, our fall is inevitable under every aspect, unless we pray for the assistance of God, which, as St. James teaches, He will not only not refuse, but communicate with abundance. Let us say, with David: "O Lord! show me Thy ways, and teach me Thy paths. Conduct me, O Lord! in Thy justice: and because of my enemies, guide my feet to walk in Thy presence. Preserve me from the snares of my enemies; be Thou my divine escort, and in Thy mercy govern all my steps, and keep me in Thy ways, that I may not wander."

2. The second thing is to have a good guide to conduct us over these perilous roads; and this we must also ask of God, because a capable director is a great gift, and a powerful means to prevent our wandering, and to enable us to advance a great deal in a short time. Ask this with earnestness, for, if God should not give you such a guide, or guide you Himself, you would follow your own movements; and these, no

matter how learned or experienced you may be, could not conduct you well. If you should choose your director without prayer or reflection, all your mutual intercourse may end in nothing : your time will be lost in useless discourses, his instructions will not be suitable for you, he will neither exercise you in the virtues you ought to acquire, nor lead you according to the designs the Holy Spirit has on you. A director cannot be useful to you if he have not the lights necessary for your guidance. These he cannot have of himself; it is God alone who can furnish them, and He will not bestow them on a person whom He does not design to employ as your director. Hence, if you wish to have one who is really suitable for you, ask this favor of God with earnestness and tears.

When God shall have given you a suitable director (and of this your purity of intention, and the profit you derive from him, will bear witness), regard him as your tutelary angel, look on him as Tobias did on Raphael, make your soul perfectly transparent before him, show him the secrets of your heart, and follow his orders most carefully. But beware of being inordinately attached to him ; you should regard him only as an instrument which God uses to promote your advancement ; nor should you grieve immoderately when you lose him by death, or in any other way. Confide in God's providence that He will give you another, still more fitted to guide you. We read, in the Life of St. Frances of Rome, that God changed her guardian angel for one of a superior order.

The director to whom God shall have committed the guidance of a soul, ought to be extremely careful of it. His task is a difficult one, and he should daily ask of God the light and graces necessary for the proper guidance of the soul thus intrusted to him. He ought not to make his direction consist in long conversations, but in appropriate instructions, suited to the disposition of the person whom he guides, given with order and measure, according to the grace she receives, and the progress she makes. Let him strive to animate and fortify her, to attach her to our Lord, to excite her to the imitation of His virtues, to detach her from self, to make her die to creatures, and annihilate herself before God. Let him try to discover her ruling passion, and incline her to the practice of the contrary virtue. If he perceive that she is led by extraordinary paths, he must be still more careful, because, in these roads, it is very easy to go astray. He must consider and examine everything; not praise his penitent for what is extraordinary, nor admire her visions and revelations. On the contrary, let him humble and reprehend her, as Jacob did Joseph, when the latter recounted his vision: "His father corrected him, but yet he silently considered the things which he related." The enlightened Chancellor of Paris says: "Beware of applauding such a person, as if she were already perfect and worthy of such revelations; resist her as much as possible, reprimand and humble her. Scoff at her as one who requires special ways to be marked out for her, and is not content with the great beaten paths of the Scriptures and the doctrine of the saints, of ordinary light and natural reasons, and one who desires that the angels should bear her in their hands. Admonish her to make no account of these extraordinary things, to humble and despise herself on account of them, lest, becoming proud, she become, also, a fit instrument to be duped by the devil."

If the soul does not relish these resistances of her director, or opposes her judgment to his, she resists the Holy Spirit in resisting him, and crushes in its germ a seed which, if cultivated, might, in time, have produced much fruit. She must not fear that he will deceive her, for God is not a God of division, to approve Himself what His minister condemns. Rather He will make it evident that the soul who truly seeks Him cannot be led astray in so important a matter as this is.

If she feel interior assurances that her visions are divine in their source, she may always safely be diffident of her own judgment, and suspect herself of secret pride and attachment to her own views. The safe way is to follow her director, for, in obeying him, she will acquire great merit, and cannot offend God. If she rely on her own wisdom, she opens the door to many disorders, as she herself will soon discover. "The Holy Spirit," says Gerson, "communicates Himself to the humble. He will not retire from a soul that acts in the manner we have described. On the contrary, seeing her so humble and pliable, He will communicate new favors, love her with a more special love, and raise her to the summit of perfection and glory, here and hereafter."

3. The third thing is humility, which is absolutely necessary to obtain divine lights and graces. The more humble you are, the more you will be enlightened, and the less you will be liable to be deceived. The more proud you are, the more easily will you be deluded by the devil and corrupt nature, for, as St. Paul says, "God shall send them to the operation of error who believe lying." Concerning the utility of humility, our Lord said to His Father: "I confess to Thee, O Father, Lord of heaven and earth! that Thou hast hidden those things from the wise and prudent, and revealed them to little ones. Yea, Father, for so it hath seemed good in Thy sight." "It is only to the humble," says the Abbot Moses, "that God gives this knowledge." Discretion and true light are obtained only by true humility, which we must strive earnestly to acquire, if we would possess this great good, which is of such vast importance to us.

St. Paul shows the Romans how pride deceived the pagan philosophers, and how, in consequence of it, God permitted them to fall into such strange blindness that, with all their apparent wisdom, they were real fools. St. Bernard has written on this subject: "The Spouse leaps over mountains and skips over hills; why, then, art thou proud, O dust and ashes? Consider that He leaped over His angels, because of their pride. Let the horror He showed of this sin in His noblest creatures make us wise, that the misfortune of the devil may contribute to our salvation. When I read that he was abandoned by reason of his pride, and see myself sullied with this vice, I am seized with terror. If God treated His angels so severely, what will become of me, who am only flesh and blood? Satan was proud in heaven, and I am inflated on a dunghill. Do we not know that pride is more intolerable in a beggar than in a prince? Woe to me! If pride is so terribly punished in this strong and beautiful angel, who seemed to have some reason to be proud, what shall become of me, who am miserable and, nevertheless, proud? It is not without cause that for some days my courage has been failing, and my soul growing dark and stupid. Heretofore, I went with quick steps, I even ran, in the ways of perfection, but, unfortunately, I fell against a stone, which has wounded me. This stone is pride; because God discovered in me pride and vanity, which caused Him to withdraw in anger. He is gone, and therefore is darkness found in my understanding, aridity and indevotion in my will, hardness in my heart, and extravagance in my imagination. Now, I know in truth that nothing is more efficacious to acquire, preserve, recover, or increase grace, than to renounce the good opinion I entertain of self, to humble myself before God, and to fear, according to this word of the Sage: *Blessed is the man who is never without apprehension.*

"O sad deceit!" cries out Gerson. "Who among all that make profession of piety is entitled to live without fear? O snares, everywhere spread to catch souls! who shall defend us from you? Who can walk securely in darkness? Verily, none but the humble man, who works out his salvation in the fear of God, and cherishes sentiments of his own baseness."

David said, from experience: "Because I humbled myself, He delivered me. Blessed is the man who is always fearful.

He shall walk securely through every ambush; in vain the devil rages like a lion against him, and seeks to devour him. All his cunning is vain, because Thou, O God! dost take care of the poor, and protect the orphan."

St. Catherine of Bologna relates that the devil appeared to her once under the form of our crucified Lord, and again as our Lady holding the divine Infant in her arms. Mistaking these visions for divine favors, she adored him; and she confesses that this misfortune resulted from secret self-confidence, by which she imagined that the devil had no *ruse* so subtle, no artifice so hidden, that she could not discover. This vanity cost her dearly: on account of these illusions, and other sufferings, she was often horribly tempted to despair. *Humble thyself greatly*, says the Sage; keep thy spirit abased before God, and nothing can injure thee. Men are subject to two great evils, which cause many others. One regards devotion; it consists in the illusions and deceits of which we have spoken; the other regards doctrine, and consists in the errors and novelties wherein wise men look for truth; and God, to punish their inordinate curiosity, or chastise their inconstancy, or for some other reasons of which we are ignorant, permits them to fall over this precipice: and then are verified in them the words of the Sage, "The just man perishes in his justice;" for he follows novelties in religion, which injure him as the pestiferous atmosphere of an hospital injures a sound, healthy person, who does not use the necessary preservatives and antidotes. *Let him, therefore, who thinketh himself to stand, take heed lest he fall.* The remedy against both these calamities is contained in the following words, which ought to be profoundly engraven on our hearts: *Humble thyself greatly.* Put away thy self-sufficiency, cultivate a low opinion of thy own powers, follow the advice of others, attach thyself to what God gives, here below, of the solid and immovable, and pray continually that He may never permit thee to be deceived.

CHAPTER IV.

OF THE GIFTS OF THE HOLY GHOST IN GENERAL.

THE last subjects we shall treat of in this place are the gifts of the Holy Ghost, a knowledge of which is excellent, useful and necessary. It is excellent, because of its object, for these gifts are of inestimable value; they are precious jewels, which render the soul more beautiful than the sun, and more brilliant than the stars. It is useful, because these gifts confer on us immense riches. "We ought," says the Mystical Doctor, John Rusbrocius, "to represent to ourselves the eternal and personal love of God, namely: the Holy Spirit residing in the midst of the just soul, and shedding on her, and on all her faculties, in quality of Fountain of life, these seven gifts, as seven streams, as the luminous sun enlightening the soul by seven rays, as a great fire which burns with seven flames." It is necessary, because these gifts are so essential in the spiritual life, that they alone raise the soul to the summit of perfection, as we shall presently see. Yet this knowledge is very rare; but few persons are convinced of its merit and utility. Hence, I shall be somewhat diffuse on this subject, taking, first, all the gifts in general, and then each gift in particular.

The gifts of the Holy Ghost are seven habits, communicated by Him to the just soul, some in the understanding, others in the will, to render these faculties pliable to His movements, and to enable her to perform virtuous actions, particularly such as are great and heroic. We say they are habits, that is, fixed and lasting qualities, like sanctifying grace, which they always accompany and follow. Things may exist in a man in three ways : first, by power, as when we say of a child richly endowed that he is happy. This does not mean that he possesses beatitude, since he is incapable of it, because of his age; but we use these terms to show that there is in him a great disposition to happiness. Second, by habit, as when we say of a great philosopher, who is asleep, that he is a learned man, though, at the moment, sleep plunges him in ignorance ; and, third, by act, as when this philosopher gives utterances to his beautiful ideas, or applies himself successfully to some new study. The power is the natural capacity for a thing ; the act is the effect and work of this power, and the habit is a quality attached to the power, by which the act easily becomes feasible.

These gifts resemble the different beatitudes and fruits which St. Paul mentions when writing to the Galatians. St. Thomas, teaching the difference between the gifts and the virtues, the beatitudes and the fruits, remarks that, in virtue, we consider two things : the habit and the act. The habit prepares for the act, and when this habit is general, it is called virtue ; if it work in an extraordinary manner, it is styled a gift. Beatitude is the virtue perfected ; it fills the soul with the joy which it produces, and hence it is called the *fruit*. As good fruit, when perfectly ripe, is delicious to whoever eats it, so virtue, when perfect, causes great pleasure to him who exercises it. The fruits of the Spirit are perfect works, which bestow contentment. And this is to be understood, even of actions which are grievous to nature and the senses, provided the soul exercises them joyfully. Patience and continence cannot be possessed without combats, yet St. Paul places them among the joys and fruits of the Holy Spirit. Thus they resemble virtues, in that they are habits of virtue ; hence, some Fathers speak of them as of virtues. But the opinion of

St. Thomas and others, who make a distinction between a virtue and a gift, is much more probable and better sustained :—

1. Because the Holy Scripture distinguishes between gifts and virtues, calling gifts spirits; thus Isaias says: "The spirit of fear, the spirit of wisdom," and not the virtue of fear, or the virtue of wisdom.

2. Because our Lord, having possessed all these gifts, did not necessarily possess all virtues, as faith, repentance for sin, which virtues could not be found in Him, because of the abundance of His perfections; and as these virtues suppose some want or failing, they could not be gifts of the Holy Ghost in the sense we here understand.

3. Because the virtues can, of their own nature, exist in a soul without sanctifying grace, but the gifts are inseparable from sanctifying grace : it must accompany and follow them.

4. Because it is the office of the virtues to render a person docile to reason, while, by the gifts, one yields himself without resistance to the guidance of the Holy Spirit.

5. The virtues produce ordinary acts, but the gifts elevate one to high sanctity and heroic perfection : so that the virtuous action which regards any object, emanates from such a virtue; but the high and sublime manner in which it is performed, emanates from the corresponding gift. The gifts are unlike the virtues, which do not dispose the soul to act of itself, but rather to suffer, to receive an impression, that it may afterward produce the action, not by its own movement, but by the impulse of the Holy Ghost. St. Gregory distinguishes between the gifts and the virtues, when he likens the seven sons of Job to the seven gifts of the Holy Ghost, and the three daughters of the same patriarch to the three theological virtues.

Hence, we may gather, with the theologians, that the gifts are of a more noble nature than the virtues—we mean the moral virtues, not the theological; for God has established the following order, which is the best to make us holy and perfect here below, without speaking of the sacraments: first, the theological virtues; then the gifts of the Holy Ghost; then the moral virtues. Faith, hope and charity hold the highest rank, because they regard God directly, and unite us to Him, in which union consists our perfection. The gifts hold the second rank, because they serve to make these virtues act with greater excellence. All the other virtues follow in order, according as they regard religion, ourselves or our neighbor.

The gifts surpass the virtues for another reason, which the Angelic Doctor gives: "It is necessary that the thing which receives the motion should have some relation to the thing which gives the motion; and the more excellent the cause, the more excellent will be the effect. A pupil ought to be somewhat advanced before he takes lessons in any high science. Virtues prepare the soul for the divine operations, but the gifts render the soul entirely submissive to the Holy Spirit. "The Lord opened my ear," says Isaias, "and I do not resist." I submit myself to Him unreservedly in every occurrence, great and small.

These gifts are specially attributed to the Holy Ghost, not to the Father or the Son, who produce them conjointly with Him, because the Holy Ghost is the first gift of God, His love: and love is always the best gift that can be bestowed, and the source of all other gifts. Goodness, benevolence and communication are the principles of benefits; justification, sanctification and perfection are referred to the Holy Spirit, who makes souls, in their measure, like Himself, and unites them to God, as He unites the Father and the Son by the bond of love. These gifts subject the soul in a special manner to the movements of the Divine Spirit, and fit it for receiving His inspirations and following them.

The gifts of the Holy Ghost are seven in number, as Isaias declares, when speaking of our Lord : "The Spirit of the Lord shall rest upon Him, the spirit of wisdom and understanding, the spirit of counsel and fortitude, the spirit of knowledge and piety, and the spirit of the fear of the Lord." Reason is either speculative, desiring to know truth; or practical, to execute it. If it wish to know truth, the gift of understanding aids it ; if to practise what it has learned, the gift of counsel renders it service. The gift of wisdom is speculative, that of knowledge is practical. Piety rectifies the will, fortitude and fear strengthen us against concupiscence. Wisdom, understanding, knowledge, and counsel reside in the understanding, which is their throne ; fortitude, piety and fear are seated in the will.

If you desire to know which are the more perfect,—those which enlighten the understanding or those which polish the will, I answer, with the Angelic Doctor, that the intellectual virtues are, of their nature, more excellent than the moral virtues. Among the virtues which reside in the understanding, wisdom holds the first rank, then knowledge, then counsel. Among those of the will, the first place is due to piety, the second to fortitude, and the third to fear. The gift of wisdom perfects the theological virtue of charity, and the gift of understanding that of faith.

§ 1.—*The effects of these gifts.*

The first effect of the gifts of the Holy Ghost is to render the soul more susceptible of His impressions, that He may lead it as He pleases. The Angelic Doctor says, these gifts are habits which give a man facility to allow himself to be guided by the Holy Ghost, as the moral virtues prepare his appetites to submit to the guidance of reason. The Seraphic

Doctor teaches that these gifts are supernatural habits, infused by the Holy Ghost, which render souls docile to His inspirations, which admonish the memory, enlighten the understanding and inflame the will; for it is the property of the Holy Spirit to move and excite us to love God, as Tertullian has remarked, thus: "It is a point of our faith to believe that Jesus Christ has merited for us the Holy Ghost, and has sent Him to excite the faithful to press forward to perfection." St. Gregory, explaining the miracle Jesus wrought on the deaf man, by putting His fingers into his ears, says that the Holy Ghost is the finger of God: "To put His finger into the ears of our soul, is to open them with the seven gifts of the Holy Ghost, thereby rendering it docile to his voice."

The same learned and holy pope, comparing these gifts to the seven sons of Job, says: "The sons of Job made a sumptuous banquet, at which the virtues, that is to say, the gifts of the Holy Ghost, feast the soul, each in its own fashion. Each made a feast on his own day; the day of each son of Job typifying the light that each gift communicates to the soul, and which is different from the light of the other gifts, the gift of wisdom having its own peculiar light, that of understanding having its own, and so of the rest.

The gifts of the Holy Spirit, says St. Bonaventure, are the rays of His light, the irradiations of the Divine Son of Justice To this I add, that they have been understood to be indicated by the seven eyes of which the prophet Zachary speaks. The same saint styles them gleams of fire, because the Holy Ghost is the sun from which they emanate; He uses them as fire, to work his wonders in souls. Haughty spirits are brought low by the gift of fear; hard hearts are softened by piety; the gift of science chases away darkness; fortitude confers strength; counsel brings us back when we wander, or keeps us in the right path; the gift of understanding enlightens the mind; wisdom inflames the will. He communicates, by these gifts, the lights of true knowledge and the ardors of holy love, which are His richest gifts, and which cause us to taste, beforehand, His promised felicity. These gifts aid the three theological virtues and the four cardinal virtues, to which all moral virtues are reducible. The gift of understanding sustains faith, the gift of knowledge vivifies hope, showing that we should be deceived in fixing our desires on created things. Wisdom inflames our charity. Prudence would be very shortsighted without the gift of counsel. Piety teaches justice always to use the necessary moderation, lest it should be ungrateful to superiors, or severe to inferiors. With fortitude we are sure to be victorious in all our combats. And the gift of fear is necessary to the virtue of temperance, to repress the impetuosity of concupiscence, and all inordinate appetites.

These gifts shield us from the greatest evils which can attack us. Wisdom secures us against folly, understanding prevents stupidity in the mysteries of faith, counsel hinders us from being precipitate in our actions, knowledge guards against ignorance, piety against hardness of heart, and fear against indiscreet liberties. They are not only useful, but in some degree necessary, for they accompany and follow sanctifying grace. They make us really spiritual. Without them we should be unable to resist the world, the flesh and the devil; to overcome inveterate habits, or to accomplish anything great for God's glory and our own salvation. "The great world," says St. Bonaventure, "was perfected in seven days; and man, who is a little world, is perfected by the seven gifts of the Holy Ghost." The gifts of understanding and wisdom are requisite in the contemplative life, and the five others in the active. Three things in man concur to his salvation: The first is sanctifying grace, which elevates him above nature, makes him a child of God, an heir of eternal glory: this resides in the soul. The second is virtue, which adorns and perfects the faculties, as faith the intellect, charity the will, temperance the concupiscible appetites, fortitude the irascible. Of these virtues there are three kinds, namely: first, the theological, which refer to God. By these virtues St. Augustine defines the Divinity, when he says: "God is that which cannot be explained by words or conceived by thoughts, but who can be believed, hoped in and loved." The second species are intellectual, as prudence, which is the torch to conduct us, and the other virtues, which inspire us to render to God His due, or to restrain our passions, and subject them to the law of reason. The gifts of the Holy Ghost are not given properly for the embellishment of the mental faculties, but for the virtues that reside in the soul, that these virtues may be employed in a more excellent manner; wherefore, St. Gregory calls them the helps and the perfection of the virtues.

Our reason, though fortified with all the moral and theological virtues, cannot attain to high perfection without these gifts; as appears by the daily experience of many of the faithful, who, having only the virtues, praise and love God very imperfectly, do little or nothing heroic, and make but small progress in the way of perfection. Richard of St. Victor observes that the heart of one who applies to spiritual things without the assistance of the Holy Spirit and the help of His gifts, is easily diverted from his good purposes, according to this saying of the sage: "Thy heart shall suffer the phantoms and agonies of parturition, if the Most High do not visit and aid thee." The virtues will only enable a man to reach mediocrity, but the gifts lead to perfection. The virtues sketch the picture, the gifts give it the finishing strokes. All that we read of the illustrious actions and admirable operations which raised the saints to the summit of perfection, are but the effects and productions of the gifts of the Holy Ghost in their souls.

St. Thomas compares the virtues to the light of the moon,

and the gifts of the Holy Ghost to that of the sun, which is much more brilliant and efficacious. Some birds have wings, but cannot fly, like the ostrich; others have wings, but cannot fly high, as the hen; but others can soar high, and for a long time, over rocks and mountains, even to the rarefied regions of the air, like the eagle. The infused virtues in baptized children are, like the wings of the ostrich, inactive; they enable the just to fly, but not very high, like the wings of the hen; but the gifts of the Holy Ghost confer the wings of the eagle, to make the soul fly to the summit of perfection.

The just soul navigates with great facility the ocean of this world, when she possesses these gifts, which the Scripture calls *spirits*, because they carry us a long way in a short time. New wheels turn with noise and stiffness, but when they are oiled, they move noiselessly and quickly. It is thus the Holy Ghost, by the unction of His gifts, gives motion to the wheels of our soul: hence the Church calls Him *Spiritalis Unctio.* The Royal Prophet said: *Send forth Thy Spirit, and they shall be created, and Thou shalt renew the face of the earth.* He will give us a new spirit, new affections, new senses, and entirely renew us with these gifts.

There was before the tabernacle a golden candlestick, concerning which God had given command to Moses: "Thou shalt make a candlestick of fine gold, which shall have one stem, and the branches, cups, lilies, and the bowls going out from it. Six branches shall come out of the sides; three out of one side, and three out of the other."

The Rabbins, the better to penetrate the sense of the Hebrew word which St. Jerome translates *globes of gold*, used *pomegranates of gold*. Arius Montanus remarked that these lamps were on one side shaped like the eye of man, and on the other like his ear. This seven-branched candlestick is, according to the explanation of Venerable Bede, a brilliant figure of the seven gifts of the Holy Ghost. It was of very pure gold, typifying charity, which these gifts accompany. Its lamps are likened to eyes, because the gifts illuminate and conduct us ; and to ears, because they render us docile to instruction, and pliable to the movements of the Holy Spirit, for the ear is the organ of obedience. The cups, globes and flowers represent the inestimable riches the gifts confer on the soul ; the lilies, purity and innocence ; the globes, with their rotundity, and the pomegranates, with their seeds and crowns, the multitude of good works and the summit of perfection ; the cups, the contentment and delight which the gifts produce in the soul. As we are the temple of God, according to St. Paul, we ought to have always lighted in our hearts this mysterious candlestick, that we may love and serve Him with the seven gifts of His Holy Spirit.

§ 2.—*Means of acquiring the gifts of the Holy Ghost.*

We have already said that these gifts always accompany sanctifying grace, but only in a minor degree. If you wish to receive them in a notable degree, you must first retrench worldly affections, and apply to spiritual things: "Worldly spirits and hearts," says St. Bonaventure, "being attached to earth, are incapable of possessing these precious gifts, these brilliant lights ; they cannot become the theatre of these excellent operations, because the Holy Ghost gives Himself in His gifts, and with them, *Whom*, says our Lord, *the world cannot receive*, because the world knows Him not, and, in consequence of this ignorance, loves Him not. The understanding of worldlings is stupid and blind in heavenly things, according to the words of the apostle : "The animal man cannot comprehend the things of God ; " and those of the Psalmist : " They keep their eyes fixed on earth." Their will loves and relishes only creatures, and in creatures these three things, which are so contrary to the Holy Spirit, namely: the concupiscence of the flesh, the concupiscence of the eyes, and the pride of life. These are the elements which compose worldlings, the water in which they bathe, the air which they respire, the fire which warms them, and the earth which supports them.

2. We must ask an increase of these gifts by prayer; for, as they are the *gifts* of the Holy Ghost, it is reasonable and necessary that we should ask for them; and, as they are great gifts, we should beg them with all possible earnestness and ardor.

For this purpose we should say, with great affection, the *Veni Creator*, the *Veni Sancte Spiritus*, and the Little Office of the Holy Ghost. And it would be salutary sometimes to beg one gift, sometimes another, as occasion may require.

3. We must unite ourselves intimately to our Lord Jesus. St. Thomas teaches that the most necessary thing in the Christian religion is the grace of the Holy Ghost, because it justifies and sanctifies us, and makes us children of God, and because, without it, we should remain slaves to our passions and appetites, and be sullied with vice: we could neither practise virtue nor exercise good works, and we should infallibly be lost. "Now," he proceeds, "we acquire the grace of the Holy Ghost by our Lord Jesus Christ. *The Word was made flesh*, says St. John,—*the Word, full of grace and truth.*" The Son of God has become the Son of man, and is filled with grace and truth. For Himself first, and without measure: *God doth not give His spirit by measure*, says the same saint; and moreover, not as the fruit of merit on His part, because His plenitude was communicated in virtue of the hypostatic union; and, secondly, for us, because of *His plenitude we have all received, and grace for grace; for the law came by Moses, but grace and truth are conferred by Jesus Christ;* yet with measure:

for, says St. Paul, *to every one is given grace according to the measure of the giving of Christ;* and through His merits, for, the labors of His life and the pains of His death impetrate for us all the aids necessary for working out our salvation, and all sorts of heavenly benedictions."

Among these graces and blessings the seven gifts of the Holy Ghost hold a superior rank ; and, as our Lord has been superabundantly replenished, both for Himself and for us, we ought to unite ourselves intimately to Him, that He may share them with us. St. Clement of Alexandria elegantly styles our Lord *the Breast of the Father*, after Isaias, who, speaking of Him, said : *Thou shalt be nourished with the breasts of kings.* We must recur to this sacred and amorous Breast, and, *like new-born babes*, as the Prince of the Apostles says, draw therefrom some of the milk of which it is full. We see that hungry infants, taught by nature, seek their mothers' bosom ; let us, in like manner, draw our aliment from this dear Breast of the Father. This may be done by acts of faith, believing we are destitute of these gifts, and unworthy of them ; that they are necessary for our perfection ; that it is only Jesus Christ that can give them, they being the fruit of His merits. We must ardently desire them, praying for them continually with the most pressing instance, and with acts of faith and love. Thus should we draw this divine liquor from this amiable Bosom.

§ 3.—*Of the gift of fear.*

This gift is the foundation of the other gifts, and opens the door by which they enter into the soul. There are two kinds of order among the gifts of the Holy Ghost, namely : first, the order of perfection, according to which the gift of wisdom is the highest ; and, second, the order of acquisition, according to which, fear holds the first rank. Hence, we begin the more particular explanation of these gifts, by explaining the gift of fear. St. Thomas distinguishes four species of fear : first, the fear which makes us turn our back upon God, which is called worldly fear; second, the fear which makes us go to God, through dread of His chastisements: this is called servile; third, the fear of displeasing God, which is filial; fourth, if this latter include also the two former, it is called *initial*, or fear commenced. To these St. Bonaventure adds natural fear, as the fear of death, which in itself is neither good nor bad.

This fear our Lord condescended to suffer in the Garden of Olives. Worldly fear is distinguished from human fear, in that it makes us offend God for the sake of earthly advantages, like the Jews, who put the Son of God to death, in order to preserve their country. In like manner, the fear of torments and death caused Peter to deny our Lord after the Last Supper.

Filial fear is the most perfect of all. The fear a servant has of his master is founded on the authority of the master over him; but the fear a son has of his father, and the fear a spouse has of her spouse, make, respectively, the son submit to his father by filial love, and the wife to her husband by conjugal love. Filial love engenders filial fear, and conjugal love is chaste fear. Every species of fear flows from love of some kind.

We fear death, because we love life. If a father felt no affection for his son, he would not be apprehensive of what might injure him. Hence, perfect love ought to engender the most excellent fear. "Whoever," says Cassian, "has arrived at the perfection of true charity, ought also to have attained a high degree of fear, which produces, not dread of pain or desire of recompense, but greatness of love. A good son does not fear the blows of his father, a loving spouse the reproaches of her husband, but they both respectively fear to displease father and husband, or to diminish their love. Filial fear and chaste fear are continually vigilant, lest by the least word or act they displease the object beloved."

Filial fear is properly the *gift of fear*. It imprints on us a great veneration toward God, and a correspondingly great fear of offending Him. It is communicated to the just soul, producing all the other gifts, and invariably accompanying them : *The fear of the Lord is the beginning of wisdom.* By it, as the first gift received, we arrive at *wisdom*, which is greatest, and, by consequence, at all the gifts. St. Bonaventure says that the first step in the ladder of perfection, and the foundation of all other gifts, is the fear of the Lord. St. Bernard writes : "It is with reason that the fear of the Lord is styled the beginning of wisdom, because the soul commences to taste God when she begins to fear Him. You fear the justice and power of God ; God then is sweet to you, for fear is a species of savor. Fear sketches wisdom in the soul, because, as riches make a man rich, and knowledge renders him learned, so fear makes him become truly wise. Learning prepares our minds for the knowledge of spiritual things, but vanity would easily glide into knowledge, if fear did not prevent it. Hence fear is well named *the beginning of wisdom.*"

The gift of fear is the mother and guardian of all graces and virtues, because, as nothing but sin can separate us from God, and as fear banishes sin, it disposes us to receive all graces from God, and to acquire all virtues. As fear drives away pride, which is the first of vices, it necessarily engenders humility, which is the source of all good, and renders the soul capable of receiving all divine favors. St. Bernard expatiates, as follows, on the effects of fear, in a sermon which he preached on the seven gifts of the Holy Ghost : "Fear takes the sword and shield, to defend the soul from negligence. It opens the mental eye, to examine attentively what passes within, to execute all the commands of God, failing in nothing according to these words of the Wise Man: *He that feareth God, neglecteth nothing.*"

The Cardinal James of Vitry tells how the Blessed Mary d'Oignies possessed this gift: "The greatness and sincerity of her love for God rendered her extremely circumspect, not only in her actions, but also in her words and thoughts. The belief that God held his eyes always fixed upon her, led her to fear all her works, lest she might, in the slightest degree, displease Him. This fear served as a girdle to prevent her thoughts from dissipating themselves, as a bridle to govern her tongue, as a spur to urge her forward, and prevent her loitering on the way, and, finally, as a rule to indicate limits that must not be passed. This holy fear made her so little and so humble in her own eyes, that she looked on herself as nothing, or worse than nothing."

Denis the Carthusian says that the gift of fear drives out sin, puts idleness to flight, causes wisdom to take root, and gives stability to the mind, which would otherwise waver. This is the doctrine of the Holy Scripture: *The fear of the Lord expels sin. The fear of the Lord is the root of wisdom. He that feareth God neglecteth nothing. He that is without fear cannot be justified. The fear of the Lord is glory and honor, and gives delight of heart and perfect joy. The true point of wisdom is to fear the Lord.* The Royal Prophet often enlarges on this subject in his Psalms: "All you who are holy, fear the Lord, for nothing is wanting to them that fear Him. O how great is the multitude of Thy sweetness which Thou hast hidden for them that fear Thee! Thou hidest them in the splendors of Thy face, where they are protected from the injustice of men. Thou dost protect them in thy tabernacle from the tongues of the wicked."

The principal effect of filial fear is a profound reverence, which pains even to trembling, as the Scripture remarks of the pillars of heaven and Seraphim who tremble before the Divine

Majesty. The just soul evinces intense respect before the Divinity. Isaias says of our Lord: "He shall be filled with the spirit of the fear of the Lord;" and St. Paul remarks that "He was heard for His reverence." What reverence did He not show in the Garden of Olives! How profound was His abasement! Verily the more a soul knows of the greatness and majesty of God, the more respect and honor she renders Him; and as the soul of our Lord possessed this knowledge in an infinite degree, so He was incomparably more reverential than all men and angels together. Souls that possess the true Spirit of Jesus, and a high degree of the gift of fear, are extremely circumspect and reverential in the presence of God. They revere Him with such profound humility that they are, as it were, annihilated in His presence, remembering only that He looks on them, and abasing themselves before His august Majesty.

Abraham evinced this reverence when, having received the three angels who had come in the form of young men, and spread out the food prepared for them, *he stood before them, under the tree*, to serve them; upon which St. Chrysostom makes the following remarks: "A personage so great and illustrious, remarkable for such heroic actions, venerable for his old age, stands as a valet before three young men, who are seated at the table his hospitality has prepared for them. What wonderful respect! Addressing one of them, he uses these terms: *I will speak to my Lord, though I am but dust and ashes.*" When St. Francis prayed, he did so with such reverence that he always knelt and uncovered his head. When travelling, he frequently dismounted, and stopped to pray; and if the rain surprised him in this exercise, he would neither cover his head nor omit a syllable, but finished his prayer with his customary reverence. "On whom shall I cast my eyes?" says God, by His prophet: "To whom shall I have respect but to him who is poor, of a contrite heart, and who trembles at my words."

The gift of fear not only makes us respectful toward God, but also, proportionally, toward men, as being God's creatures, on whom He has stamped His perfections in stamping His image, so that we become reserved, modest and deferential before them. "Lord," says the Sage, in the Book of Wisdom, "though Thou art infinitely powerful and wise, Thou dost conduct us with great reverence, and govern us with honor." Now, if God respects men, men have surely far greater reason to respect each other. The second effect of fear is a mortal horror of all sin, even the smallest. Sin is the sole object of the apprehension of a soul holily fearful. Such a soul would die a thousand deaths rather than wilfully commit the smallest sin. The blessed would choose to quit heaven, and endure the torments of hell, rather than commit the least deliberate sin. Hence we read of women and little girls who, to preserve their chastity, disfigured their faces, destroyed their beauty, and often buried themselves alive in sepulchres, and lived hidden from all. St. Macarius of Egypt says: "Men truly spiritual are not exempt from fear; not that they are molested by that fear with which the devil tempts beginners and novices; they fear only lest they should offend God in the slightest degree, or abuse the least of His graces. Ypres relates that our Lord having said to St. Teresa, "Fear not, my daughter, it is I: I will not abandon you," the saint felt a wonderful courage, and laughed at the power of the devil, saying, "that the soul sincerely desirous of going to God should have no fear, save that of offending Him, else she would wrong so good and gracious a Lord."

The third effect of this gift is, that when one has offended God, even slightly, the soul is covered with shame and confusion. She cannot rest till the stain be effaced. Souls profoundly struck with this filial fear have a lively horror of the least faults, and gladly suffer all things to obliterate them. "I have seen men," says St. Climacus, "humble themselves deeply for their sins, and beg forgiveness with such lamentable cries as would almost melt the heart of a rock. They might well say with David, 'Every night I water my bed with my tears. I did eat ashes as bread, and did mingle my drink with weeping.' They passed days in extreme affliction, forgetting to take food, or, when they took it, mingling ashes with their bread, and tears with their drink. There remained of them only skin and bone, and they were more like mere skeletons than living men." Without this gift we should take undue liberties with God, comport ourselves irreverently before Him ; we should become too audacious and familiar when we speak to Him, and commit other vulgarities in His regard, which would testify our criminal ignorance of Him and of ourselves. Not that this gift prevents the caresses of a son toward a father, of a spouse toward her beloved ; it banishes only insolence, audacity and irreverence. Abraham, notwithstanding his great respect for the angel, asked him six times, consecutively, for a great favor, namely, the pardon of the Sodomites. Reverence, far from being opposed to love, invigorates, purifies and perfects it. A young princess, perfectly well bred, will not fail to show great respect to her spouse, who is a powerful king, while she renders him also an ardent love, and uses toward him most tender familiarities. The failings that proceed from a want of this gift, result from secret pride and a disesteem of the Divine Majesty. They make a person act with too much license, not only toward God, but even toward men. Hence proceed usurped authority, petty tyrannies, haughty, rude and most ungracious manners. The soul makes no account of small faults ; relying on her own strength, she does not avoid occasions of sin ; she uses negligently the graces of God, and even abuses them, as if grace were a thing of small consequence, which she was certain of always possessing. Far from being ashamed to offend God, she becomes a prey to the misfortune which

Jeremias describes, when he says: "They were not confounded with confusion, and they knew not how to blush."

To prevent these great evils, let us earnestly beg of God the gift of His fear, saying: *Pierce Thou my flesh with Thy fear.* Replenish my will with Thy fear, that it may flow on my soul and body. Let us every day produce acts of this virtue, according to the advice of the Royal Prophet: *Serve the Lord with fear, and rejoice unto Him with trembling.* However great your elevation of spirit, whatever sentiment of piety melts your heart, whatever degree of love inflames you, never fail in the reverence you owe to Him, who is your King and your Judge, as well as your Father and Spouse. Nobles and royal favorites are never on terms of equality with their prince. God is the King of kings and the Lord of lords, before whom the greatest monarchs of earth are but atoms. Hence a little after the Spouse, transported with love, had cried out: "Let Him kiss me with the kiss of His mouth," and, "Show me, O Thou whom my soul loveth! where Thou feedest," our Lord says to her: "If thou knowest not thyself, O fairest among women! go forth and follow after the steps of the flocks:" for, with all thy beauty, shouldst thou forget my greatness and thy own littleness, thou must retire from my presence.

§ 4.—*Of the gift of fortitude.*

When we speak of fortitude as a certain constancy of mind to resist temptation, and subject the passions to reason, it is not under this aspect a special virtue, but, generally, all virtues, because each possesses the property of fortifying the soul in the practice of good; hence William of Paris remarks that the name which virtue bears signifies *strength.* Virtue is cognizable as force and power; but the fortitude, which is a gift of the Holy Ghost and a cardinal virtue, lies between two of our passions, namely, fear and audacity, and gives them respectively their just temperament. It regulates the fear of death, that we may not fear it excessively, or think of it with too bold a blindness.

This virtue has two offices, namely, to attack and to resist, to act and to suffer; it is like the sword of the soldier to give a blow, and the shield to receive a blow. In its office of shield, it is peculiarly necessary, for the devil attacks us on our weaker points. It is true that suffering is the effect of infirmity, as action is the effect of power; and when we say that the martyrs were invincible in their combats, this is to be understood of their courage and their soul, which would never yield to the will of the tyrant; not of their bodies, which were really vanquished by death. Hence St. Thomas teaches that those who suffer grievous things are the most valiant of the valiant, and the Holy Ghost says that the neck of the Church is like the tower of David, on which hang a thousand shields—not swords nor arrows, which are made to inflict injury, but shields, which sustain injury. St. Thomas, after St. Augustine, teaches that a man can do great actions without doing them through a motive of virtue: first, when he does not esteem them difficult, and easily does them well, through skill, or because of his experience, or by good luck; second, when he does them through excitement, not with consideration and light; and, third, when, though great in appearance, they fail of being truly great, because of the end he proposes to himself, such as, hope of gain, ambition, inordinate self-love, which are not virtues, but vices, and cannot, therefore, be the mother or source of virtues. But, as a gift of the Holy Ghost, fortitude is a supernatural habit, communicated to the will of the just man and to his irascible appetites, to perfect the will in the theological virtue of hope, that it may bravely undertake all things necessary for the accomplishment of its designs; and also to perfect in the irascible appetite the cardinal virtue of fortitude, when, of itself, this virtue would be too weak to suffer painful things courageously.

The gift of fortitude does all that the cardinal virtue supposes, but accomplishes it in a more excellent manner, namely, by the direct movement of the Holy Ghost Himself. As corporal things are often types of things spiritual, the prodigious physical strength with which God endowed Sampson is the figure of the strength which God confers on the soul by means of this gift. No man, before or since, ever equalled Sampson in this physical perfection. The Bible tells us that he tore a young lion, as if he were a kid; that, being bound with strong cords, he burst his bonds as easily as if fire consumed them; that he slew two thousand Philistines with the jaw-bone of an ass; that he carried away the gates of Gaza to a neighboring mountain, as readily as if they had been little sticks. The Holy Ghost works similar effects in the soul of the just man. Of him Isaias says: "It is he that giveth strength to the weary, and increaseth power and might to them that are not. They that hope in the Lord shall renew their strength; they shall take wings as eagles, they shall run and faint not." Certainly, this gift may be compared to certain elixirs and cordials, of which six or seven drops suffice to revive invalids who are half dead.

St. Bernard, speaking of this gift, says: "Fortitude renders a man fearless in adversity; hence Solomon says that the just man is confident as a lion, and that he fears nothing." The great souls that lived without reproach, as St. Paul testifies, were animated with this spirit, since with invincible courage they endured mockeries, prisons, scourges, and all sorts of calamities. "Remain in the city," said our Lord to the apostles; hide yourselves as weak and imbecile, "till you be endowed with power from on high." The Holy Ghost bestows an interior vigor, a divine courage, which renders things impossible to nature not only possible, but easy. Without this savor the fasts, watchings, and other mortifications of religious, would be painful indeed, but with His assistance we find them sweet and delightful. The apostles, after they had received this gift, were no longer faint-hearted. "They went out from the council," says St. Luke, "rejoicing that they had been accounted worthy to suffer for the name of Christ." "It is an admirable work of God," says Cassian, "that man, who is composed of flesh, can despoil himself of its inclinations, and be firm and constant in the divine service, under such varied and difficult circumstances." This a holy old man declared when, after being much tormented by the populace of Alexandria, who scoffingly asked, "What miracle did Jesus Christ do, that you should adore him?" he answered: "The miracle He has wrought is this: that the insults you give me, and the injuries you do me, though they were many times greater, are not capable of offending me." The learned Cardinal of Vitry attests that God opened his treasures to Blessed Mary d'Oignies, and drew from them the precious jewel of fortitude, with which to adorn her; hence she was neither dejected by adversity, nor elevated by prosperity; she received abuse and outrage with tranquillity of mind, and, far from being offended with those who injured her, she loved them with cordial charity. She was unshaken in her holy resolutions; she undertook bravely great and heroic things for the honor of God, without troubling herself about their probable issue; she waited patiently for the misfortunes which she foresaw, and, when they came, she received them without a murmur. One day being tormented by a grievous sickness, a pious person who happened to be with her, touched with pity, besought God to grant the sufferer some relief. This prayer was instantly heard; but the saint, after thanking her friend, entreated her not to pray for that intention again, as she wished to suffer her pains without any comfort whatever.

This gift regulates the interior and the exterior man, giving to the one and the other a wise constancy, banishing all levity and precipitation, restraining natural impetuosity, preventing many little agitations of mind, retrenching useless and superfluous movements of the head, the hands, the eyes and other members; watching over the heart, that it may not be grieved by untoward occurrences; foreseeing and enduring patiently and sweetly the many trials which are inevitable, and strengthening soul and body in every emergency. It confers supernatural strength to fast long, to keep weary vigils, to pass many hours, and even whole nights, in prayer, like St. Anthony, who complained that the sun rose too soon, because, when day dawned, he was obliged to finish his prayer. It enables the soul and body to endure strange and terrible sufferings. It supported Simon Stylites on his pillar, and St. Lidwina in her long and painful sickness. But what shall I say of the martyrs? Can anything be more glorious than to see queens and princesses, young girls and tender children, resist the threats, the persuasions, the promises of tyrants, and all the endearments of fond fathers and mothers, brothers and husbands, and yield up their delicate bodies to the most horrible torments which the fury of men, or the rage of the demons, could invent, with patience and even with joy? The Church says of St. Agatha that she went to prison with as much joy as others go to a banquet. Verily, this gift rendered the martyrs indomitable.

God said to the prophet Jeremias: "Thou shalt arise and speak to them all that I command thee; be not afraid in their presence, for I will make thee not to be afraid of their countenance. I have made thee a pillar of iron and a wall of brass. And they shall fight against thee, and not prevail, for I am with thee, to deliver thee." By this gift, while the body suffers grievous maladies, the mind is calm, and the spirit becomes ready to go to God. This is a signal operation of grace, for great torments naturally make a great impression on the soul as well as on the body, because of the mysterious bonds between soul and body, and the wonderful power pain has of drawing to itself all the attention of the mind. Blessed Angela Foligno relates of herself that being, by the special grace of God, animated with this heavenly fortitude, she ardently wished to die the most cruel death that could be devised, and to feel in all her members the most excessive rigors. She was not astonished at what the martyrs suffered, since she experienced within herself a desire to suffer still more. When assailed by injuries, and overwhelmed with opprobrium, she prayed for those who injured her, and tenderly loved them ; nor did she think that the saints who had prayed for their persecutors had done any great thing, since she did the same herself, with uncommon fervor and earnestness. These wonders show that, weak though we be by our nature, we become invincible by the grace of God and the succor of the gift of fortitude. A Japanese Christian, who had a natural dread of fire, in order to prepare for the persecution which she knew was coming, used often to go close to the fire, to inure herself to heat ; but as soon as it burned her a little, she was constrained to withdraw, not being able to endure the torture. This grieved her much, for she feared that she could not suffer so dreadful a martyrdom ; but God appeared to her, and told her that she would assuredly be martyred, and by fire too, adding that He would give her such powerful help that she would suffer with amazing constancy, which accordingly happened. In short, this gift raises us above riches and poverty, above contempt and honor, above pleasures and sorrows, above life and death, and makes us victorious over all enemies, in every encounter. The great things which this gift enables the soul to do and suffer, do not inspire pride : she refers to God all the glory and praise of them, and thanks Him a thousand times for the succors He has given for their accomplishment. When St. Peter the martyr, who suffered under Decius, was asked by the proconsul whether he was a Christian, he answered, "Yes, I am a Christian;" and when the executioners broke his bones on a wheel, he looked at his judge, and then raising his eyes to heaven, he exclaimed : "Thanks be to Thee, O Lord Jesus Christ! who hast given me courage to defy this impious tyrant." When this gift fails us, we become weak and tepid; we fear everything, the smallest trifle is capable of annoying us. With it, reeds, like Agnes and Agatha, are pillars; without it, pillars, like David and Peter, become reeds. Peter, after all the instructions and examples of our Lord, after pledging his solemn word to remain faithful, denied his Master at the voice of a simple servant-maid. With this gift one does not burn in the furnace or drown in the sea; one does not fall in slippery places, or sicken in pestilential atmospheres. Without it, we become weak in the most salubrious atmosphere, we stumble on the safest road, we are drowned by a few drops of water, or reduced to ashes by a spark. With it, a person can be recollected in the most distracting business; without it, he is dissipated in the depth of solitude. With it, we are chaste in the most infamous places; without it, the flesh rebels against the spirit during the holiest conversations. With it, one is humble in the midst of applause; without it, one glories even in his defects or vices. With it, nothing can disturb a man; without it, a straw is enough to torment him. As Isaias says : "The most vigorous become weak without fortitude, and the weak become invincible with it."

The first means to acquire this most necessary gift is, to ask it of God. For this purpose the ancient Christians had incessantly in their mouths these words with which the Church begins the canonical hours : "Incline unto my aid, O God! O Lord! make haste to help me;" and those others: "Restore unto me the joy of Thy salvation, and strengthen me with a perfect spirit:" a generous spirit, ready to suffer and to die for Thee. When we undertake any particularly difficult action, we must pray in a more special manner, as Judith did when she was about to cut off the head of Holofernes. For these she prayed with tears: "O Lord! fortify me now to do what I believed I could accomplish with Thy assistance. Strengthen my arm in this dangerous circumstance;" and taking the sleeping heathen by the hair of his head, she continued: "O God! confirm me in this hour, that I may free my nation from the tyrant. Humility must ever accompany these prayers, as well as self-distrust, and unshaken confidence in God, by whose grace we can do all things.

The second means is the worthy participation in the body and blood of our Lord, for, in the blessed Eucharist, we are united to Him who is strength itself, the arm of the mighty, the Omnipotent, as His holy Mother called Him, the Lion of the tribe of Juda, as He is styled in the Apocalypse. We read that Chiron, tutor of Achilles, fed this young prince with the marrow of lions: and this it was which gave him such extraordinary bodily strength. When we receive the divine Eucharist, we feed on the marrow and flesh and blood of the Lion of Juda, which should confer on us supernatural courage. "We come from this holy table," says St. Chrysostom, "like lions; and by the celestial banquet we are rendered terrible to the devil. Hence the Eucharist is called by David the bread of angels and the food of the strong, because it renders those strong who receive it with requisite dispositions. To produce these effects, it is administered to the sick as a *Viaticum* to a happy eternity, to fortify them for their last passage; and the martyrs would not face their judges till they were divinely nourished with this heavenly bread. This was the source of that admirable constancy of which St. Augustine speaks, when he says: "The martyrs who had drunk abundantly of this mysterious wine, marched bravely to death, heeding neither wives nor children, fathers nor mothers;" and, speaking of St. Lawrence, he says: "This invincible martyr, during his long and horrible torments, showed that he had worthily eaten the body and drunk the blood of our Lord, and fattened on this celestial food, for he lost the sentiment of his sufferings, and smiled joyfully, though stretched on his gridiron."

The third and last means is to use faithfully the natural courage God has given us, sustained by His ordinary grace of the cardinal virtue, and the gift of fortitude, as far as we possess it, to perform our daily actions well, that we may receive from Him the gift in a more eminent degree. For this end we must accustom ourselves to overcome nature in little things, to subject the soul daily more and more to grace, to destroy bad habits, to resist the passions, to regulate the imagination, to act with more reflection, to constrain ourselves to be more attentive at prayer, more recollected during the day, more docile to the movements of grace; to speak less, to evince less curiosity, to close the ears to news, to inure ourselves somewhat to hunger and thirst, heat and cold; to accommodate ourselves to the humors of others, to endure a cold look, to receive tranquilly a little contempt, to covet a slight abjection, to endure some opposition to our will and judgment, and, moreover, to strive, in all the little daily trials of life, to increase this gift in our souls: for a man does not become a good general without having been first a good soldier; he must practise the lowest degrees of warfare to fit him for the highest, passing through all the intermediate grades.

We very frequently err by neglecting to do for our perfection that which it is in our own power to do. We desire to fight against giants, before we can measure swords with persons of our own stature. David, while young, combated the wild beasts that would have destroyed his flocks, else he had not been worthy to gain the victory in his encounter with Goliath.

When we shall have vanquished lions and bears, that is to say, our passions, we shall get grace to do more. The abundant communication of the gift of fortitude is the recompense of the good use we make of the virtue of fortitude which resides in our souls, in the annoyances that happen every day.

§ 5.—*Of the gift of piety.*

The word piety signifies, first, a natural affection; second, a particular virtue; and, third, a gift of the Holy Ghost,—the gift of piety.

1. It signifies a tenderness and affection toward our parents, which our nature has imprinted on our hearts, and, in order, to those who have some relation to us, as our friends, our neighbors, our countrymen, and those who are afflicted and miserable. This affection is a passion of the sensitive appetite, neither praiseworthy nor censurable, since it is found in beasts and in birds, especially the swan, which is called the *pious bird*, because it takes care of its parents. Filial affection is another name for this natural piety.

2. The piety which is a virtue, has reference to justice; by it we give to God *latria*, the supreme honor which is His due; we acquit ourselves of our duties toward our parents, our country, and all that belong to us.

3. The piety which is a gift of the Holy Ghost, unites us to God as to our Father, and to all things which relate to Him, in proportion as they are dear to Him. "As the gifts of the Holy Ghost," says the Angelic Doctor, "should render us supple to His movements, He gives us the gift of piety, and the heart of a child toward God, according to that saying of the apostle: 'You have received the spirit of adoption whereby we cry, *Abba, Father.*' The gift of piety prepares our

souls for this illustrious spirit, and binds us to God with the golden chain of filial love, for He is our true Father."

This gift is the source of all other gifts, because it honors God as a true Father, it cultivates great affection for Him, and for all that appertains to Him. It defends Him with zeal, and receives His words with veneration. It consoles in adversities, it strengthens in combats. It accepts from the hand of God riches and poverty, honor and contempt, health and sickness. Its only fear is lest it should offend Him; and, should this happen, it is deeply afflicted, and earnestly strives to obtain pardon as soon as possible.

This gift imprints on the heart great love and zeal for the Holy Roman Church, our mother, teaching us to submit to her with the simplicity and docility of children; to revere all her ceremonies, to be grieved at the persecutions and slanders that come upon her, and to pray to God, with sighs and tears, that He would remove them. It impels us to honor the saints, especially the Queen of Saints, our Lady, as being the creature most intimately connected with God, the Daughter of the Father, the Mother of the Son, the Spouse of the Holy Ghost, and to respect her as our true Mother, in all that regards our salvation. It makes us love all human beings, because they belong to God, and are truly His by many titles. Piety makes it easy for us to address all with gentle and gracious words, in a manner at once frank and cordial. It also inclines us to pardon faults, to be merciful and compassionate, to look upon human miseries with tearful and pitying eyes. It puts upon the tongue words of kindness and consolation, and urges the hands to works of mercy and charity. It makes us love to assist all who require our assistance, compassion or sympathy, for sake of our common Father. In short, piety makes us regard all creatures as belonging to God; as, when we see the pages and valets of a king, we know them by their royal livery, and cannot think of them without thinking of their master. "This gift," says Harphius, "engenders in the heart a natural inclination for benevolence, a love for all creatures, because of their bond of union with their Creator. Without this gift, man would comport himself differently, because he would not remember that God is his Father. He would speak to Him, not as to a father, but a stranger. He would not regard that paternal Providence that regulates all things for his good, as the ordainer of events, but refer all events to chance, the ignorance of creatures, or the malice of enemies. And toward his fellow-man he would be without affection, of a cold, ungracious demeanor; devoid of compassion for the miserable, indifferent to the necessities of his neighbor: men, as St. Paul says, *full of love for themselves, without friendship, haughty, disdainful, rough, cruel and unpitying.*"

As this gift is very necessary, being, as it is, a stream flowing from the infinite mercy of God, a ray of His bounty, a participation in His charity, which inclines us to communicate ourselves according to His example, let us ask it earnestly of the Holy Spirit, since it is His gift, and of the Son, that we may love God with a filial spirit, like Him, in our measure. Let us recite the Lord's Prayer in a filial manner, and remember that its first words assure us that God is our Father, and that we should entertain for Him the sentiments of true children; and let us, moreover, continually exercise ourselves in works of piety and mercy, according to the counsel St. Paul gave his dear disciple, Timothy. Let the delightful thought that God is our Father be familiar and habitual with us. Let us think of Him, and speak to Him, and receive all things from His hand, as from our father. Let us fly sin, because it displeases Him, and grieve over our failings, doing all this with a filial spirit, thereby executing what God commanded by Jeremias: *Begin, at least now, to call me thy Father.* Let us strive to treat with men in this excellent and divine manner, regarding them as the children of God, with eyes of respect and honor, and never suffering anything to lessen our esteem for them, remembering the excellent prerogatives that make them lovable.

§ 6.—*Of the gift of counsel.*

This gift, being the first of the seven which perfects the understanding of the just soul, is very important in the many emergencies of this life. It is a supernatural light which the Holy Ghost sheds upon the soul, to empower it to discern good from evil; to judge rightly in difficult cases, where reason would not suffice; to teach us what to do, and what to avoid, when to speak, and when to be silent. Solomon, by this gift, was able to judge between the two women who each claimed the living child as her own. This gift is a means, not an end; hence St. John Damascene observes that it is not found in God, who knows all things, but is necessary for us, who are ignorant and short-sighted. Yet as our Lord, the Incarnate Wisdom, possessed it, according to Isaias, we must remember that counsel may be considered in two ways, namely: in him who gives it, and in him who receives it. A man who ordinarily gives good advice, and suggests proper expedients, is said to be a man of good counsel: thus was St. Antoninus commonly styled at Florence, even while he was a simple religious. If we regard counsel merely as an abundance of light, capable of directing men in doubtful and difficult conjunctures, it is found in our Lord; but when we regard it otherwise, it belongs only to an imperfect mind, as the mind of man.

The gift of counsel conducts the just man by a supernatural rule, namely, the movement of the Holy Ghost, in the selection and the application of the means which lead to his eternal end, as the infused virtue of prudence guides a man by another supernatural rule, which is faith in the truth of our Lord, while acquired prudence governs the daily actions by the rule of reason. This gift instructs and guides us in important and difficult conjunctures; it directs the gift of fortitude, and hinders it from degenerating into temerity. In undecided matters, this gift is especially necessary; and here it differs from that of knowledge, which conducts a man by things already determined by the law of God. St. Thomas says that God, while governing His creatures with sovereign wisdom and infinite goodness, does not destroy the natural inclinations He has given them, but, on the contrary, preserves and perfects these inclinations, using them as ways by which to reach the end He has marked out; and man, being endowed only with reason, does not know the truth of things all at once, as angels and as souls detached from matter do. The wisest are obliged to consider both sides of a question, and in these considerations and researches God assists us to discover the right path by the gift of counsel, having previously infused the cardinal virtue of prudence, which is the eye of all the other virtues, and the guide of their operations. This noble virtue exercises three acts, to which all its other acts are reduced: the first is, to deliberate, consult, and seek expedients; the second is, to judge and pronounce on the things deliberated and suggested; and the third is, to command the execution of the things which appear the best. Prudence is defined by philosophy to be the just rule by which to do things, and to act in all emergencies. Prudence has two sorts of parts: the first are integral, because they compose its integrity, as the members constitute our body; and the others are potential, or organic, because they are the organs by which it is produced, as we say that the understanding and the will are the potential faculties of a reasonable soul, because they are the faculties which produce its operations. The potential parts of prudence are three, namely, three intellectual virtues: the first of which

St. Thomas calls *euboulia*, whose function is to give a good counsel; the second is called *synesis*, judicious, whose function it is to judge wisely of common things; and the third is called *gnome*, judicious by excellence, which judges rightly in the extraordinary and unforeseen things that sometimes happen. *Synesis* attaches itself only to what the law has already determined; but if the fulfilment of a law in some extraordinary case would be ruinous to the republic, *gnome* penetrates the *intentions* of the legislator, which are to defend the republic, and acts accordingly. These three virtues are necessary to the high perfection of prudence. There are eight integral parts in prudence: memory, understanding, docility, vivacity, reason, foresight, circumspection and precaution; the first five belong to passive prudence, and the three others to prudence directing. Prudence receives a knowledge of things past from the memory, of things present from the understanding, and, from the memory and understanding combined, is sometimes able to presage the future. The Latin word, *prudens*, like *providens*, signifies one who sees things at a distance, one who looks forward.

We acquire knowledge by ourselves, or we learn it from others. If we acquire it ourselves, or by our own invention, subtlety and vivacity are necessary; if another gives it, docility must render us capable of receiving it. And when we have acquired this knowledge, by ourselves or others, reason instructs us how to use it in the occasions that present themselves. For prudence in action, the first ingredient is foresight, to select wisely the means best fitted for the end proposed; the second is circumspection, to examine attentively all the circumstances of a thing; and the third, precaution, to avoid all that might hinder its success, to foresee the obstacles likely to be raised. Six vices combat this excellent virtue by excess of prudence, namely: prudence of the flesh, which seeks its own ends by crooked ways, and thinks all means good that can bring about the desired end; *finesse*, which seduces the simple, under pretext of serving them; fraud, which executes *finesse* by action, and deceit, which executes it by words; excessive care for temporal things, and too eager solicitude for the future. Prudence is also combated by want of prudence, namely: by precipitation, inconsiderateness, inconstancy and negligence. Precipitation is opposed to good counsel, inconsiderateness to sound judgment, inconstancy and negligence to sensible direction.

God has given us prudence for a guide, but all our prudence, infused or acquired, is often too weak to dissipate the thick darkness of our understanding, to teach us to discover the wiles of nature, to guard us against the deceits of the devil; hence He used prudence, to prepare us to receive the gift of counsel, which perfects the virtue of prudence in all its parts, illuminates us in the ways of salvation, and teaches us the most excellent means to attain virtue. Speaking of Blessed Mary d'Oignies, the pious Cardinal James of Vitry says: "The servant of Jesus Christ, being enlightened by the spirit of counsel, did no action precipitately, but always acted with care, circumspection and deliberation, omitting nothing through pusillanimity, and performing nothing through impetuosity or over-eagerness. The Holy Spirit with this gift animates us powerfully to perfection, and gives us excellent counsels of sanctity. It unceasingly urges the soul, teaching her to act, not by passion nor by mere reason, but divinely. It overflows the memory with the thought of God, the understanding with His light, the will with His love. It propels the soul to God as to her centre, as the river to the sea, the stone to the earth, the flame to its own sphere. It teaches the practice of patience and humility, goodness, charity and meekness, and spurs on the soul to the degree of perfection which God wills her to attain. Sometimes the Holy Spirit inspires with this gift chosen souls, exciting them to perform extraordinary and heroic actions. Thus some of the saints have counterfeited the idiot; others have suddenly been endowed with wonderful gifts. Those who are really directed by the Spirit of God walk under the conduct of a guide incomparably more excellent than reason; hence we may gather that :—

1. Without this gift we should easily miss the right path, fall over precipices, become inconstant and impetuous in all things. If we lose it, or its predecessor, the cardinal virtue of prudence, we shall be compelled to walk without a torch through perilous places, and surely fall. Some men are blind in all things, so that it seems as if they were delivered up to *a reprobate sense,* as St. Paul says. Princes and monarchs have been found in all ages, from whom God has withdrawn His Spirit, and who, by their strange errors, almost ruin their states. The possession of this gift is so useful that the Wise Man says : *Counsel shall keep thee, and prudence shall preserve thee* from false paths. Let us, then, often demand earnestly of God this rich gift of His Holy Spirit, and dispose ourselves to receive it by humility, submission of mind, and disengagement from creatures. Let us do nothing rashly, that is to say, without begging the divine aid and light. Let us beseech Him to teach us how to act in every emergency, saying with the Royal Prophet: "Show me, O Lord! Thy paths, and lead me in Thy ways. Direct me in Thy truth, and teach me." Josue failed in this matter, when he permitted himself to be duped by the Gabaonites; hence the Scripture remarks in this instance, that *the mouth of the Lord had not been consulted.* Neither Josue nor his counsellor had asked the light of God, and therefore they were deceived.

§ 7.—*Of the gift of knowledge or science.*

There are three sorts of knowledge : the first is that of philosophy, which regards a thing in its source, and discovers it by its effects; the second is theology, which is drawn from the Scripture and the articles of faith, and teaches us to instruct the ignorant, and to defend religion against heretics and others who combat against it. This science is generally acquired with labor and study, though occasionally it is a gratuitous gift. It may, like philosophy, exist in the vicious as well as the virtuous, and therefore it has often happened that men of loose morals learnedly defended the faith, and persuaded their adversaries, with more success than virtuous men could, because they were more learned.

The third is the science of the saints, which the Scripture often mentions. This is the *gift of knowledge*, which the Holy Ghost infuses into the soul, to teach us to regard all things in the designs of their creation, and use them as steps to reach Him. It does not depend on reasoning, as philosophy and theology do, but on the light of the Holy Spirit, which, in a moment, irradiates the whole soul. Its objects are all created things, which it uses as faith teaches; its dwelling is inferior reason, as superior reason is the dwelling of wisdom. It produces salutary effects on the just soul, teaching her that creatures are drawn out of nothing by the infinite power of God; that they are preserved by the hand that produced them, that their perfections come from Him, outside of whom there is neither wisdom, nor essence, nor beauty. It teaches us what we are, what we have been, and what we may hope, by the grace of God, to become. It makes us regard all things as ladders to reach Him, as mirrors to reflect Him, as books to instruct us in His perfections, and, in general, as means to draw us to Him.

As the things of the world ensnare and captivate us with a sort of magic, the gift of science unmasks them and manifests them as they really are. It views them with reference to death and eternity; it shows that they are not worth the pains and troubles with which they are acquired; that they cannot content our hearts. It is only our littleness of mind that makes us esteem them great, just as children value their dolls and playthings. This gift confers discernment of spiritual things, showing us how to root out our passions, to acquire virtue, to arrive at perfection, according to the attraction of the Holy Spirit, to recognize the deceits of the devil and the *ruses* of nature, and to show how to discern the movements of grace. When this gift is wanting in the soul, she is easily deceived. The wisest man, if devoid of it, sees the mysteries of nature, but cannot decipher them correctly ; like a boy who looks at a Latin book without knowing the Latin language. He may distinguish the letters and form them into syllables and words, but he cannot comprehend what they signify. Clever men know natural things by their properties and effects, but they do not recognize the purposes they are created to serve. After the Royal Prophet had declared that all creation furnished him with motives for loving God, he added : "Thou hast delighted me, O Lord ! in Thy works ; and in the works of Thy hands I rejoice. How magnificent are Thy works, O Lord! But the ignorant man knoweth not this ; and the fool cannot understand it."

"All men are vain," says the Book of Wisdom, "in whom there is not the knowledge of God, and who, by the good things that are seen, could not understand Him that is ; neither by attending to the works have they acknowledged the workman." The saints without any tincture of letters, as St. Anthony, knew how to regard the world as a great book always open, which taught them to honor, adore and love God. "My mouth," says David, "shall show forth Thy justice and Thy salvation all day long. Because I have not known, I will enter into the powers of the Lord. O Lord ! I will be mindful of Thy justice alone :" it will suffice to teach me.

But without the succor of God, not only are men ignorant of the true end of all creatures, but use them to offend the

Creator. Some know them only as ministering to the pleasures of the body, others as ministering to those of the mind ; as St. Paul recounts of the ancient philosophers, who, despite all their knowledge, used creatures against God, and defrauded God of the honor due to Him, to give it to beasts ; and unenlightened by Him, became slaves of the most execrable vices and passions. Hugh of St. Victor well said that creatures are like the strings of a lyre. If you do not touch them, they are silent ; if you touch them unskilfully, they produce discords ; but if you touch them scientifically, they give forth a sweet melody. If you do not touch creatures, if you consider them not, they are silent for you ; if you make a bad use of them, they will give forth discordant sounds ; but if you handle them virtuously, and with the gift of knowledge, they will sing in your ears delicious melody, and excite in you the knowledge, praise and love of God. St. Lawrence Justinian says : "Sometimes man is attracted to the love of God by the contemplation of created things, in which he recognizes visible traits of the Divine wisdom and goodness; he hears as many voices praising God as he perceives creatures, and the beautiful concert their spiritual harmony makes, resounds in his heart, and renders it impossible for him not to praise God when he sees all creatures employed in publishing His wonders. Transported with a singular pleasure by these ravishing harmonies, he is impelled to exclaim : *Lord, who is like unto Thee?* St. Denis explained this mystery by the beautiful word *Theophania*, which implies that the view of creatures should carry us to God, as a portrait reminds us of the lineaments of a friend. St. John Climacus speaks of a spiritual person who could not look on a beautiful face without shedding tears of devotion ; so that, what might have been to others the cause of destruction, was to him a source of merit and a means of high perfection. Verily, the first thing that ought to strike us when we regard creatures is, that they are divine. When we see a king, we are struck with awe, even though he be still a babe; his infancy and weakness do not hinder us from making a most profound obeisance. When the priest elevates the Host, we do not think of its color or form; we reflect that it veils our Lord Himself. In natural things, let us not regard merely the beauty and other perfections, but look on them as works of God, created for His glory and for our salvation. To God we must refer all His admirable works. Of this our Lord is an excellent model, because He is the Word and the knowledge of the Father, and is infinitely glorious to Him, this glory being the esteem and perfect praise of Him : "A Word and a fruitful knowledge," says St. Augustine, "who with His Father produces the Holy Ghost, who, being the personal love of both, is the principle of all sanctity and perfection. As man, He always proposed as His only end the glory of God and the salvation of souls, and He spoke only words of eternal life. Now, as our knowledge is a ray of His, His science being the source of ours, we must, in order to be perfect, take God for the rule and measure of ours, and avoid the dangers of which our Lord warned us when He said : *If the light that is in thee be darkness, the darkness itself, how great will it be!*—a text which specially refers to science.

Let us strive earnestly for this grand gift, and often ask it of the Holy Ghost, saying with David : "Divine Spirit, *teach me goodness and discipline and science.*" O God! enlighten me with this precious gift, without which all other science is useless and even hurtful. Everything is vain which is not referred to its true destiny. Is it not a strange and lamentable fact that the devil who has prodigious science and skill, occupies himself in cursing God? But he is now in a state of reprobation, and his gifts serve only for his chastisement. Well, before his fall, he possessed these gifts as helps to his salvation, and, nevertheless, he fell. It is, then, an easy matter for us to fall, how rich soever our science may be ; and hence we should earnestly beg this great gift which will purify, sanctify and deify our minds and our studies, by referring them to God, and daily discovering in all things new motives to love and serve Him. There are four sorts of knowledge, namely: 1, that which enters through the senses ; 2, that which comes through the medium of reason; 3, that which emanates from the light of grace ; and, 4, that which the light of glory produces. The knowledge given by the senses is imperfect, and is common to all animals. The knowledge communicated by reason is more perfect, showing an object according to its nature, its effects, its feeling, and other qualities ; it extends not only to things present, but also to things absent, but it gives information in a merely natural manner. The knowledge by grace is incomparably nobler, because supernatural ; this is properly the gift of knowledge of which we have been speaking. Finally, the knowledge gained by glory appertains to the blessed, and forms their beatitude in heaven. I will conclude this section with these beautiful words of the apostle : *Beware lest any man cheat you by philosophy and vain deceit ; according to the tradition of men, according to the elements of the world, and not according to Christ. For in Him dwelleth all the fulness of the Godhead corporally.*

§ 8.—*The gift of understanding, or intelligence.*

The name of intelligence is given to pure spirits, as the angels, and to God himself, who is the first Intelligence. Understanding, or intelligence, is the noblest faculty of our soul, which serves for a mental eye. It teaches us the first principles of things, as for example, that the present is not the past, that a whole is greater than a part ; and in practice it teaches us to avoid evil, to honor our parents, and similar things. But the understanding, which is a gift of the Holy Ghost, is a supernatural habit conferred by grace on the soul of man, which illuminates for him the mysteries of faith and the things of salvation. It is speculative; for, though all the gifts of the Holy Ghost tend to the exercise of good works, some do this by irradiation, and others by practical influence. The Angelic Doctor teaches that the word understanding signifies a strong and intimate knowledge: "For," says he, "*intelligence* comes from *intus legere.*" Among things, some are veiled, as substances under accidents, truth under figures, thoughts under words, and understanding is necessary to discover them; but as our understanding is often weak, and as faith teaches things obscurely,—for faith is to believe, not to see,—man, in order to know the secrets of God's mysteries and the sense of the Scriptures, often requires a more particular light with which God favors him in the gift of intelligence.

The first degree of understanding is, to manifest to the soul the truth of one mystery by reasons which make it evident; for, every man in the state of grace is always provided by God with understanding enough to believe and know all things necessary for his salvation. Hence we see many who, being very ignorant, are unable to give the reasons for the various points of faith, and who, nevertheless, believe them with invincible firmness; not so much because of a distinct light, as by a divine impression, which renders them so immovable in their belief that riches, honor, pleasures, threats, promises, torments or death cannot shake their constancy. The second degree of understanding is when this gift confers a high degree of knowledge of the mysteries; and the third, when it unravels them clearly, as when David said of himself: "The secret and hidden things of Thy wisdom Thou hast manifested to me. Thy testimonies are wonderful: therefore my soul hath sought them. The declaration of Thy words giveth light, and giveth understanding to little ones. I opened my mouth and panted, because I longed for Thy commandments."

Thus it happened to St. Augustine, who, before his conversion, could not, with all the subtlety of his learned and powerful mind, penetrate the mystery of the Incarnation; but after his baptism the door was opened to him, for he had become humble: "I could not be satiated," says he, "in these happy days of my spiritual infancy with reflecting on the depths of Thy counsels and Thy wonderful operations for the salvation of the human race. The mysteries of faith are secrets, the exterior of which often repels; but what they contain is admirable, like the famous *Silenes* of Alcibiades in Plato, of which the appearance was ordinary and even gross, while they contained within ravishing beauty and invaluable treasures.

This gift manifests the excellence of grace, it shows the beautiful order and perfect symmetry of all the parts of our holy religion; that it is august and venerable, that its least ceremonies have been wisely instituted; how the old law corresponds to the new, as the body to the soul; how there is nothing contradictory in the Holy Scriptures; how the articles of faith, if not *according with* reason, are not *against* it, but *above* it. It discovers to the just man the causes of the things that happen to him; how sickness, loss of honor and of friends, should conduce to his salvation; why he has not received more talent or judgment, more memory or knowledge; why things do not succeed which he has undertaken for good purposes. It shows him what God hid in the commencement to give him means of exercising faith, hope, charity, obedience and fortitude, of which the recompense is the gift of intelligence, which is conferred in proportion to the acts of these virtues made by him; for, the more faith, submission and respect we evince with reference to the conduct of God, the better shall we be disposed to receive His lights, and understand the secrets of His providence.

This gift illumines the understanding like a torch, discovering things that were before invisible, as the curiosities of a cabinet are displayed best in a strong light. With this gift, a peasant or a villager, a servant or a beggar, knows more about the secrets of salvation than do many great philosophers and erudite theologians, who, not having this gift, are dry and destitute of unction, and are influenced by vanity rather than charity. Without it we should discover but little of the things of God; they would be sealed books to us, and we might apply to ourselves these words of our Lord to His apostles: "I see well that you are without understanding."

We should resemble those little children who see the priest at the altar in his sacerdotal vestments going through the most mysterious ceremonies, but are ignorant of what all this signifies: while with it the simplest persons are capable of contemplating mysteries of faith, and can spend with delight whole hours in the consideration of God and His works. "Then you shall see and abound," says Isaias, "and your heart shall be enlarged:" the mysteries of faith shall be the fruitful sources of your contemplation, as happened to Blessed Brother Giles, who said, speaking of himself, that he knew a person who received a hundred lights and a hundred interpretations on every verse of the holy Psalms he daily recited, every one of which was capable of exciting wonder and delight. Certainly, those who have received this gift in a high degree can easily close their eyes to earthly things, as people nurtured in the pomp of courts despise the feasts and dances of plebeians.

God is the rule and measure of all created things. His truth is the truth of all things, His goodness the goodness of all, His beauty the beauty of all, His felicity the happiness of all: the more closely things approach Him, the more they participate in His perfection; the farther they retire from him, the more imperfect they grow. As things corporal have the least share of His being, which is purely spiritual, so things spiritual approach Him more nearly, and consequently are incomparably more excellent. What can be conceived more beautiful than our Lord in all the particulars of His life and death, when He is pleased to execute in us the words of the prophet Isaias: "I will give thee intelligence, and I will instruct thee"? "The Son of God has come on earth," says St. Bernard, "when He works such wonders that our mind may well withdraw its attention from earth to observe them, to meditate on them, to converse about them. Truly He has given to our understanding a vast field for consideration, a torrent of meditations so deep and so high, that it is simply impossible to realize their profundity, or comprehend their sublimity." As this gift is of such immense utility, it should be earnestly desired and prayed for. "Blessed is the man," says David, "whom Thou shalt instruct and shalt teach in Thy law."

Let us then beg unceasingly for this great gift. Let us ask it of the Father whom St. James calls "the Father of lights;" let us implore it of the Son who is the knowledge of the Father, and of the Holy Ghost, to whom properly appertains the distribution of it. Let us say to God with David: "Give me understanding and teach me Thy law, that I may keep it with my whole heart. Lift up my eyes to consider the wonders of Thy law: I am Thy servant, give me understanding, that I may know Thy testimonies. Enlighten me, that I may live." It is impossible to obtain it without firm and simple faith, for God says by Isaias: "If you will not believe, you shall not understand." Humility is also necessary, and it was want of this virtue that rendered the conversion of the Gentile philosophers so difficult, as St. Augustine remarked, when speaking of the Platonic school: "They are ashamed," says he, "wise as they are and disciples of Plato, to become disciples of Jesus Christ, who has inspired an ignorant fisherman to utter these memorable words which a Platonic philosopher said ought to be engraved in golden letters on the most eminent places in every church: *In the beginning was the Word, and the Word was with God, and the Word was God.*"

§ 9.—*The gift of wisdom.*

The last and most excellent of the gifts of the Holy Ghost is the gift of wisdom, of which the Holy Scriptures say such beautiful and such marvellous things: " I have preferred her to kingdoms and thrones," says the Book of Wisdom, " and I have despised riches when compared with her; gold in her presence is only as sand, and silver in respect of her shall be counted as clay. She is more beautiful than the sun, more brilliant than the stars."

I know that whatever is said of wisdom in the Old Testament is understood, by many Fathers and Doctors, of the Incarnate Wisdom, Jesus Christ, our Lord; but I know also that, according to others, it refers likewise to the gift of wisdom, which the Holy Ghost infuses. The nature of this gift is that it imparts the *savory* knowledge of God and of divine things. "*Sapientia,*" (wisdom) says St. Bernard, probably takes its name from *savor*, a relish, that, being added to virtue, which was previously somewhat insipid, seasons it, and makes it agreeable. But we may lose this flavor or taste of good by the poison which the infernal serpent has spread in our hearts (to a certain extent we *have* lost it in the fall of Adam), and by the tyranny of the flesh and the senses. Wisdom is the savor of good, malice is the taste depraved by the savor of evil, and folly is disgust for good. The gift of wisdom is a savory and delicious pleasure which the soul feels in thinking of God, according to these words of the Psalmist: *Taste and see how sweet the Lord is.* It is a certain affection, good and holy, dry perhaps, but strong, sweet and full of unction,—the salt that preserves the savor of heavenly things, and makes them sweet to us."

St. Bonaventure says: "The gift, as regards its splendor, is like light; and, as regards the sweetness with which it fills the soul, like honey, or rather sweeter than honey." "It is," says Denis the Carthusian, "a supernatural brilliancy which illumines and deifies the human understanding, and which is among the most beautiful rays that emanate from the sun of the Divinity." "The gift of wisdom," says another doctor, "is a sun which drives away darkness, turns the spiritual night into day; it is the eye of the heart, it is a delicious fruit, it is the paradise of the soul, which changes a mortal, miserable man into a god. By means of it the soul becomes all light, all visage, all eyes, like the mysterious animals of which Ezekiel speaks, and which had each four faces, and were *full of eyes;* because there is no faculty of the soul which is not enlightened with this divine light. The material objects of this gift are the works of nature, grace and glory, which are all divine, considered in their source and in their end, inasmuch as they have come from God, and conduct to God." The formal object is to know them in their first principles, and to know them with relish and pleasure. Its three acts are: first, to know with great clearness things divine; the second is, to judge wisely of them; and the third, to taste and relish them. We may judge soundly of a thing by our assured knowledge of its truth, and again by a certain sympathy we feel with it. A sick man judges of his malady otherwise than his physician does: the patient judges of it by his feelings, and the doctor by science. The chaste man and the libertine know what chastity is, but each knows it in a different manner: the first by experience, the second by mere knowledge.

The gift of wisdom teaches us to judge of divine things in the highest manner, that is to say, with taste and relish: we not only know things by the gift of understanding, but we relish them, they become savory to us ; and by this savor we know that they are truly excellent, and distinguish them from false and despicable things, as we distinguish by our taste whether the food we use is sweet or bitter, pleasant or unpleasant. This gift is closely allied to that of understanding. Wisdom and intelligence are the most perfect of all the gifts. They dwell in the highest region of the soul, their objects are divine things, and they are rather speculative to enlighten, than practical to operate. Intelligence conducts to wisdom as to its fruit, as knowledge precedes judgment, and speculation, taste. The pleasures we find in the operations of the gift of understanding are not so great as those conferred by the gift of wisdom, which unites the soul more intimately to God. "Lord," says the Scripture, "those who from the commencement have pleased you, have been healed of their evils by means of wisdom. All sorts of good come together with her, and innumerable riches come to me through her hands, for she is an infinite treasure to men, which they that use, become the friends of God."

The effects of wisdom surpass all that can be said. Aristotle remarks, in his *Morals*, that the contemplative man who occupies himself with considering the nature of things need not seek any contentment outside himself, because the study of wisdom is to the mind a sort of marvellous satisfaction. Plato strives to show this at greater length in his *Phædon ;* yet these great philosophers spoke only of natural wisdom, which alone they knew, not of the supernatural gift of the Holy Ghost, which is immeasurably more elevated and excellent than mere natural science.

The gift of wisdom replenishes the understanding with admirable light, and the will with matchless happiness. All the operations of mystical theology refer to it. Of this gift the Royal Prophet says : "The law of the Lord I have desired above gold and precious stones; it is sweeter to me than honey and the honeycomb." And St. Augustine, in the beginning of his conversion, used to consider the mystery of the Incarnation with wonderful pleasure. "How often," says he, "have I not wept with tenderness when listening to the sweet harmony of the Canticles of Thy Church! The voices, flowing agreeably in my ears, distilled Thy truths in my heart; I felt my will inflamed; and my eyes shed torrents of tears, which overpowered my soul with joy."

The Cardinal of Vitry says of blessed Mary d'Oignies: "This holy woman, by means of the gift of wisdom, tasted and saw how sweet the Lord is, when her soul fattened on the honey and milk which flowed from the divine lips of her adorable Spouse, and she consumed in a paradise of delights this hidden manna. This savory gift put upon her tongue sweet and gracious words, and embalmed all her works with precious ointment. It rendered her calm in her interior, affable in her discourse, amiable in her actions, and inflamed her with charity toward all. It inspired such contempt for the honors and pleasures of this life, that she turned from them with disgust, as one who is accustomed to delicious meats experiences nausea when stale and disgusting food is given him."

Speaking of wisdom, St. James affirms that it is modest, pacific, sweet, full of mercy, and fruitful in good works. *Modest*, because it makes those who possess it chaste, temperate and sober; for, after having once tasted of the delights of the spirit, one ceases to be enamored of sensual pleasures. *Pacific*, because it puts all our affairs in order, and consequently in peace: "For wisdom is orderly," says Aristotle; "it being the property of a wise man to arrange things, put them in their own places, and by this means give them repose." *Modest*, because, being the mother of order, it is also the mother of discretion and modesty. *Susceptible of good counsel*, for it renders the soul docile to all the movements of the Holy Ghost.

Full of mercy, because full of resemblance to God. *Fruitful in good works*, to render it holy and replete with pure delights. Finally, it is not rash, because it goes to God with great simplicity, and acts in His presence with all possible innocence.

John Rusbrocius, speaking of this last quality, says: "We ought to hold ourselves before God in simplicity, and love Him, reflect on Him, and act for Him, in a simple spirit. The most simple are those who are the best regulated, who have the most interior peace, who go down deepest into God, who are the most illuminated, richest in good works, and endowed with the most universal charity; and as they are more like to God than others are, fewer obstacles arise to hinder or divert them." The gift of wisdom perfects the three theological virtues: faith it perfects with its knowledge, which wonderfully fortifies this virtue; hope and charity, with its sweet savor of God, which renders them more constant, and increases their ardor. Faith believes on the Word of God, but it sees not; hope is often faint and weary, and charity in this life experiences great hindrances in the performance of its interior and exterior acts: wisdom, as it carries light and heat, knowledge and joy, is the remedy for these deficiencies.

With its help we know and relish the things of God, we love all that regards His service, we find no contentment but in Him. There is more pleasure in doing mean actions through love of Him, than in bearing crowns and sceptres for any other motive. St. Teresa relates of herself that when, after great struggles, she entered religion, she felt intense delight in sweeping and performing the menial offices in the convent. All the grandeurs of earth, all the beauties of nature, all the delights of the senses, are by this gift changed into gall; what before was bitter to the soul, now becomes sweet, as St. Augustine experienced, particularly with regard to chastity. Poverty becomes more desirable than riches, austerity more sweet than sensual pleasures, and contempt is more delicious to the saints than all the honors and dignities of this world are to the ambitious. But without this gift the things of God are not esteemed, because they have not been tasted. One prefers to them the toys of children, the smoke of honor, the excitement of sin, and the riches of earth. The exercises of devotion become dry and insipid; the most touching objects, the most lively representations, the most devout songs, the most pious books, the strongest reasoning, the most pressing considerations, are sometimes unable to move the soul; while with one ray of this sun, with one drop of this honey, with one spark of this sacred fire, the most common things, the least ceremony of the Church, an ordinary prayer, some words one may have already heard a hundred times without effect, strike, enter, pierce. "Wisdom," says St. Bernard, "stifles the sentiments of the flesh, destroys the delectations of sense, purifies the understanding, cleanses the palate of the heart, that it may taste rightly of things. He who loves all things with a well-regulated love, despising earth, esteeming heaven, using this world as if he used it not; knowing, by a delicate and refined taste, how to distinguish between the things he may enjoy and those he must only use, between the end and the means; applying himself to eternal things with entire and continual affection,—such a man is truly wise, because he knows things as they are, and he may truly say : *God has set in order charity in me*, and taught me to love things according to their merit, bestowing on each the degree of affection which it deserves."

These singular advantages and admirable perfections of wisdom ought to urge us to esteem it highly, and desire ardently to possess it, saying with the Sage : *I have loved her, and sought her for my spouse*, because her attractions have made a powerful impression on my heart. This ardent desire is the first means to acquire wisdom, according to the experience of the Sage himself, who says : "*I wished*, and a right understanding was given me; *I called*, and the Spirit of Wisdom came upon me."

To desire we must add invocation and prayer, the second means of obtaining it, praying with most pressing instance that God would be graciously pleased to communicate to us this great gift in a high degree, and saying with the Wise Man: "Give me wisdom that sitteth by Thy throne, and cast me not off from among Thy children. Send her out of Thy holy heaven, that she may be with me, that I may know what is pleasing to Thee;" praying our Lord, who is the Incarnate Wisdom, and the Holy Ghost who is its proper donor, to communicate to us this immense gift. Undoubtedly so sublime a grace merits to be asked. "If any one want wisdom," says St. James, "let him ask of God who giveth to all men abundently and upbraideth not, and it shall be given him." "Give me," says the holy man, Job, "that I may be according to the days in which God kept me; when His lamp shone over my head, when God was secretly in my tabernacle."

If you wish to possess wisdom, ask grace, not science; desire, not understanding; weep, sigh and pray earnestly, for you will not find it in books. Ask God, not man; it is not mere light, but a fire that consumes the soul with its flames. Entreat wisdom of God, not of creatures, and let your prayer be made with recollection of mind, not with dissipation—in grace, not in speculation.

The third means to acquire wisdom is profound humility, of which St. Bernard says: "Whoever thou art that desirest to realize what it is to enjoy the Word and to possess the gift of wisdom, prepare not thy ear, but thy mind and heart, because it is grace, not the tongue of a master, that teaches this science; and it is not shown to the wise and prudent of this world, but to the little and the humble. O my brethren! how great a virtue is humility, which deserves to understand and see what cannot be taught! It is worthy to conceive of the Word by the operation of the Word Himself, which it is impossible to explain with all our words. But no person must attribute this grace to his own merit or dignity, but to the good pleasure of the Father of the Word, who has willed so to bestow it.

The fourth means is increased purity of soul and body, and a great elevation above the flesh and the pleasures of the sense : "For," says the apostle, "the sensual man is incapable of tasting the things of God ;" and the Sage had said before him : "Wisdom will not enter a malicious soul, or dwell in a body subject to sin." "Where," asks Job, "is the house of wisdom, where does she make her abode? Man knows not the price of her, for she is above all price, and she is not found in the land of them that dwell in delights."

Having thus treated of the spiritual man as far as we judged necessary for our purpose, it now remains for us to pass to the principles of the spiritual life ; and before elucidating those which regard it, in particular, in its three different stages, the purgative, the illuminative and the unitive state, we shall treat of it in general, by giving its general principles.

GENERAL PRINCIPLES

OF THE

SPIRITUAL LIFE.

Vol. II.

GENERAL PRINCIPLES
OF THE
SPIRITUAL LIFE.

CHAPTER I.

FIRST GENERAL PRINCIPLE OF THE SPIRITUAL LIFE.

That it is necessary to have general principles.

HAVING treated of the spiritual man as far as we considered necessary, we will now pass to the principles of the spiritual life, the subject of the second part of our work. To proceed with order, we shall speak, first, of its general principles, and afterward of those which regard it in particular. The first general principle of the spiritual life is to *have* general principles. Here, as in the sciences, we style certain propositions which hold the first rank, and certain great and important truths which are the origin of all others, *principles*. "A principle," says Aristotle, "is that whence a thing flows as from its source, or which is an ingredient in its composition, or which is the means whereby it comes to be known. Principles are the basis, the sustenance of the thing, and are, consequently, of the greatest importance." In the science of salvation and in the spiritual life, principles are certain fundamental truths of Christianity which contain all others, and are the most capable of making an impression on our minds and touching our hearts; of withdrawing us from vice, and inducing us to practise virtue. They are, for example, the following truths:—There is but one God, the Creator of heaven and earth; this God has made us for His glory, He recompenses our virtues and punishes our vices; He has not only universal, but particular, care of all that happens in the universe, and especially of man, His noblest and dearest work; He is present everywhere; His ears are always attentive to what we say; His eyes are always open to see what we do. The Son of God came on earth and clothed Himself with our nature to save us, and to become our model. There is only one important affair in this world, namely, our salvation: a happy or a miserable eternity invitably awaits us, according as we shall have lived here below. These and other like truths are denominated *principles*.

Any one who desires to give himself to virtue, and to make great progress in the spiritual life, ought to know these principles, and know them well, at least some of them. To this end, he should study them till he shall have obtained as much knowledge of them as his capacity admits of, and till they are solidly established in his mind. He must not complain if it should take a long time to imprint them on his heart and memory; for he can never know them too well, or penetrate them too deeply. They are the roots of a tree destined to bear fruits of life, the foundations of the spiritual edifice which he has planned, the sources of humility, patience, charity, and all the perfection which he can possibly acquire in this life.

In philosophy and in speculative sciences one cannot know too well the principles of a given question, and consequently cannot examine them too closely. The more clearly one sees them, the more clearly will he see their consequences, and the better will he be able to sustain them against those who attack them : otherwise he should be easily discomfited. Well, it is the same with the great principles of salvation.

When a person is attacked by the world, the flesh, or the devil, he will easily be vanquished if he have not these great maxims of religion as an arsenal, and as arms to defend himself. According as he shall consider or withdraw from the thought of the presence of God, His celestial Providence, and the example and love of our Lord, during the time of temptation, he shall be victorious, or be conquered. Even after making strong resolutions, these arms will not be of much advantage, if he be not familiar with their use. When he knows and can use them well, they become, at the moment of attack, a sword in his hand and a shield on his neck. A soldier may be readily captured and put to death, if he encounter his enemy far from the fort ; but he laughs at him, if he meet him near a strong citadel, the door of which is always open that he may seek shelter therein. To vanquish our adversaries in the temptations and combats we shall have to sustain, it is very important to have always ready some of these principles of Christianity which are capable of doing for us the office of a sword and shield. He who acts in this manner is like the Wise Man in the Gospel, of whom our Lord said that "he built his house upon a rock. And the rains fell, and the floods came, and the storms beat upon that house, and it fell not ; because it was founded upon a rock." On the contrary, he who does not govern himself in this manner imitates the foolish man that built his dwelling upon sand, and when the rains and floods came, they ruined that house, and it fell. God, as David sings, enlightens and fortifies souls on the eternal mountains, that is, in high and sublime virtue, when they have a good knowledge of it ; but those who are destitute of this knowledge are like poor fools, easily discomfited, who know not what to do, nor where to go, nor how to defend themselves when attacked. Therefore, as the same prophet sings, let us cast the foundations of our salvation in the holy mountains; let us establish the design of our perfection on these great and important truths, these *principles* of the spiritual life.

In the first Psalm, David elegantly compares the just man who thinks day and night of the law of God, and carefully weighs His mysteries, to a tree planted by running waters, which is always beautiful with verdure, and never fails to bring forth its fruit in due season. And persons whose souls are not enlightened with these lights, he compares to clay and dust which the wind blows in all directions. For these miserable beings, unable to make the considerations which alone can bestow constancy on their minds, are without any firmness, and not knowing which side to take, easily become the sport of every wind that assails them.

To acquire perfection, we ought to act by reason and not by sentiment, for reason endures, while feeling passes away. If you hate sin, despise the world, and love God to-day, because He gives you consolations; to-morrow, when these consolations are converted into bitterness, when your lights are extinguished, when the waters of sensible grace are dried up, you will no longer love God, you will feel drawn to sin, and the world will appear very agreeable to you. But, if you love God because He is worthy of your love, and hate sin because it deserves your hatred, and despise the world because it merits your contempt, you will do to-morrow and always what you do to-day. The reasons are always the same; they contain eternal truths which cannot change. We must, then, act by reason, and by the strongest reason, that is to say, by the principles of which we speak; for, besides being of greater consequence than others, they are also more powerful to move our hearts, and to keep us within the bounds of duty.

CHAPTER II.

SECOND GENERAL PRINCIPLE OF THE SPIRITUAL LIFE.

IGNORANCE of the things of God is the most universal cause of all the evils in the world, and the source whence flow nearly all the sins which men commit. The knowledge of the things of salvation is to us what the sun, by its sweet and vivifying light, is to the earth; and as its absence, total or partial, would ruin or greatly injure all nature, so ignorance of divine things entails upon us many evils. This truth was in the heart of the prophet Jeremias when he said: "With desolation is the land made desolate, because there is no one that thinketh upon these things in his heart." Before him. David had said: "They have not known nor understood; they walk on in darkness; all the foundations of the earth shall be moved." And before David, Job had said: "From morning to evening shall they be cut down, and, because no one understandeth, they shall perish forever." The prophet Osee expressed the same truths with still greater energy, saying: "Hear the word of the Lord, ye children of Israel, for the Lord shall enter into judgment with the inhabitants of the land : for there is no truth, and there is no mercy, and there is no knowledge of God in the land. Cursing and lying, and killing and theft, have overflowed, and blood hath touched blood. Therefore shall the land mourn ; and every one that dwelleth in it shall languish, and the people that doth not understand shall be beaten." Such are the evils which spring from the want of knowledge of heavenly things.

The reason of this is that man, by a movement which is common to him with all creatures,— but which is greater in him because of his excellence, and the intense love he bears himself,— has a strong and violent instinct for self-preservation. Hence he earnestly endeavors to avoid misfortune, because he regards it as the cause of his ruin, and he does all he can to procure himself prosperity, as being a means of his preservation. No one will deliberately insert a thorn in his arm, or chop the nail off his finger. Even when it is necessary to endure something, nature tries, if possible, to avoid it, or, at least, to lessen its pain. Experience also teaches that men will take great trouble in procuring a little pleasure; and hence we may justly conclude that they would take more pains for a still greater good, if they knew of such. Why do they not take great pains to secure the immense treasures, the sovereign delights, the unspeakable goods of soul and body, which God has prepared for them in heaven? Why do they, by their bad lives, precipitate themselves into the horrible torments of hell? The true reason of this blindness is, that they know nothing of the joys of heaven and the torments of hell.

Why does a child put his finger into the flame of a candle, and you will not do so? Because he is ignorant that the flame will burn him, but you know it. If you knew what damage a single idle word would cause you, there is no evil, no sorrow in this world, which you would not choose to suffer rather than speak it. If you knew the immense advantages the observance of the commandments and the performance of good works would procure you, you would observe the first and perform the second, despite all obstacles; and you would not fail in the least iota, even though your parents and friends besought you, on their knees, to desist from your holy undertaking. Why, then, do you abandon works that are easy? Why, not to speak of your graver sins, do you daily waste your time in idle and frivolous discourses? If you rightly appreciated the joys and horrors of eternity, you love yourself far too well to risk losing the first, or deserving the second.

But, besides this reason drawn from the natural love we bear ourselves, there is another not less strong. The truths of our holy religion are so great that, if rightly considered, they are capable of vanquishing the most haughty spirits, and breaking the hardest hearts. This is so true that we may say, without the least exaggeration, that there is not in France or elsewhere any person so wicked that, if he understood a single mystery of religion, not in a sublime fashion, but in an ordinary manner, he would not be converted and change his life in a quarter of an hour : " For," says St. Paul, " the word of God is living and effectual, and more piercing than any two-edged sword : and reaching into the division of the soul and the spirit, of the joints also and the marrow, and is a discerner of the thoughts and intents of the heart." David says to God : " Thy words are all fire." And God Himself, by Jeremias, asks : " Are not my words as a fire, and as a hammer that breaketh the rock in pieces?" Now consider the effects of fire,—how it heats and enlightens, destroys or fortifies, or rejoices. The eternal truths have similar powers over our heart, and work similar operations in our souls, if we diligently reflect on them.

In effect, as Christian truths are emanations of the first truth, and rays of the eternal Sun of justice, they participate in His nature, who is not only the living Word of the Father and His truth personified, but also a principle of the Holy Spirit, and, consequently, the source of the goodness and sanctity of men. These truths have most wonderful power : they contain things of great consequence, as the losing or gaining of God forever, the beatitude or damnation of soul and body,— affairs of such paramount importance to us that the gain or loss of all the kingdoms of this earth is merely child's play in comparison These great truths have made the martyrs and confessors, they have brought kings and queens and princesses from their thrones, and excited them to trample under foot their gorgeous crowns. Yes; if we ask Agnes, or Catharine, or Agatha, or other tender maidens of illustrious birth, who gave them courage to despise, as they have done, the pleasures of this life, to suffer so willingly the most frightful torments, and to go more joyously to the fire and to the block than others go to their nuptials; if we ask the illustrious prince, Josaphat, what persuaded him to renounce his magnificent kingdom of the Indies, pass his days in the most frightful solitude, and practise austerities the most rigorous,—all will answer that it is the firm belief in Christian truths. Esdras speaks of a courtesan of Darius, who, being asked what was the strongest of all things, answered: "It is truth."

If, then, the truths of our religion are so efficacious in touching the mind and changing the heart, why have they so little weight with us? It is because we do not really know them. And why do we not know them? Because we will not consider them; we prefer to employ ourselves in thinking of the merest trifles. "The people have devised vain things," said David; "for all our days are spent, and our years shall be considered as a spider." No animal works with greater application than the spider; she performs her task with incredible diligence, activity and eagerness. She draws her web even from her entrails, and yet a stroke of the dusting-brush will destroy the labor of her years. It is the same with men who consume their days and nights, weaken their bodies and torment their souls, to acquire the honors, riches and dignities which death can deprive them of in a moment, and will destroy with a single stroke. I ask a man to do only one thing, which if he does, I will promise him heaven. It is, that he will take leisure to think somewhat seriously on the things of salvation; for, if he knew only one of them as he ought, no matter how badly he might be disposed, he could not resist, he would immediately change his life. After all, nobody wishes to be lost. If a man be engaged in a lawsuit upon which much of his property depends, he will, if he have a grain of common-sense, leave his pleasures for a few days to apply himself unreservedly to his business. If, while this suit remains still undecided, a neighbor or friend should come to ask him any favor that involved labor or time, he would excuse himself from granting it, and even complain of any one indiscreet enough to propose it in such a critical conjuncture, when he had enough to do to think of his own business without distracting himself with that of another. Well, properly speaking, we have only one affair in this world : it is to save our souls. All other affairs are only the amusements of children. You have already lived twenty, thirty, fifty, or sixty years, during which you have had this important business to conduct to a good end, and yet perhaps you have not thought of it at all, or, if you have, you have thought of it but little. Look abroad upon men, and you will see that the greater number of them resemble dreamers. When you rouse a man out of a lethargy (and this requires great force), he opens his eyes a little, he stares about with a troubled, languishing air, he hears imperfectly, he says two or three incoherent words, and then falls back into his lethargic slumber. Thus it is often only by force that a man thinks of his salvation, and even then he thinks of it but very slightly. When we say that Christian truths are calculated to operate wonderful effects, we mean, if they are known ; for it is a maxim with all philosophers and theologians, that our will cannot be touched by anything of which we have no knowledge. The most beautiful object in the world can make no impression on us, if it be unknown to us. Place a blind man in the midst of a museum of all the wonders of art and nature, and they will excite no admiration, no surprise, no love. Hide a treasure in the garden of a poor villager, and what use will it be to him unless he knows that it is there? Alas! we possess immense treasures in heaven; we are surrounded with the mysteries of our holy religion, with the presence of God, with His providence; we have learned the history of the Incarnation and death of His Son, and we know that His sacred and adorable body and blood are veiled in the sacrament of our altars; we know that death is coming upon us, that eternity awaits us, and the least of these things contains secrets enough to ravish our souls,—yet they work nothing, or little more than nothing, in us, because we are ignorant, or nearly ignorant, of them. Thus our Lord said: "You shall know the truth, and the truth shall make you free." It shall deliver you from the power of your enemies, it shall aid you to gain over them glorious victories. If you be tempted to pride, to anger, to avarice, or any other sin, it will strengthen you powerfully to vanquish the temptation. If occasion or necessity requires you to practise patience, sweetness, charity or any other virtue, it will give you invincible courage to practise those virtues with a high degree of perfection. But, first, it is necessary that you should *know* the truth, otherwise it cannot assist you to overcome obstacles.

It is necessary to know the truth, and to know it well; for, if one should know it only superficially, it will work weakly, as appears by experience. Every Christian knows that there is one God, Creator of the universe, who is present everywhere, and who will reward the good and punish the wicked; nearly every Christian knows the principal mysteries of religion, and yet these truths, so great, so striking and so powerful, do not withdraw people from their vices, or force them to practise virtue. How comes this? It is because they have not sufficient knowledge of them to produce these salutary effects. We can easily know them as the objects of our belief: for this purpose we need only hear and consent to them. But, if we would make them the rule of our conduct, we must have some further knowledge of them. A tree may be planted in an hour or less, but it requires two or three months to take root; and it cannot bear fruit unless it be firmly rooted, because it is the root that supplies the leaves and branches with sap. In like manner, Christian truth is easily planted in our hearts, but, in order to bear solid and lasting fruit, it must be deeply engraved on our hearts. It must be well known, and consequently well considered, otherwise it will always remain unfruitful.

We know enough as regards things concerning our salvation, but we do not know these mysteries so well that they make us change our lives. We ought to know them in such a manner that they will make a lively impression on our hearts. "How long a time have I been with you," said our Lord to Philip, "and you have not yet known me!" It is many years since we learned the existence of a God full of goodness, wisdom and power, whom we ought to serve, love and honor with our whole hearts, to whom we are infinitely indebted for the benefits He has conferred upon us; and, nevertheless, we do not render Him the service we owe Him, we do not live as He desires. Why is this? It is because we know these great truths imperfectly. It is necessary, then, that we know them well, and appreciate them as they deserve.

A little of this real knowledge would speedily change us. When a great lord decides on going to war, he will separate from his wife and children, abandon the riches and comforts of his home, and bid adieu to his pleasures, from one single motive, namely, the desire of glory; and if this desire failed to replenish his mind and heart, he would soon turn his back upon the enemy. Thus the sole motive of the presence of God, of the infinite gratitude we owe our Lord Jesus, of eternity, or any other truth already spoken of, will suffice, if we comprehend it well, to make us abandon what is dearest to us, overcome the greatest obstacles, give ourselves perfectly to God, and serve Him zealously during the remainder of our lives.

Let us consider ourselves. Every day we produce a great number of various actions, whether of the vegetative life, or the sensitive life, or the reasonable life, and yet all these operations have but one cause, namely, the soul which animates the body. In the same way, one single truth possessing and animating our soul may be in us the source of many dissimilar actions. It is even wise to apply the mind to one, or at least to choose but very few of these fundamental truths, that we may be the better able to understand them, and that they may aid us with greater facility. For we have not leisure to penetrate a great many, and our mind is not capable of retaining and studying them with the energy necessary to produce the effect desired. Our own experience shows us that we have not penetrated even one truth in this salutary manner, since we do not change our lives. But if we do not know one as we ought, how shall we learn a dozen? This would hardly be possible, for one would drive the others out of our minds. Thus it is a salutary, and even a necessary advice, to take only a few, one, two or three; and in order that your mind may be efficaciously touched, you should consider them continually, in public and private, in the fields and in the city, as Moses said of the commandments of God. You should never lose sight of them; they should be the first spring of all your movements, the universal principle of all your actions.

Now, if you ask how you can know a truth in so high a degree, that it may act thus powerfully on you and become the principle of all your actions, I answer, by any one of the three following means:—

1. To consider this truth. Consideration produces knowledge, and knowledge produces affections, and affections produce works. Here below we cannot know things if we do not consider them; and in this we differ from angels, for these spirits see things to their depths and in all their bearings, the moment they look at them, or think of them. We, enveloped

as we are in matter, cannot understand things so quickly. Except when accidents strike our senses, as color, quantity, figure, we arrive at knowledge only by degrees. We ascend by consideration and discourse as by a ladder : one thing conducts us to the knowledge of another. Thus we know causes by their effects, and effects by their causes ; the substance by its accidents, and accidents by their substance ; the nature by the property, and the property by the nature ; fire by its smoke, and smoke by the fire. Hence, if we desire to know, we must use considerations, discussions and researches. This is particularly true with reference to eternal things, because they are less accessible by our senses, and consequently more difficult to be learned. Without serious and deep examination, we cannot acquire a profound knowledge of them. What spoils us is, that we do not think of them at all, or think of them but slightly—we wish to know all things at a glance, like the angels ; we wish at first sight to grasp their nature, their importance and their consequences. But this cannot be ; we must have patience and turn them up and down, and examine them slowly in all their bearings.

A single consideration comes to nothing. A truth can act on us only in proportion as it penetrates our mind ; it can penetrate our mind only by repeated considerations, and the more deeply we consider it, the greater will be its impression on us. The prophet Jeremias does not attribute the desolation of the land to want of knowledge, but to want of attention and deep reflection. St. Paul, exhorting the faithful to suffer with patience, and not to lose courage in the midst of their misfortunes, suggests, as a lenitive and antidote, the thought of the passion and death of our Lord ; but he is not content that they should think of these mysteries only once or superficially, but that they should think seriously of them, for, by force of repetition, the remedy will doubtless operate successfully.

Hard though stone may be, the constant dropping of water

wears it away by little and little. The first, nor the tenth, nor the hundredth drop does not produce this effect, but many others will in time surely accomplish it. Though our mind does not understand a truth in the commencement, though nature resists it and the senses contradict it, nevertheless, after many reiterated considerations, it enters into the soul and the soul into it, the understanding is convinced, and then, by degrees, the will is excited, softened and broken, no matter how hard it may have been. The truth then becomes to the soul a *principle*, and through the soul governs the whole man.

2. If you object that you have not sufficient capacity to penetrate these mysteries in the manner I have recommended, I shall prescribe for you a second means which is easier, shorter, more efficacious and more perfect than the first: it is faith. By faith you will believe firmly the truth you shall have taken for a principle; you shall penetrate it, not by your own mind and industry, but by the Spirit of God, and by His infallible knowledge of it; you will repose on Him in an unshaken manner, holding His truth in the way in which your mind is capable, and thus it will become the motive and principle of your actions. But we shall speak of this at greater length elsewhere.

3. The third means is the gift of the Holy Ghost called *understanding*, of which we have already spoken. This ineffable gift discovers the mysteries of faith, it draws back the veil that hides them, it surrounds them with all the brightness they can possess in this life, and which enables us almost to touch them. We must imitate the Royal Prophet, by often asking this gift of God, saying with him: "Lord, give me understanding; enlighten my mind that I may know Thy law, and keep it with all my heart. I am Thy servant; give me intelligence that I may know Thy testimonies. Give me understanding, and I shall live."

CHAPTER III.

THIRD GENERAL PRINCIPLE OF THE SPIRITUAL LIFE.—THE END OF MAN.

AMONG our mental faculties there is a natural order, in consequence of which some necessarily rank higher than others, as our understanding goes before our will, carrying the torch to enlighten its steps, and manifest what it ought to love, and what it ought to hate. Among the objects of our knowledge, there is also a certain natural arrangement, by which some present themselves, and therefore require to be considered, before others. But among all these objects, that which concerns a thing most nearly is undoubtedly its end. Hence Aristotle calls the end the first of principles,—that principle the knowledge of which regulates all. "Look at an archer," says he, "and observe how the movements of his eyes, his arms, his whole body, tend only to his desired end. The end is the cause of causes; because it puts causes in action, and, as the first mover, it gives them their bent, and because all employ themselves for it." So, the efficacious intention and resolution one has to attain an end, necessarily include the use of all suitable means. This we see in a sick person, who refuses no remedy which is likely to restore his health. Hence the search for, and the application of, means always bear proportion to the affection with which an end is desired.

We must therefore conclude that the knowledge of an end is of extreme consequence, that it must be studied with care, and perfectly well understood. Now, as nothing in this world concerns us more nearly than ourselves, and as there is nothing more important to us than our end, so we must examine attentively what that end is, and how we may reach it. Our end is God and His glory. God has created us to give Himself to us in this life and in the next, and by this means to render us happy here below and in eternity; and to put us in a state to procure Him glory, the last end for which He has created all things, according to this saying of Solomon: "The Lord has produced all His works for Himself," that is to say, for His glory, as the noblest end He could propose to Himself: and in fact it was necessarily His only end. For, as He is infinitely above all that is and all that can be, being in Himself infinitely amiable, He could therefore have in all His works no end but Himself. And when we speak of His glory, we should understand only His exterior glory, for His interior glory cannot be increased: it is His esteem of Himself, it is Himself. In this thought He said by St. John: "I am Alpha and Omega, the beginning and the end,"—the beginning of created things, the end of their creation. He had previously said by Isaias: "It is for myself, it is for myself that I shall do all my works, and my glory I shall not give to another." I am the First and I am the Last: the first to confer being on my creatures, to be the cause of their production; the last, because I am their end. "I have created all men who invoke my name:" I have made them for my honor and glory. St. Augustine, in acknowledgment of this great truth, often said: "Lord, Thou hast made us for Thyself." As the sheath is made for the sword, as the glove is made for the hand, so man is formed for God, to procure Him glory.

Therefore, man is created to glorify God, in and by himself; and that he may accomplish this, God designs to make him happy in this life and in the next, and, for this purpose, to unite him to Himself. Assuredly, God being infinitely wise in all that He does, and doing all, as the Scripture says, by number, weight and measure, it would not be seemly that He should make man, the most perfect of His creatures, to be miserable. He designs that man should be happy now as far as he is capable of happiness, and for this end He wishes to unite him to Himself: for, as a thing cannot be white unless whiteness be added to it, neither can a man be learned or rich unless he be endowed with science or possess riches; so man cannot be happy of himself, since of himself he is nothing : he can become happy only by uniting himself to his beatitude, and his beatitude is God, his Creator and his last end.

Man can be united to God by grace in this life, and by glory in the next. Union with God by grace consists in loving and serving Him here; the vision of glory consists in seeing Him as He is, and possessing Him. When a man loves and serves God, this love and service are bonds that attach him to God; and being united to God, he possesses Him, and by consequence he possesses beatitude as far as he can possess it here below. He glorifies God, he fulfils the end of his creation, for all things have been formed for the glory of God.

Let us then hold for certain that the end of man in this life is to love and serve God, and by this means to glorify Him. Behold the great principles, a knowledge of which is so necessary for man, and ought in fact to regulate his whole life. This is the end to which he should tend with all his strength, and refer all that he is, and all that he does, because for this alone he has been placed in the world. "Fear God and keep His commandments," says Solomon, "for that is the whole man;" it is that which renders man perfect, and bestows on him all the felicity he can enjoy in this life.

§ I.—*Signification of the word "end."*

1. The word *end* necessarily has two significations, namely, the perfection of a given thing, and the beatitude of a given

thing. The end of any thing is so surely its perfection, that, outside of that end, it can never be perfect, whatever other advantage it may possess. If God had placed the perfection of a man in becoming a painter, he could never be happy without practising his art, though he had immense riches, were very learned, a powerful king, or a Sovereign Pontiff; on the contrary, he would become happy and perfect in proportion as he became expert in his art, though he possessed neither riches, nor glory, nor honor. The very name *end* implies all this, for it signifies the thing finished, accomplished, that it has acquired its highest perfection, and can therefore be brought no farther.

2. The end of a thing is also its repose and beatitude; it is there it finds its rest; outside of that it can experience only agitation and trouble. Hence *morals* teach that the *end*, the *good* and the *beatitude* signify absolutely the same thing.

The power of the end to confer repose does not necessarily imply that this end is excellent, or beautiful, or rich, but only that it is the end. Had God created us to look at the sun or to enjoy the company of an angel, we should be perfectly happy in fulfilling our destiny. The ox and the ass which were present at the birth of our Saviour and saw Him in His crib, preferred to look at the grass and hay scattered about them, because they were not created for higher things. So true is it that in the end, and only in the end, and precisely in the end, consists the happiness of all beings, rational and irrational.

§ 2.—*God, being our end, is, consequently, our perfection and beatitude.*

Since the end of a thing is necessarily its perfection and beatitude, we must conclude that, as the end of man in this life is to love and serve God, and thus unite himself to Him, man will be perfect and happy if he love and serve God, and in proportion as he loves and serves Him. On the contrary, if he do not love and serve Him, he shall be miserable and imperfect, for it belongs to the end to perfect and content a thing ; and if our end is to love and honor God, nothing else can confer happiness on us.

All persons agree on this point : a poor beggar, stripped of all the goods of this life, will be judged more perfect if he be humble, patient and virtuous, than a rich prince who is vicious and a blasphemer. The devils are wise, strong and endowed with singular advantages, yet they are esteemed the opprobrium of the universe, because, separated from God by their sin, they are far from their end, and consequently from their perfection and happiness. In the service of God and in His love, as in our end, we must seek and find our perfection. Here, too, we shall find our beatitude, our earthly paradise, but, outside of this, only bitterness and troubles await us. "Behold," says David, "they that go far from Thee are overwhelmed with misery and perish without resource, but as for me I will adhere to my God:" I entertain no other lights, no other thoughts, for I know that my good and my happiness consist only in uniting myself to my God. David had reason to speak in this manner, for, as St. Paul says, "He who is united to God is made one spirit with Him," and by this union becomes wise, powerful, rich and happy.

"When I shall be entirely united to Thee," says St. Augustine, " when all that is in me shall be joined to Thee, then I shall be free from sorrow and trouble ; my life will be full of joy, because it will be full of Thee. But now, because in many things I am void of Thee, I lead a languishing life, I am a burden to myself." "Why hast Thou set me against Thee," says Job, "and I am become burdensome to myself?" Let us, when we feel pains, afflictions and weariness, consider whence these inconveniences come, and we shall find that they proceed from our not being well with God,—we have withdrawn from Him by some sin, or by some resistance to His will, which withdrawal, separating us from our end, separates us also from our beatitude.

When we live united to Him by grace and love we enjoy unbounded satisfaction, and receive abundance of the sweetest pleasures. This sometimes happens even to the imperfect when they approach the holy sacrament. In the union of the soul with God they feel their hearts leap with divine joy, and they taste delights to which nothing here below is at all comparable. Now, if so short a time of union with God produces fruits so delicious, what will not a long period of union, as that of the saints and the perfect, produce! What torrents of joy must inundate their hearts! With reason, then, do we commonly say that true joy and solid content are found in the soul of the just man. The great St. Augustine said: "God forbid that I should be so blind as to look for content out of Him. There is a certain joy which is not given to the wicked, but only to those who serve Thee with a good heart. This joy is Thyself, for the life of beatitude consists in rejoicing in Thee, from Thee, and for Thee. In Thee is true joy found, and not elsewhere." "Say to the just man that it is well, and that he shall eat the fruit of his doing," says God by Isaias. Yes, but, Lord, if he be poor, afflicted, persecuted or sick, what shall we say to him under these distressing circumstance?

Say that with his poverty, his afflictions, his other evils, he shall be perfectly content; and tell the rich man that, if he be wicked, he shall be sad and miserable, though he were a monarch. Because, as the apostle says, "Tribulations and anguish are upon every man that worketh iniquity, but glory and honor and peace upon him that worketh good."

The wise son of Sirach writes: "The way of sinners is

made plain with stones, and in their end is hell and darkness and pains." And David had said before him: "Sorrow and pain are in their paths, and the way of peace they have not known." "There is no peace for the impious," saith the Lord by Isaias. "Lord," said St. Augustine, "Thou hast made us for Thyself, and our hearts can never find true repose till they rest in Thee. Woe to the soul who is bold enough to separate from Thee!" Turn, perverse soul, in every direction, seek every delight, possess riches, honors and pleasures, and thou shalt everywhere find thorns and weariness, for there is no true rest but in God alone.

The dove flying from the ark is a figure of the soul that seeks happiness among creatures. The Scripture remarks that she found no rest for the sole of her foot, and was therefore constrained to return; and Noah, who is a figure of God, took her in his hand, and placed her again in the ark. The true repose of the creature is God: all else will, sooner or later, inspire displeasure or disgust. Verily, a crown of gold cannot cure the headache, nor can a mantle of brocade assuage the pain caused by a broken arm. Antisthenes, Prince of the Sybarites, displayed prodigious ambition by causing a robe of triumph to be made for himself, on which the whole world was represented in embroidery: Asia on the right side, Africa on the left, Europe on the borders, and the heavens on the centre. The Carthaginians afterward purchased this robe for two millions of gold, and preserved it in their treasury. Rich and precious as it was, it could not even heal a grievous ulcer that this prince had in his back. The elements can be tranquil only in a certain condition; when that is interrupted, we have storms, floods, and earthquakes. It is the same with the soul; it must be in God in order to have repose, because that is its natural place, its centre and the term of its movements; and nothing but God can ever satisfy it. If He should give you the heavens and the whole universe, a perfect knowledge of all arts and sciences, and the empire of all the worlds it is possible for Him to make, neither this, nor any other means that He is wise enough to invent and powerful enough to execute, would render you happy, for these things are not your end; and a thing can find its contentment only in working out its destiny. Therefore, man, though he possess all that it is possible for him to possess, shall always be miserable if he possess not God, because God alone is his end, and, by consequence, his repose, his joy, his beatitude.

§ 3.—*Another reason of this truth.*

God has created the soul of man to his image. He has given man so vast a capacity that Himself alone can fill it, because He alone is infinite. "Thou hast made him little less than angels," says David, or, as others translate the Hebrew, a little less than God, because all created things are as nothing in comparison to God; and whatever God gives man, outside of Himself, is as if one should cast a fly into the mouth of a starving lion, or a drop of water into an abyss. "The avaricious," says the Sage, "shall never be content:" however great his gains, he always wishes for more. Gold and silver may fill his coffers, but his cupidity can never be satiated. It is the same with the ambitious concerning honor, the voluptuous as regards pleasure, the curious with reference to sciences, and, in short, with all who seek satisfaction among creatures. Their hearts shall be always empty. "The reasonable soul," says St. Bernard, "may be amused and occupied with trifles, but cannot be filled or satiated except by God." "In the miseries those suffer who are far from Thee," says St. Augustine, "it clearly appears that Thou hast made the reasonable creature very great, since nothing less than Thyself can satisfy his desire; for Thou art his beatitude."

Undoubtedly, our great avidity, our unquiet eagerness, our insatiable curiosity always to see, to hear, to know and to possess something new, are evident marks that created things are not our end; for it is the property of the end to calm the heart and appease the desires of the soul. "I know with full certainty," says St. Augustine, "that without Thee I am most unhappy. I can find repose neither within nor without, and the greatest abundance is to me the most wretched poverty, if I possess not my God." Sinful men know well the bitterness and chagrin of a soul that possesses not God. They may forget or stifle their remorse for a while, but the sentinel is soon awakened, because the heart that is not well with God cannot be well with self: happiness is banished therefrom.

§ 4.—*Conclusion of this subject.*

To love, honor and serve God,—this is the end of man. By this he unites himself to God. By uniting himself to God, he possesses God; and, in possessing Him, he is perfect and happy, and glorifies Him in the manner He requires. For this end He has drawn man out of nothing, and continually preserves him. This is the noblest design, this is the most perfect end, He could have in view; because it is His own end. He has no felicity but in loving and glorifying Himself, and in this He has made us like Himself. Creatures cannot content us: they are like the broken cisterns of which the prophet Jeremias speaks. But God is the fountain of living waters, the inexhaustible source of all good. And will He not satisfy us? He is all-sufficient for His own glory, and riches, and blessedness, though He is infinite; and will He not suffice for us whose capacities are created, and therefore limited? We must imprint profoundly on our own minds, and often repass in our memories, that our end in this life is to love, honor and serve God; and if this is our end, it is also our perfection and our happiness. We have come into the world for this purpose, and for this purpose alone. We ought then apply only to this, thus delivering ourselves from the blindness to which the greater part of men are subject. They think but little of the end of their creation, they pass their lives in unfruitful labors, in vain intrigues, in trifling occupations. "After having sought," said the Sage, "I found that God made man right;" and yet he amuses and embarrasses himself with an infinity of useless questions and most frivolous amusements. Extreme folly! which an author of the past century well represented by an apt emblem, in which a man carries on his back the whole universe, and, charged with this burden, often rests his hands on his knees, and perspires profusely, but for the rest acts like a fool in the midst of his work; he wears a fool's cap, and has the ears of an ass. At the foot of the picture the designer wrote these beautiful words, spoken for our instruction by the wise son of Sirach: *Seek not the things that are too high for thee, and search not into things above thy ability: but the things that God hath commanded thee, think on them always.*" (Ecclus. iii, 22.)

After all, said our Lord, "there is but one thing necessary," and that is our salvation. "I paint for eternity," said an ancient artist. As we are created for eternity, we ought to think, speak and act for eternity. Whatever we do, without this view, will be lost. In place of tending to our happiness, our labors will be the source of new trouble. Hence we must firmly determine to tend to the end of our creation, and employ all our care to attain it. Let us now treat of the means of doing this.

§ 5.—*Means to attain this end.*

God is infinitely wise in the production of His creatures; He always gives them means proper for attaining the respective ends which He has assigned them. Having designed birds to fly, He gave them wings; having designed other animals to walk, He gave them feet; and so everything in creation is endowed with what is necessary to reach its perfection, its end. Now, since the end of man in this world is to serve, love and honor God, we must conclude that God has provided him with all things necessary for the accomplishment of this design : for it would be a strange thing if God, who gives to a horse, or a fly, or a serpent, all that is required to perfect its nature, would refuse this to man who is the richest of His works, and for whom all other creatures were produced. O, certainly, He will give him the means of attaining his noble destiny, and give these means more abundantly in proportion as man is nobler and more excellent than other creatures!

These means are natural and supernatural. The natural means are : the heavens, the sun, the moon, the stars, the elements, stones, plants, animals, and all the creatures of the universe. God has not made these immediately for Himself, since they are not at all necessary to Him ; He has not made them for the angels who are pure spirits, and who for their conservation and felicity require only God ; He has not made them for themselves, for they are incapable of realizing their existence. It is for man, then, that He has given being to these things; it is for him He preserves them. Other natural means God has given him, too, in order to compass his end : such as, riches and poverty, health and sickness, honors and contempt, pleasures and pains, life and death, and generally all that happens in this world. Sin is the only thing that can become a real obstacle to our perfection or salvation.

Of the supernatural means of attaining our end, our Lord is the principal, and hence He is styled, by excellence, the Mediator. The others are: our Lady, the sacraments, habitual and actual graces, the Holy Scriptures, good books, sermons, particular instructions, and all that is contained in the order of grace. These means are excellently well adapted to the proposed end. Moses remarks that God, on considering the works He had made, said they were good; and the son of Sirach proclaims that the works of God are very good. This must be understood, not only of the natural goodness that is opposed to nothingness, but also of a certain moral goodness which renders them entirely suitable for the ends which God respectively assigned them at the moment of their creation.

§ 6.—*Signification of the word " means.*

To understand perfectly the knowledge and practice of this important truth, it is necessary to comprehend well the signification of the word *means*, and what it is to be the means of any end. The means is, first, a help to reach an end; secondly, all the goodness and excellence of a means is relative, not absolute, as Aristotle remarks; and this goodness and excellence consist in the power the means has to conduct to an end. It is good only when it conducts to the end; and the more powerfully it conducts to this end, the better it is. A medicine which restores health is good, though it be very bitter; a medicine that has no beneficial effect is useless, though it be sweet and pleasant. A knife which is made only to cut, becomes useless when it will not cut. I say, thirdly, that the means is the *means* only when we use it as such. Its nature is perverted when it is badly used; a bad use makes it a hindrance instead of a means. If a strong medicine should not cure you, it will certainly injure you. The best bread in the world is only a means of health, but it ceases to be such, if you do not use it as nature requires: if, for example, you should swallow it without chewing it. If you want a knife to be of service to you, you must handle it rightly: otherwise, instead of cutting your bread, it will cut your finger, and the sharper it is, the deeper will be the wound; it may even render you incapable of ever cutting anything again. So, then, the means, to be a means, to be capable of producing its effect, must be rightly used, that is, with reference to the desired end.

§ 7.—*All creatures should be to us means of salvation.*

Since God has given us all things, since it is He who sends us riches and poverty, honors and dishonors, health and sickness, and everything else of good or bad fortune that can come to us, as means to attain our end, we must necessarily conclude that they all have power to conduct us to it, if we use them rightly as they come. There is nothing in this world which may not conduce to our salvation. Certainly, we cannot doubt that the sun and the rose and all other creatures are what they are, through the power and bounty of the divine Creator; but His first and chief intention in creating them was that they might serve as helps to man, and become to him as steps of the ladder which conducts to happiness and perfection here and hereafter.

Philosophy teaches that less perfect things always have reference to such as are more perfect; and hence we may conclude that corporal things are produced for spiritual things, and temporal things for those which are eternal. God has not created the sun merely to be the sun, to rise in the morning, and gladden our eyes with its beauty; nor has He created the rose merely to exhibit its delicate tints and embalm the air with its perfume, but to become to man means of reaching his end: as an artisan never made a knife or a sword merely *to be* a knife or a sword, but to be instruments with which to cut or wound. Therefore, all things, sin excepted, are, by the institution of God, instruments, means, and aids to operate our salvation. Nothing comes to us in the guise of an enemy: neither hunger, nor thirst, nor persecution, nor anything else,—everything wears the face of a friend coming to assist us. It is true that sickness seems like an enemy to health, and want looks like an enemy to abundance; but neither can come as an enemy to our beatitude, which consists in loving, serving and honoring God.

It is sweet to think that in Christianity all things can be useful to us, if we please. Our vessel can steer toward the port in a calm or in a tempest, with a favorable wind or with a contrary wind; poverty can bring us riches, opprobrium can crown us with glory, pains and pleasures are equally potent to open for us the gate of happiness; or, rather, pains are the more potent. Verily, it is a great and solid consolation to think that there is nothing in the universe which can be an obstacle to our salvation, if we do not make it such; and that all things may become most powerful means of perfection, if we wish to make them such. The Angelic Doctor beautifully says: "God makes all His works, even the least, even a grain of sand or a drop of rain, with all possible perfection; so that, even in imagination, they could not be better adapted to the design of their creation."

Consequently, all the adversities that befall us, all the persecutions that we can sustain, hunger, thirst, war, pestilence, and all the other evils that can assail us, are means exactly adjusted to the designs which God has upon us, and selected with infinite wisdom to perfect and save us, though our corrupt nature would not choose them as such. The traveller who desires to have fine weather for his journey does not like rain; the vine-dresser who sighs for a good vintage dreads the hailstorm, but the one and the other answer the designs of God. "It is the property of a perfect cause," says St. Thomas, "to act perfectly, and to give to its work all the excellence of which it is capable." If Michael Angelo or Raphael could not make a bad picture, because neither could use his pencil otherwise than in exact conformity to the perfect ideas he had of his art,—how should God err in the means which He furnishes us to attain our end? He chose them all according to the rules of His infinite wisdom and goodness, so that all that comes to us from Him, strange or ill adapted as it may appear, is, nevertheless, in itself the most proper means to conduct us to Him.

So, then, since all things in the universe, especially what our nature deems afflicting, are, in the unerring designs of God, means to attain our end, we must regard them as such. The first idea that ought to strike us concerning things, is their quality of leading us to God. When we see the sun and the stars; when we cast our eyes on trees, flowers, rivers and animals; when we speak of wars, famines, pestilences, we ought each to say: These are means of my salvation if I please; they are instruments of my perfection, and ladders by which God designs that I should reach felicity here and beatitude hereafter. As all things can conduce to our salvation, we ought to be indifferent to all, and use them as they come, only as instruments of our perfection. It is with this view, and in this manner, we ought to love all created things: this is their chief excellence in our regard, that they are destined to become to us means of salvation, if only we are willing to use them as such.

§ 8.—*Discernment is essential in the selection of means.*

Though all things may become conducive to our salvation, it is nevertheless true that all are not equally so; and, as inclinations and dispositions are different, so, what might be very serviceable to one person would be deleterious to another. Health is good for one who uses it well; sickness is bad for one who will not patiently endure it. Adversity conducts some to paradise, and prosperity brings others to hell. Riches have saved St. Louis, while they have damned those whom God called to a state of poverty. Dignity and honors have made St. Gregory the Great more holy and more humble, but they have rendered others insolent and haughty before God and man. Thus the armor of Saul was good for him; but it was bad for David, who found a shepherd's sling and a stone more useful in conquering Goliath. Hence the Book of Wisdom says that creatures are, to weak minds, snares and sorcerers by which the devil entraps them, and that the smallest trifles have charms for self-confident souls, who despise what they ought to esteem, and esteem what is deserving of contempt, and who, thus fascinated as if by magic, yield to the impetuosity of concupiscence and the ardors of unbridled passion, and fall into an abyss of misfortunes. It is, then, necessary that the means of our salvation be suitable to our character and condition.

As some means are better adapted to accomplish an end than others, it is the part of prudence to select such as are in each case most proper and efficacious. Of two knives equally good, a wise man will take either; but of two, one of which cuts a little better than the other, he will certainly choose the latter. We ought to select what is most conducive to our salvation, though it be painful. A sick man who is truly desirous of recovering his health, will not be arrested by the bitterness of the medicine: it suffices for him to know that it will heal him, and in this belief he swallows it directly. A traveller meets with two roads, one of which is broad, shady and pleasant; the other is stony and unsheltered: he will choose the second rather than the first, if it lead more directly to his journey's end. Thus, in our use of creatures, we must not select what is most agreeable to our nature, but what seems best adapted for attaining our last end, which is our eternal salvation.

§ 9. *The good use is essential to the means.*

The use we make of a thing renders it a means or a hindrance to the end we have in view. As there is nothing in this world which may not become beneficial to our perfection, so there is nothing which may not become injurious to it. The things which, when rightly used, are capable of being the most beneficial, are, when otherwise employed, the most pernicious. The utility of a means in our regard depends entirely on the manner in which we employ it. God gives you riches, He raises you above others in power and dignity,—all that will sanctify you, if you make a good use of it; but, if you do not, it will become your ruin. You are afflicted, persecuted, sick, imprisoned; well, afflictions, persecutions, maladies and imprisonment shall produce in you effects exactly conformable to the use you make of them. If you accept these misfortunes with patience and resignation to the will of God, they will advance your salvation considerably, acquire you immense treasures of merits, and unite you more intimately to God, who is to be found in a prison as well as in a church. But, if you receive them with murmuring and impatience, they will separate you from God, and become very prejudicial to your salvation.

"To the pure, all things are pure," says St. Paul, but to the bad all things are bad; because the pure of conscience use all things according to the designs of God, but the wicked pervert and sully them, as a man who handles a beautiful vase of gold with soiled fingers. Ecclesiasticus had said long before him: "In the beginning God produced all things necessary for the life of man: water, fire, iron, salt, wheat, honey, oil and raiment." All these things are holy to the good; but the impious abuse them, and change them into means of accomplishing their temporal and eternal ruin. And, seized with admiration, David had, before either, exclaimed: "Great is the Lord in His works, and exquisite in His designs. O Lord! how great are Thy works! Thy thoughts are exceeding deep. But the senseless man shall not know; nor will the fool understand these things." Therefore holy Simeon, when speaking to Mary of her divine Son, who is the greatest means that God has given for our salvation, said : "Behold this Child is set for the fall and for the resurrection of many in Israel : " not by the design of God who sent Him to ransom all nations, and to enlighten the whole world, but by the bad use which people would make of Him. It is the use made of a thing that decides all, as a painter sketches good or bad figures according as he uses his brush; and a writer forms good or bad letters according to the manner in which he applies his pen. Anything becomes salutary when we use it well; everything becomes hurtful that we use ill. There is nothing in heaven or on earth more holy than the most adorable sacrament; yet, if we receive it unworthily, it becomes to us a source of death.

The bad use of a means consists in perverting its nature, and applying it in a manner different from that in which it ought to be applied. Everything in the universe is capable of conducting us to God; but, if we use things otherwise than as God has willed us to use them, they must have a contrary effect. All the vicious attachments and disorderly affections we entertain for creatures change these creatures into obstacles to our perfection; we amuse ourselves with them and rest in them, while we ought to advance toward our end by means of them, instead of suffering them to retard our progress. Therefore, in order that all means, natural and supernatural, which God has given for our salvation and beatitude, may become truly means, not obstacles, let us always regard them as such, and use them only for the designs for which God has furnished them. The end for which all means are given us is, to possess God, and, in possessing Him, to be happy; and, in being happy, to praise and glorify Him in the manner He desires. Let us now see the admirable effects which the acquisition of this end will produce, that we may be encouraged to use all our efforts to attain it.

§ 10.—*Effects of the acquisition of this end.*

The acquisition of our end will produce in us many excellent effects, among which are : first, sanctity of soul ; second, light in our understanding ; third, peace in our will ; fourth, a just and generous contempt of created things ; fifth, a composed exterior. These five effects are five delicious fruits of the tree of life, which render us as perfect and happy as it is possible for us to be in this world, and which put us in a position to glorify God in a manner worthy of Him.

FIRST EFFECT.

The first and principal effect that the union with God will operate in us is the perfection and sanctity of our soul ; for perfection and sanctity necessarily flow from this union with God, and increase in proportion as this union augments. "He who is united to God," says St. Paul, "is one spirit with Him." Now, as God is sanctity, purity and perfection by essence, it is impossible that the soul which is united to Him should not be holy, pure and perfect.

The soul by this union becomes beautiful and brilliant with the irradiations of the Divinity, as the cloud becomes beautiful and is gilded by the rays of the sun, or as iron becomes pure and sparkling in the furnace. "By means of this divine union," says the pious Louis Blosius, "the soul that was previously cold becomes hot ; she is led from obscurity to light, from hardness to pliability ; she becomes tinctured, as it were, with divine coloring, imbued and pierced with God with whom she becomes one spirit, as gold and brass become in the furnace but one mass of metal." O who can describe the ravishing beauty and sovereign glory of a soul which has arrived at this blessed state! The Holy Scriptures speak of her as decked with the glories of Lebanon, and the beauty of Carmel and Saron. "O fairest among women!" cries out the sacred Spouse, "thou art all beautiful, lovely as the morning rising, fair as the moon, brilliant as the sun. Adorned with gold and silver, clothed with fine linen and embroidered work of many colors, thou art made exceeding beautiful." These magnificent eulogies the Holy Ghost bestows on a soul united to God; but of a soul which does not possess this union He says: "How exceeding base art thou become, going the same ways over again! Abominable is the man that drinketh iniquity like water!"

The just soul is incomparably the most beautiful creature on earth. Gold, precious stones, plants, the sun itself, cannot compare with her. Were it possible to concentrate all the beauty of the universe in a single face, it would not still be as lovely as a soul in the state of grace, although that soul may be sullied with venial sin and imperfections. All imaginable corporal loveliness is but the shadow of beauty when compared to such a soul. There can be no comparison between the beauty that is produced in the body by the vivacity of sweet coloring and the finest proportions of the figure, and the divine beauty produced in the soul by grace, which is a ray of the infinite beauty of God.

Plato said that, if virtue could show itself as it is, its charms would attract all men and ravish all hearts. Hence his illustrious master, Socrates, made this prayer: "O Pan, great God of the universe! and all you blessed spirits who are in his company! grant me this favor, that I may be *interiorly* beautiful." And speaking of this hidden beauty, St. Augustine says: "What is all justice and virtue but the beauty and the ornament of the interior man?" Socrates asked it as if it were the only true beauty, in comparison with which physical beauty was nothing. And yet he spoke only of the beauty of moral virtues, because he was unacquainted with supernatural virtues and grace, which infinitely surpass all other beauty. Such is the excellence which the soul attains by union with God. Undoubtedly we ought to strive eagerly to attain it, for we should be extremely desirous to see in ourselves these glorious and precious qualities. How greatly corporal beauty is desired! What care is taken to preserve and increase it! What grief is occasioned by its loss! If it were for sale, what enormous sums rich men and women would give to purchase it! Half of their wealth would seem little for such a treasure. Yet, physical beauty is like that of the rose, which blooms only for a season; or a sunbeam, which soon vanishes. It is incapable of making its possessor better, and, alas! often makes him worse. How many who are hunchbacked and crosseyed, and blind, would give all they possess to be delivered from these deformities! Let us do as much to become beautiful of soul, which is in our power, and which is incomparably more desirable.

It is impossible that we be perfect without union with God: we ought to use all necessary diligence to acquire it. All creatures teach us this lesson, for there is not one of them which has not a violent inclination to attain its perfection, and which does not for this object tend continually to its end. Whatever is imperfect strives, and even seems to pray, for its perfection. Matter would have form, rivers run toward the sea, the stone seeks the earth, plants, trees and animals grow, and our bodies, which are half of ourselves, increase continually till they acquire their proper dimensions.

What, then, ought not the soul to do which is our nobler part! St. Augustine says: "If God had made us beasts, we might justly love the life of the body and the pleasures of sense, for these would suffice to content us." If we were trees, waters, stones, wind or flame, it is true we should have no feeling, but yet we should have a violent inclination to accomplish our destiny. Therefore, since we are men, formed in the image of our Creator, let us cast our eyes on this image which is within us, and return, like the prodigal child, to Him from whom our sins have separated us. When we see the stone descend with such impetuosity to the earth, the rivers roll so rapidly toward the sea, our bodies increase steadily till they have attained their destined size and consistency, and all things tend directly to their respective ends, regardless of obstacles,—ought we not to be ashamed that our soul, the masterpiece of God's hands, created for the noblest of destinies, should loiter on the road, and make no effort to press forward? Let us, therefore, apply from this moment to that which alone is worthy of us; let us do by reason what flies and pebbles do by instinct and nature. Let us go toward God with rapid strides, let us run to Him, fly to Him, and promote our union with Him by every possible means.

§ 11.—*Second effect of the acquisition of our end.*

LIGHT OF THE UNDERSTANDING.

God, being the Eternal Wisdom, and the source of all true light and holy knowledge, will, when our soul is united to Him, replenish it with the splendors of His light, and, as Isaias remarks, "He shall be as a sun to enlighten you always, and to guide your steps." "I am the Light of the world," says our Lord; "whoever followeth me walketh not in darkness, but dwelleth in the light of life." The lights which union with God communicates to the understanding are immeasurably more beautiful, more pure and more sublime, than those which the greatest human minds can otherwise procure, because God is their cause and their object. They come gently into the mind, and confer happiness upon it. "O how quickly is that learned," exclaims St. Leo, "which God Himself deigns to teach!" "Under such a master we taste that hidden manna, which," says St. Bernard, "is given, not by erudition, but by unction; and which, not science, but a good conscience, can comprehend." On the contrary, how much time and pain has it not cost us to acquire the little tincture of letters that we have, for there is nothing more certain than that saying of Solomon: "In much learning there is also much trouble; and he that increaseth his knowledge addeth labor."

These divine lights teach the soul the greatness, the goodness and the other ineffable perfections of the Divinity; they exhibit to her her inherent nothingness and her continual need of God; they make palpable the vanity of creatures, and their inability to confer real happiness; they discover to her the snares and perils that beset her paths; and at the same time indicate the road she ought to take, and that which she ought to avoid. The divine Master secretly instructs her in everything. He teaches her to read the book of grace which He places in her interior, and to which she can recur in all her doubts, for He has promised this by David: "I will give thee light, and instruct thee in thy steps. I will fix my eyes firmly on thee that thou mayest not wander." The soul united to God becomes very wise without much labor, and in a little time. "When the soul has attained this union with God," said Louis Blosius, "she sees clearly with the rays of eternal truth, she grasps her faith with certainty, her hope with strength, her charity with ardor." Hence, though all the wise of the world should say to her, 'Poor wretch, thou art deceived, thy faith is an illusion,' she would answer firmly: 'No, I am not deceived; it is yourselves that are deluded, for I am perfectly certain of my faith.' And she would speak thus, not because of her reason, but from her union with

God, which gives her an unshaken certainty of the mysteries of our holy religion."

Such a soul, says the same Blosius, has more knowledge of the Divinity than many learned and profound theologians, who, not having entered the sanctuary of the living God, nor been admitted to the secrets of the King of eternal glory, are not so highly illuminated with the lights of grace. God gives her the intelligence of the Scriptures, and relish for the Gospels. He enables her to acquire true wisdom, more by the irradiations of the Holy Spirit, than by the reading of many books. He shows her clearly how she ought to comport herself toward herself and toward others; what she ought to do, and what she ought to avoid. A man whose soul is thus illuminated becomes capable of governing others as well as himself. Often with two words, and two ordinary words, he will make more impression on his neighbor than others can make with long and well-studied discourses. Do we not read of some saints who had neither eloquence nor human science, and who could, nevertheless, with a few words work wonders? This is not unlike what the son of Sirach relates of Elias: "And Elias stood up as a fire, and his words burned like a torch." "The words of the wise are as goads," says Solomon, "and as nails deeply fastened in;" for the word derives its power, not from the mouth that utters it, but from the heart that has conceived, and the mind that animates it. Now, as God, the Omnipotent and All-Holy, resides in these divinely-enlightened souls, and as it is He who speaks by their mouths, their words savor of this divine origin. Hence they are capable of touching, illuminating, inflaming and sanctifying those who hear them. But the words of the worldly wise come from a pestilential source, from the human spirit, or some salutary effect. To produce fruit among men, we must be less careful of what we say than the disposition and manner in which we say it.

Let us, then, sigh, and sigh continually, after this reunion with God, which produces such wonderful effects. "Blessed is the man, O Lord!" said David, "whom Thou shalt instruct and shalt teach" the things concerning Thy law and his salvation!

§ 12.—*Third effect of the acquisition of our end.*

PEACE OF THE WILL.

The lights of the understanding are a great disposition to this peace of the will, for, says St. Augustine, "the contemplation of truth pacifies the whole man," banishing troubles, and filling the soul with delicious tranquillity. "God is in the midst of my heart," says David, "and I shall not be moved." "The fruits of the Spirit are charity, joy, peace," says St. Paul. And God has said by Isaias: "Behold I shall bring upon her, as it were, a river of peace. Joy and gladness shall be found therein; thanksgiving and the voice of praise." "In Thee is found perfect repose," writes St. Austin. "Whoever rests in thee enters into the joy of his Lord; he shall not fear, for he is united to the source of good. But I, O my God! wandered far from Thee in the blindness of my youth. I passed from creature to creature, and made for myself thorns and misery."

"Many ask," says the Psalmist, "Who showeth us good things? The light of Thy countenance, O Lord! is signed upon us. By the fruit of their corn, their wine and their oil, they are multiplied. In peace, in the self-same, I will sleep and will rest." "O Peace, always the same!" cries out St. Augustine, "thou changest not, and in thee alone I find repose." "Men united to God," says Louis Blosius, "enjoy the sweetest liberty of spirit. They are raised far above all the cares and fears which would raise a storm in their heart."

According to David, *a multitude of peace* is given to those who love His law, and nothing shall be able to embarrass them, or even scandalize them. The reason why the soul that is united to God enjoys this profound peace is, because she has attained her end; and it is therefore impossible that she could be disturbed. The man who is well with God cannot but be well with himself; he must be content, because he is united to God, his last end. "The more closely a man is united to God," says Taulerus, "the greater is the peace he enjoys; and the farther he is separated from God, the less peace he finds. All in him that is united to God is in repose; all that is separated from God is in agitation."

The man who has attained this union must always be tranquil, because he will make a right use of everything that happens. He regards all the accidents of this life, painful though sometimes they be to nature, as excellent means to promote his salvation: for, taken in this manner, they bring joy, not trouble. He considers some as affording him occasions of patience, others of humility; some give him occasions to practise obedience, others reanimate his faith and hope in God; others excite and inflame his charity, and all contribute greatly to his advancement in perfection, and, consequently, to his beatitude: and so he derives from them solid consolation and true delight. The soul that sees things in this light cannot be otherwise than tranquil. Sin is the only thing which can oppose our perfection; still, when we have the misfortune to commit it, we can make this also turn to our profit by the repentance we conceive for it, and draw from the viper which has bitten us the salve which is capable of healing our wounds.

Since, then, union with God produces a fruit so delicious as peace, we ought to use all our efforts to attain it. Nothing is more sweet and desirable than peace. "Turn, O my soul!" said the Royal Prophet, "turn to thy repose. Seek for peace and pursue it." "Return, O man!" exclaims St. Cyprian,—"return to Him who is thy repose, and out of whom thou meetest with nothing but pain and sorrow."

It is strange that there is nothing more universal among men than the desire to be happy, and yet nothing more rare than to see a man who is truly content. Kings make war, soldiers bear arms, merchants traffic in commerce, mariners cross the seas, artisans work day and night, laborers till the soil, vine-growers prune their vines, the learned study books,— all in general strive to find repose; and yet but few find it. Why is this? Because they seek happiness where it is not. They wish to find it in creatures, but it can be found only in God. In Him, then, it must be sought. We are very unfortunate, and we have almost lost our senses: we have the strongest inclination to procure peace, and yet we will not seek it where alone it can be found. God Himself, with all His power, could not enable us to find our happiness in created things, unless He were to change the end of our creation; yet we pass our lives in a thousand cares and pains to seek it where it cannot be; we have it at our doors, in our houses, in the depth of our hearts, for Eternal Truth has said, "The kingdom of God is within you," and we will not even take the trouble to recognize it, much less to enjoy it. Let us, then, enter into ourselves, and seek our peace and felicity in God, who is within us; let us unite ourselves intimately to Him: this union will give us the repose which others seek in vain; it will render us happy even in this world, despite all obstacles.

§ 13. *Fourth effect of the acquisition of our end.*

A JUST CONTEMPT OF CREATED THINGS.

The fourth effect of union with God is a just contempt of earthly things; it enables the soul to experience the truth of these words which God said by Isaias, "I will lift thee above the high places of the earth." And, as He says by the same prophet, the soul, enlightened with divine lights, "shall see the King in His beauty, and discover the land afar off;" and consequently earthly things will appear very insignificant to her, or rather will entirely disappear from her view. An untravelled villager thinks there are fine houses in his village, but when he travels to great cities and sees the magnificent mansions and palaces of kings and lords, he soon changes his first opinion, and acknowledges that he was deceived.

The soul, when united to God, easily loses the remembrance of all that is beautiful and brilliant here below, because she possesses God. It is easy for a powerful monarch who has superb mansions in town and country, to despise the poor cottage of a laborer; and for a millionaire to be careless about a crown-piece. "When once the soul has found God," says Blosius, "she freely bids adieu to created things, and sings with the Psalmist: 'It is good for me to adhere to my God;' and with holy Job: 'I shall die in my little nest, and as a palm, I shall multiply my days.' The possession of God quenches her hunger and thirst for created things, and hinders her from wandering after creatures in search of the wretched content they can give; for she is united to Him who is a torrent of delights, and an inexhaustible source of beauty and sweetness, and all that can rejoice the human heart."

"If thou hast God," asks St. Cyprian, "what more canst thou want? If God is thy treasure, what more canst thou have; and if He is thy possession, what can be wanting to thee?" When Anna, a childless wife, wept because of her sterility, her husband, Elcana, said to her: "Anna, why weepest thou? Am not I better to thee than ten children?" God, with far greater reason, can say to the man who grieves to see himself without wealth, without reputation, unknown and persecuted, "Why do you weep, why are you sad? Am not I better for you than all the riches and dignities, and glory and goods of earth?"

"If," says St. Augustine, "we desire to possess anything in this world, we ought, first, strive to possess God, who is the creator and possessor of all that is, and, in possessing Him, we shall have all." But, as no one possesses God who is not mutually possessed by Him, we must give ourselves to God that He may become ours. And what can be conceived more glorious than the heritage of him who has the Divinity for his own? If this is not enough, what can suffice? What more can he seek than his Saviour, who is his joy and his all?

Therefore, since union with God makes us possess God, and thus enriches us with the most precious treasure imaginable, this alone ought to be a powerful motive for us, who are naturally so wedded to self-interest, to employ all our strength to acquire it. But, though this employment be so worthy of our cares and labors, men, nevertheless, are so foolish and miserable, that they prefer to think of amassing temporal goods, attracting to themselves the vain smoke of honor, and other foolish trifles which they must soon relinquish. The Royal Prophet said, and we have already said the same with him, but it will bear repetition: "We pass our years in weaving webs to catch spiders." For, if we weigh in a just balance the riches, pleasures and other things for which men exhaust their mental energies and wear out their bodies, what better are they than the labored webs of spiders, which a servant with one stroke of a broom tears down; that is to say, which death shall certainly tear from us? Yet for such fine things men work, they are eager, they disturb themselves.

What does man accomplish with all his care and toil? He wastes his days, says the same prophet, in seeking the shadows and phantoms of true riches and honors. For this he torments himself, but in vain; for nothing of these things could ever satisfy him. "Men seek their contentment sin creatures," says St. Augustine, "and they lose themselves in these vain researches." They amuse themselves with visible things, subject to change; they seek images of happiness, which can never satiate. But, though they had all they desire, they must be in the midst of their false grandeurs, like statues of wax which, being richly adorned, are visited and admired by many persons, but, when they are exposed to the sun, gradually melt. Such is the life of men in the midst of their temporal prosperity: their inherent corruption, and the venom hidden in their mortality, gnaw it continually, and soon drive off the joys of this worldly felicity. Let us, then, be more wise, and not lose our time and our pains in running after shadows, but pursue our true good which is God, not in His images, but in His truth and in Himself, and strive earnestly to possess Him.

§ 14.—*Fifth effect of the acquisition of our end.*

A COMPOSED EXTERIOR.

The body even is influenced by the soul's union with God, and this is the fifth effect the divine union produces. It appears full of grace, diffusing a sweet odor of sanctity, a modesty and cheerfulness, as the Book of Judith expresses it, sweet and agreeable as the saints. The interior peace which the soul united to God enjoys, and which moderates all inordinate promptitude, sallies, impetuosity, and all that is too *brusque* and lively within, passes outside and regulates the movements of the body.

As a glorified soul shall, after the resurrection, communicate to its body the qualities of its glory, light, agility, subtlety and immortality, because it shall animate it and give it motion; so the soul in the state of grace, and in high grace, as when closely united to God, gives to the body impressions of grace, and causes its motions to be accompanied with reserve, sweetness, tranquillity, and all requisite moderation.

REMARKABLE EXAMPLE OF THIS TRUTH.

The celebrated spiritual director, Taulerus, one day met at the church door a poor man covered with rags, without shoes, and apparently very wretched. Taulerus having addressed him, saying, "Good morning, my dear friend?" he replied: "I thank you for your good wishes, sir, but I have never had a bad morning." "I pray God," pursued Taulerus, "that He may make you content and happy." "I have never been otherwise in my whole life," answered the mendicant. "God bless you, then, my friend," continued the director; "explain yourself a little more clearly, for I do not quite comprehend you." "Very willingly," said the beggar. "You wished me a good morning, and I told you I never remembered to have had a bad one. When pressed with hunger, I praise God; if I am cold, I bless Him. Whether He sends rain, hail, snow or fine weather, I equally thank Him, taking all that happens in a spirit of benediction and praise to His divine Majesty. In this manner all days are good to me, and I cannot have a bad one. All are referred to the end for which God has given them, which is to praise, love and bless Him; and they can be bad only when we employ them for other purposes. You have wished me contentment and happiness, and I replied that I never knew what it was to be discontented or unhappy, because nothing can happen to me against my will, which is perfectly united to the will of God. As I wish only what He wishes, nothing can sadden or grieve me. Therefore, in absolute submission to the will of God, and in the conviction that He ordains all things for the best, I always live in perfect tranquillity."

"Well, my friend," said Taulerus, "who are you, and whence do you come?" "I am a king," said the happy mendicant; "and my kingdom is my own soul, where I rule my passions by reason, and submit my reason to the law of God. And you must admit that my kingdom is more rich and noble than any kingdom on earth. If you wish to know whence I come and whither I go, I shall tell you that I come from God and I go to God. Nothing less than God ever possesses my mind and heart. In quitting the creature, I have found the Creator, and with Him perfect repose and unalterable peace."

Every one will readily conclude with us that this poor man, notwithstanding his apparent misery, was among the most perfect and happiest men of his age; for he was intimately united to his end which is God, and served Him in hunger and cold, using all the accidents of this life as steps to attain beatitude. We are all certain of the same happiness, if we walk in the same traces.

CHAPTER IV.

FOURTH GENERAL PRINCIPLE OF THE SPIRITUAL LIFE.

Union with Jesus Christ.

THE fourth general principle of the spiritual life, which I regard as the chief and most important of all, is the intimate and inseparable union which we ought to contract with Jesus Christ. On this subject we must observe four things: the first is, why we ought to have this union; the second, the manner of attaining it; the third, the place; and the fourth, the exercise of this union. To proceed:—

1. Our Lord Jesus is the true and only repairer of God's glory, and He came into the world to teach us by His instructions and examples, and to give us the means of loving and serving God. He is also the meritorious cause of our predestination and sanctification, the foundation of our salvation, and the source of all the grace and glory we can ever possess. Without Him we should be eternally miserable, and with Him we must be eternally happy. "We find in our Lord Jesus," says St. Ambrose, "all we require, and He is all things to us:" our treasure, our honor, our glory, our joy, our wisdom, our justice, our All.

We have all in Him; we find in Him our soul's beatitude, for He is God, and the beatitude of our body in a future life, because He is also man. He is the means by which we can acquire all these goods. First, He is our means, exteriorly, by His doctrine and His example, which teach us what to do and what to avoid, what to esteem and what to contemn, what to love and what to hate. From this divine exemplar we must learn to speak, to converse with God and man, and how we ought to act in all circumstances. Secondly, He is our means, interiorly, for He furnishes us with the graces necessary for us. Hence He says of Himself: "I am the way, the truth, and the life." I am beatitude, and the means to acquire it; I am the term of the voyage, and the way that conducts to it. Being life, I am your felicity; and since I am the way and the truth, I am also the means of attaining life. "No one cometh to the Father but by me. I am the door: whoever enters by me shall be saved." And St. Augustine, explaining this, says: "Jesus shall be forever our life and our sovereign beatitude." But He is also the means to attain these blessings; for God could not testify His affection for us in a stronger manner, nor make us feel the effects of His goodness with more sweetness and charity, than in sending His only Son on earth to assume our nature without relinquishing His own, and devising a way by which men could come to Him who is as immeasurably distant from them as immortality, immutability, sanctity and beatitude can separate their possessor from poor creatures, mortal and changeable, sinful and miserable. Men possess in Jesus Christ, and by His merits, justification, sanctification of the soul in its inferior and superior parts, and in the whole man. Jesus Christ has become a perfect man, without sin, that He might heal the whole man from the pestilence of sin."

But to put man in a state to enjoy these advantages, Jesus Christ assists him with His grace, according to these beautiful words of Peter, Abbot of Moustier: "Jesus, with a goodness and largess truly divine, recompenses not only our good actions, but even our good desires. He walks before us, His hands charged with gifts; He walks at our side with a beautiful countenance; He walks behind us with extended arms. He walks before us, to smooth the rough places of our paths;

He walks at our side as a faithful companion, to cheer, encourage, console and defend us. He walks behind us, to receive us if we fall. He walks before us, that we may follow and imitate Him; He walks beside us, that we may not grow lonely on the road, and He walks after us, to be the remedy of our evils. In following Him we cannot wander; in travelling in His company we shall be strong and vigorous; and in keeping us intimately united to Him, He takes care to prevent the slightest suspicion that, with such a support, we cannot do and suffer all things."

This truth being so clear, we must infer that, whether we desire to glorify God, the principle and end of our creation, or whether we are moved by self-interest and our salvation, we ought to have in view the glory of God, as He Himself wishes and intends we should have. We ought to strive earnestly to join those sensible people of whom St. Luke says: "All the crowd strove to approach Him, and to touch Him, because virtue went out from Him, and healed all." As we have amply discussed this great truth in other places, we shall now pass to the second thing, which is, to seek the manner of uniting ourselves to our Lord.

§ 1.—*The means by which to acquire union with our Lord.*

The first means of attaining to divine union is sanctifying grace. This is the true and the closest means of union with Jesus Christ, and hence we ought to labor continually to increase it in ourselves. In the second place, we can augment this union by acts of all virtues. Such acts are so many bands to attach us to our Lord. But the acts of the theological virtues of faith, hope and charity, are peculiarly efficacious for this end.

1. We must produce acts of faith in our intrinsic nothingness, believing that we are nothing by essence, by power, by

operation; nothing in the order of nature, grace and glory. Afterward we may produce similar acts regarding the domination of sin in us, of our captivity in its chains, of our weakness, our inclination to evil, and our inability to do any good. "The law of God is spiritual," says St. Paul, "and I am carnal; I have within me the source of evil desires, sin dwells in me." "There is nothing sound in me," said Isaias sorrowfully; "from the sole of my foot to the crown of my head all is diseased:" for my cure nature is too weak, she has no remedies equal to my distempers. Ezekiel says to us as well as to Jerusalem, on the part of God: "Thy root and generation are in the land of Chanaan. Thy father was an Amorrhean (a rebel), and thy mother a Cethite (a fool). And when thou wast born in the day of thy nativity, thou wast not washed with water nor salted with salt, but wast cast out upon the face of the earth in the abjection of thy soul, in the day wherein thou wast born. And passing by, I saw that thou wast trodden under foot in thy own blood."

After this we must make acts of faith in our necessity of possessing Jesus Christ, to free us from all our evils. "There is no distinction," says St. Paul, "for all have sinned, and do need the glory of God." And speaking of himself, he says: "I am delighted with the law of God according to the inward man. But I see another law in my members, fighting against the law of my mind, and captivating me in the law of sin which is in my members. Wretch that I am, who shall deliver me from the body of this death? The grace of God, by Christ Jesus our Lord." It is from Him alone I expect my deliverance from servitude, and my freedom from all miseries.

Hence this divine Saviour said: "Without me you can do nothing." And this is so true that the apostle St. Paul attests that no one can say the Lord Jesus but by the Holy Ghost. Of ourselves, we are so incapable of doing any good that it was necessary He should purchase with His blood our least holy thought, and even the permission to present ourselves before His divine Majesty, of which honor we were utterly unworthy. We would judge a person very weak who had not strength to lift up a straw, and still weaker a person who could not move any of his members, even his eyes. Behold our own condition. It is absolutely impossible for us to move our foot toward God, to reach a finger toward performing a good action, to raise our eyes to heaven, or to do the least good work, of ourselves. Paralytics are not so powerless as we, for they are never wholly paralyzed; while, without our Lord, we are entirely impotent in what concerns our salvation and perfection.

Men, with all their strength, could not, before the time of Moses, observe the law of nature; the Israelites were unable to observe the law of Moses, and this general inability of men to avoid evil and do good proves that they had need of a new spirit, and of a Saviour to give them what they wanted. Behold the necessity we have of a Saviour, and the acts of faith we ought to make in this our necessity.

2. After these acts, we come to those of hope, which, like charity, flows from a lively faith as a river flows from its source, and as a ray emanates from the sun. If we firmly believe that our Lord is to us all that faith teaches, it will be easy for us to hope in Him and love Him; it will even be impossible not to do so. Hence faith is well styled the foundation of all virtues, and it is very important that it be well cultivated. We should produce acts of hope toward our Lord, founded on His goodness, on the love He bears us, on His wisdom. His power, His mercy, His liberality, and His fidelity to His promises: for all these august qualities, being in Him in infinite perfection, merit infinite hope. We found our hope also on His life, His passion and His death, upon which we ought particularly to lean.

We have, then, immense reason to confide in Him, and to

rejoice that our salvation is in His hands, not in those of another. Can we desire our salvation, or procure it, with as much love, or wisdom, or power as He? He has given proofs of His goodness, by becoming man for us, by laboring three and thirty years, and by dying in horrible torments for our salvation. We cannot do for ourselves the thousandth part of what He has done for us. Alas! we will not even conquer our passions, or eradicate one defect which displeases Him. I may therefore say to Him with the most lively affection, as David did: "O Lord! Thou art my hope. Thou art my helper and my protector, and in Thy word I have very much hoped."

We must produce these acts in the assurance that He will have a particular care of us, of our spiritual and temporal prosperity, of our employments, our dwellings, our health and our sickness, our life and our death, and of all that can concern us in this world or the world to come. From hope we pass to love.

We should love our Lord with our whole heart, because He is infinitely amiable in Himself, and because He is infinitely amiable to us, for the immense benefits He showers on us every day, and those others which He has prepared for us in time and eternity. "If any one love not the Lord Jesus," says St. Paul, "let him be anathema," for our Lord has assumed human nature for him. What! He has done and suffered so much, and with so ardent a love died to deliver man from misery, and purchase beatitude for him, and yet he will not love Him! If any man refuse to acquit himself of so great and reasonable a duty, verily, let him be anathema.

The eternal Father by His own example teaches us to love our Lord Jesus Christ. He twice declares the love He bears Him, saying: "This is my beloved Son in whom I am well pleased," and whom I love. Hence St. Paul calls Him the Son of the Father's love. "God hath subjected all things under His feet," says David; "and let all the angels of God adore Him." "The Father loveth the Son," as we read in St. John, "and hath given all things into His hands." He has given His attributes to the holy Humanity to be employed at its pleasure; His power to work miracles; His wisdom to teach men; His mercy to pardon their sins, and His justice to judge and punish them. In this manner God has, so to say, despoiled Himself of His authority, to honor Jesus. For love of this divine Son, the Father forgives the injuries we do Himself, gives us entrance into His house, makes us partakers of His felicity. To Jesus He has given the key of His treasures, that they may be distributed as He pleases. In fine, He is the object of all His love, so that the Father loves all created things with reference to His Son.

We ought to imitate Him in this: for the love of the Father is not guided by passion but by reason, and He, being equity itself, can love only what is deserving of love. Let us, then, with all the affection of our heart, love Him on this model, producing often toward Him acts of love, of choice, of complacence, of contrition and of desire. Let us sigh for union with Him, saying with David: "As the hart panteth after the fountains of water, so panteth my soul after Thee, O God! My soul thirsteth after the strong and living God. When shall I come up and appear before the face of my God? I have desired thy salvation, O Lord! My flesh hath fainted away after Thee." And with Isaias: "My soul hath desired Thee in the night: yea, and with my spirit within me, will I watch to Thee in the morning early." And with the holy prince, St. Josaphat: "My soul hath adhered to Thee. O Christ! receive me at Thy right hand. Wounded with desires of Thy love, I burn to possess Thee, to drink of Thy salutary waters, O Fountain of life!"

3. The sacraments are the third means to unite us with our Lord. He has instituted them to confer grace upon us,

particularly the sacrament of penance, and, above all, the Eucharist, for this unites us intimately to Jesus Christ, and is hence called *communion*. In receiving this august and adorable mystery, we must unite ourselves to Him by acts of faith, hope and other virtues, but especially charity. We must strive to kindle a great fire of love in our heart, and reduce it to flames, by the consideration of what He gives us; for, with more than royal profusion, He gives us Himself entirely.

Ah! well did St. Thomas call the holy Eucharist *the sacrament of love*. If the passion and death of our Lord were the effects of the infinite love He bore us,—since He Himself declared that greater love than this no man hath: to give his life for his friend,—yet all this was necessary, because He died to appease the justice of His Father, and to satisfy for our sins. But He has established the adorable sacrament of the altar to testify in a new and wonderful manner His immense love, and to give Himself entirely to us. Undoubtedly, in this sacrament He renders Himself infinitely amiable to us. In the other life, when we shall have been purified in the highest degree, He will communicate to us the joy of His Humanity and Divinity; but He cannot wait so long, His love presses Him to anticipate in our regard this union, though we have rendered ourselves so unworthy of it by our sins and imperfections. O what love! what excess of goodness! And how immense are our obligations to love Him ardently in this divine sacrament!

4. Fourthly, we can unite ourselves to Him by mental and vocal prayer, and particularly such prayers as are most efficacious for this pupose, as the Litany of Jesus, the Office of Wisdom, composed by Henri Suso; by inflamed ejaculatory prayers, by thinking ordinarily of Him, of His perfections, of the benefits we have received and hope to receive from His bounty, and by familiar entertainments with Him as if we saw Him present near us. We must be with Him

as a child with his parents, as a spouse with her beloved, a brother with his brother, a friend with his friend, a patient with his physician, a subject with his prince, remembering that beautiful saying of the Abbot Moses: "The soul ought to judge that she is guilty of infidelity toward her Spouse, if she quit for a moment the thought of Jesus Christ." Pious reading is very conducive to this divine union; and among the Sacred Scriptures, we ought to be particularly familiar with the New Testament; above all, with the Gospel of St. John and the Epistles of St. Paul.

§ 2. — *Where we ought to make this union, and how it should operate.*

3. The heart is the place in which we must particularly unite ourselves to our Lord. We know that He loves us, and love always places the person beloved in the heart as his peculiar domicile. We can dwell in the heart of Jesus by our thoughts. It is there we must establish our abode. Religious profess rigid poverty, yet they have their cells; hermits and recluses have caves in which to perform all their exercises. Our Lord lodges us in His heart; and we can have no better dwelling. This home is more magnificent, more pleasant, and more holy, than all the palaces of kings, nor can all the boudoirs and cabinets of queens approach it in beauty. Hence St. Bernard exclaimed: "O my Lord! Thou hast willed that Thy sacred side be opened with a spear, that we may have an entrance to Thy heart. It was love rather than the lance that pierced Thy heart, to the end that we might enter it and be shielded from all dangers. Let us then joyfully enter this house, and never leave it. O how good and pleasant it is to live in the holy heart of Jesus!"

4. It is in this heart we must work, as the scientific man works in his laboratory. We ought to do here all that we do, exercising in it all the actions of the purgative, the illuminative, and the unitive life. Considering, examining, and bewailing our sins, asking pardon of God for them in this heart, which in the Garden of Olives conceived inexpressible sorrow for them, let us hate and avoid the least offence, in this infinitely holy and sovereignly pure heart, which has an extreme horror of the very smallest imperfection. Let us, in this heart, combat generously our vices and perverse inclinations, resist courageously the assaults of our enemy, and gain, as we easily may in so renowned a fortress, many glorious victories. Let us perform, in this penitent and afflicted heart, our mortifications and austerities; and when we experience dryness and weariness, let us suffer these trials in this heart, which in the Garden of Olives was overwhelmed with sadness even to agony.

Certainly, tribulations, hunger, thirst, heat, cold, pains of body and mind coming to us in this heart will be very sweet, and will easily lose their natural bitterness, and become most salutary, as waters passing through mines become highly medicinal by the contact. While the illustrious martyr, St. Palemon, was horribly tormented, being torn with iron hooks and burned with torches, by order of the Emperor Maximin, he heeded not his wounds, but thought only of Jesus Christ who was able to aid him in this extremity. He was not disappointed, for the murderers soon lost the use of their arms, and the fire ceased to burn. Then the tyrant furiously cried out: "By what enchantments dost thou wrest the power from the executioners of my justice, and from the fire itself? These are the proofs of thy magic." "My magic and my spells," replied the saint, "are Jesus Christ, who assists and strengthens me to overcome the sufferings thou dost inflict."

2. The illuminative life. We must exercise virtues and

good works in the heart of Jesus, practising faith in this heart, which is infinitely wise ; hope in this heart, which is infinitely loving, and which is liberal and merciful beyond all our thoughts. In this heart so humble, so patient, so sweet, so gentle, gifted with all virtues in a sovereign degree, we must produce our acts of humility, of patience, of sweetness, of gentleness, and of all virtues. There we must make our mental and vocal prayer, our thanksgiving after communion ; we cannot choose a more holy oratory. As this most sacred heart has always been elevated to God, so we shall be more recollected and less distracted there than in any other plaec.

In the heart of Jesus all burning with love for man, we shall love our neighbor, bear with the vices and defects of his body and mind, and endure the sufferings he may cause us. St. Paul wrote to the faithful of Philippi : " God is my witness, how I love you in the entrails, in the heart, of Jesus Christ." Consider where St. Paul loved the Philippians. He loved them not in his own heart, in his own nature always attached to self-interest, in his own weakness and corruption, but *in the heart of Jesus.* From this he spoke and wrote, and instructed and admonished them, and consequently he acted toward them most piously, perfectly and divinely.

Whence comes it that we show so little true love, so little cordiality, goodness, meekness, tenderness, affability and sweetness, toward our neighbor ; so little condescension to his humors, so little patience with his defects, so little allowance for his natural character? It is because we do not look at him, and receive all things from him in the heart of Jesus, that loving, suffering and merciful heart; but in our own hard, fiery, unloving and impatient heart, which makes all things difficult. In His heart all duties would become very easy and very sweet.

The pardon which our Lord, when on the cross, asked of

His Father for His murderers, furnished St. Austin with this reflection: "Our Lord shows this extreme goodness toward His persecutors, because He did not regard that they were putting Him to death, but that He was dying for them." In like manner when any person offends us, we ought not to make the reflection that we are offended by such a man, nor in what, nor wherefore, nor that he is reckless, ungrateful, malign, perfidious, and that we have never injured him; but to remember that we are in the heart of Jesus, that it is there we receive the offence, that we dwell there with him who has insulted us, since we are both Christians, that this charitable heart loves him, and has been pierced for love of him. Such ought to be our reflections; and those will rob the injury of its thorns and sweeten its bitterness.

Doing all our interior and exterior actions in the sacred heart, we ought to perform them with the moderation, meekness, suavity, and even the intentions of this heart, that is to say, in perfect conformity and entire submission to all its inspirations and movements.

Finally, as regards the unitive life, this divine heart which was continually united to God, not only by the hypostatic union, but also by acts of love and all the other virtues; this heart which was infinitely elevated above the things of earth, and burned with charity for us,—this divine heart is the true sanctuary of the unitive way; there we may practise it in an excellent manner. There we should produce acts of love, preference, complacency, benevolence and aspiration; there we must exercise adorations the most pure, oblations, homages, thanks and abandonment of self; annihilations, abasements, and disengagement from all inordinate affection to creatures, elevation above all earthly things; and there we shall possess and experience repose and joy in God, as in our centre. Such is what we do in the heart of our Lord, and how we must unite ourselves to Him.

§ 3. *Conclusion of this subject.*

I add, in conclusion, that we ought to adopt this exercise of union with our Lord, in preference to all others, and make it our special devotion. It happens often, and very often, in the spiritual life, that persons divide their minds on many little practices, and undertake a quantity of different things. This proceeding is not good. It is embarrassing, and much more likely to retard the soul's perfection than to advance it; it is to amuse one's self with leaves and branches, and not notice the trunk and root. The soul should, as far as possible, reduce its operations to unity, adopting but few practices; and these, good and solid, and such as unite the excellencies of many others. Besides, we have not mind enough to comprehend, nor memory enough to retain, too many, even of pious things, and our will does not always relish spiritual exercises : it is then much more prudent and salutary to adopt one single exercise, of a very important nature, and which includes in itself many others. The exercise which contains all these advantages is that of union with our Lord Jesus Christ. Hence we ought to undertake it with affection, not tormenting ourselves with many other exercises, but striving to cultivate and perfect this union by all the means which have been given, and to fasten every day more closely the bonds which bind us to Him ; for, after all, He is the only cause of our predestination, and our sole good, so that we shall be saved and covered with glory according to our union with Him, and the degrees of this union will be the rule and measure of our eternal beatitude. And, then, as He knows, better than we, what is calculated to forward our perfection, and desires it more ardently than we can, so we may believe that, if we are united to Him, He will not fail to give it, and to put us in the state best suited to promote our perfection and our happiness.

We need only, then, employ all our efforts to unite ourselves intimately to Him, without caring for the rest. All the economy of spiritual direction is reduced to four things: first, the mysteries of His life and death; second, His virtues and the exercise of good works; third, all things according as they shall happen to us; and fourth, the designs of God. As in the body, our hands and feet move by the direction of the head, which applies the hand to the works it does, and conducts the foot in the way it should go, so that the hand and foot, and all other parts, ought to have but one care, which is to keep themselves well united to the head, and be absolutely submissive to it; so, properly speaking, we ought to have but one thing in our minds, which is, to unite ourselves intimately to our Lord. With His goodness, His wisdom and His power, He will afterward apply us Himself to do what shall be necessary for our salvation and perfection.

1. And first, to His mysteries: by the knowledge of them, and the affections they produce; by the communication of their spirit, by a firm and simple faith, by a high esteem and respect which He will give us for them, and especially by the imitation of the virtues He has exercised, to give us an example.

2. He will apply us to His virtues, to His humility, His patience, His meekness, His obedience, His intentions, His prayer, His love toward God and man, His conversation, and His contempt of transitory things; giving us grace to know them, to esteem them, to love them, to resolve to practise them in occasions. In applying us, for example, to humility, He infuses the knowledge of the humble thoughts that He entertained, of the abnegations which He practised as man toward the Divinity, and of the love He bore this virtue. Afterward, He will give us strength to practise it in our thoughts, our judgments, our opinions, our affections, our words and our actions; also, when we shall be praised or blamed, wounded in our honor, our goods, our body and our

mind ; when we shall be opposed and contradicted, He will be our guide and our support. As the mariner's compass does not turn to the pole till it is touched with the loadstone, so our will does not of itself incline to humility, to contempt, to opprobrium ; it must first be touched with the humility of Jesus Christ, who, communicating His virtue, makes us perform cheerfully what we had previously held in horror.

3. Our Lord will apply us to all things as they present themselves, to all accidents which can happen to us : to hunger, thirst, cold, riches, poverty, health and sickness, life and death, that we may use them according to His will, that is, in a manner wholly spiritual and divine, as means of our salvation, perfection and union with God ; for He has merited that they should produce these effects, and has given us grace to use them in this spirit.

4 This is the principal. He will apply us to God's service, and unite us to God, in our measure, as He Himself was applied and united to God. He will unite us to God as our first beginning and our last end, as the Sovereign Goodness and Infinite Wisdom, as the First and only Fair, and excite in us affections suitable to His different perfections. Thus He will open to us the door to the unitive life ; we shall exercise its acts and taste its delights, according to the degree of union we shall have contracted with Him.

Behold what our Lord will accomplish in us, if we are united with Him ! Hence we ought to apply ourselves entirely to the acquisition of this divine union. "Martha, Martha," says He to us, in the person of that holy woman, "thou art careful and troubled about many things, and yet but one thing is necessary." You give yourself to various practices which are good, you apply yourself to different exercises of piety with care, often with eagerness, and sometimes with trouble ; yet one thing is necessary above all others : it is to unite yourself intimately to Jesus Christ, our Lord. All have need of this advice; for Jesus Christ is the only source of the salvation and perfection of all. But those have most need of it who labor for the salvation of souls; because souls belong to Him, because He has His particular designs on each, and He alone can give the director grace and light to help them. O how easy it is to our Lord to convert the most abandoned when He pleases, and how well He can select the means! He need only give to monarchs and princes a little of the zeal of St. Louis, to powerful ecclesiastics a share in the spirit of the apostles, and we should soon see kingdoms changed, and the Church assume a new aspect.

How admirable are the works He wrought for the advancement of His glory and the salvation of souls by St. Catharine of Sienna, a simple maid of medium rank, who lived only thirty-three years! How wonderful the power He gave the words of St. Lutgarde to change hearts! How forcibly could the words of St. Gertrude and St. Bridget impress the minds of men! "I am the divine Power," said the Holy Spirit to blessed Angela Foligni, "who give thee this grace, that all those who shall see thee, or who shall even think of thee, or repeat thy name, shall receive profit toward their salvation." To which the saint replied: "Ah! Lord, I beseech Thee not to give me this favor, for, being useful to others, it might be prejudicial to me by exciting vanity." "No, no," said the Holy Spirit, "it shall not injure thee. Thou shalt be only its guardian and depository. Thou shalt attribute nothing of it to thyself; and, if it serves others, I know how to ordain that it will not injure thee."

O how well a man united to Jesus Christ contributes to the salvation of the human race, though he be all alone in the midst of a desert! "Those united to God," says Louis of Blois, "who give Him full power to operate in them all He pleases, are very dear to Him, and bring more profit to the Church and to souls in one hour than others, who have not attained this divine union, could in several years." Let us, then, strive to unite ourselves intimately to Jesus Christ, to procure by all means, and to increase continually, this divine union; let us beg this grace incessantly, without putting ourselves in pain about any other, because the rest will assuredly come, and, if only we are united to Him, we must soon become rich, virtuous and perfect. "It is easy for God," says the Sage, "to raise a poor man from his misery, and crown him with riches and honors." And the Prince of the Apostles, writes: "The God of all grace, who hath called us into His eternal glory in Christ Jesus, after you have suffered a little, will Himself perfect you, and confirm you, and establish you. To Him be glory and empire, for ever and ever. Amen."

CHAPTER V.

FIFTH GENERAL PRINCIPLE OF THE SPIRITUAL LIFE.

Purity of intention.

THE fifth general principle of the spiritual life is purity of intention, which holds a rank so elevated, and reaches to so high a point of excellence, that it gives value to all our actions, and by a spiritual alchemy converts all into gold, pearls, diamonds and rubies. The intention for which we perform an action is of the same importance to the action as the root is to the tree, the soul to the body, form to matter; so that our action is noble or vile, eminent or abject, laudable or blameworthy, deserving of recompense or chastisement, according to the nature and quality of the intention, which renders it good if it be good in itself, and perfect if it be very good, according to that saying of St. Paul: "If the root be holy, the branches are also holy." On the contrary, if the intention be vicious, it extends its virus to the action, and corrupts it entirely, good though it apparently be, producing in it an effect similar to that which a diseased eye produces on a beautiful face.

Properly speaking, nothing in this world is, of itself, great or small before God, and consequently nothing that we do can be called great or small. An alms of a hundred thousand crowns appears very great before men, and an alms of a farthing very small; nevertheless, a bad intention can render the first contemptible before God, while a good intention can render the second praiseworthy in His sight. Show me the best actions in appearance : the renunciation of all your wealth, the most rigorous austerities, life-long fasts on bread and water, and works most useful to your neighbor's salvation. Well, if you exercise these with an evil eye, that is to say, with a crooked intention, regarding in them the applause of creatures, or your own satisfaction, or any other selfish motive, they lose all their lustre, and, in place of the reward they might have merited, become deserving of punishment. "Thy gold and silver," said God by Isaias, "are changed into brass ; thy wine is mixed with water :" it has lost all its strength. A little before He had said, in the same thought: "To what purpose do you offer me the multitude of your victims ? I am full, I desire not holocausts of rams, and the fat of fatlings, and the blood of lambs and goats. Offer me no more sacrifices in vain ; your incense is an abomination to me." See how obliquity of intention ruins the best actions, while rectitude of intention elevates the lowest.

We ought to engrave this truth deeply on our minds, that, as there is no action, lowly though it appear, which a good motive cannot ennoble, so there is no action, magnificent though it look, that may not become abject and vicious, if it have vice for its object ; because it is the object and the motive that qualify our actions, and give them their real value.

Hence the devil, who knows well that all our advancement and riches consist in the goodness of our intentions, uses a thousand artifices to sully them, and like Naas (whose name signifies a serpent), King of the Ammonites, to tear out our right eye and leave us only the left (1 Kings, xi, 2), that is, to excite us to perform our actions through sinister motives; or if he cannot persuade us to this, he strives to divert our minds, hinder us from forming a good intention, and make us work through mere routine. If he cannot prevent us from producing acts through good motives, he tries at least to induce us to be satisfied with such as are less perfect.

By these *ruses* he hinders all Christians, particularly such as profess to lead a devout life, from advancing in perfection; he robs them of inestimable treasures of grace and glory which they could easily have acquired. If we want to perform good actions, we must direct our intentions, for, as Christians, we shall labor in vain unless we practise purity of intention. If your actions be not virtuous, what praise and glory can you merit? Do we praise a man for bad, or even for indifferent, actions? And if you do not refer your actions in some manner to God, what recompense can you expect from Him? Would you pay wages to a man who, without ever thinking of you, tilled his own field in the middle of Turkey?

Hence God demands of man, above all things, the heart and the will. "My Son, give me thy heart" and thy love; let me be the end of all thy labors. "O God," exclaims the Royal Prophet, "Thy desires are fixed on me," and I ought to give Thee all things, but chiefly myself, without whom all other presents would be odious to Thee. As it is impossible that anything outside of God can content you, if you do not also possess Himself, so it is impossible that you should satisfy Him unless you give yourself entirely to Him.

2. The second remark we have to make on this subject is, that the best of all intentions consists in having God alone for the object of all we do. Intentions concerning our spiritual profit, the pardon of our sins, the avoidance of vice, the victory over any passion, the acquisition of some virtue, deliverance from hell, the gaining of heaven,—are all very good, and as such are taught by the Doctors, received by the Fathers, fully authorized by the Holy Scriptures, and have been practised by the saints; but those, which adopt for their end neither our profit nor our loss, paradise nor hell, but only the glory and interests of God, are certainly, and beyond comparison, the noblest, the most elevated, and the most excellent of all intentions.

3. The last remark I make on this point is, that we ought most carefully to propose to ourselves, always and in all we do, these last intentions, to the end that they may animate all our works. This we owe to God, and we owe Him still more. After all He has done for us, it is but little if we give ourselves to Him, if we breathe only for His love, and if we hold ourselves in readiness to do and suffer all things for His glory, which, being the end of our creation, is the most sublime design we can conceive, and renders our actions most meritorious, though we do not think at all of merit.

St. Chrysostom elegantly says: "We should do all our actions for our Lord Jesus, rather than for the reward. Our chief recompense and delight, our joy and beatitude, consist in loving our Saviour, and laboring for Him, in this disinterested spirit. We ought to refer all our thoughts, designs and works to the greater glory of God." Father Nicholas Serrarius, of the Society of Jesus, a man of great learning and greater virtue, sought, in his studies, in his communications with his neighbor, and in all that he did, the honor of God, with as much ardor as the ambitious evince for honors, or the avaricious for riches. It is impossible to describe the transport of mind and joy of heart which appeared on his countenance when he said or heard the doxology, *Gloria Patri*. When, as sometimes happened, the musicians sang it better than usual, he would leap for joy, and seemed unable to contain himself.

"True adorers," said our Lord to the Samaritan woman, "shall adore the Father in spirit and in truth, for the Father also seeketh such to adore Him." And what is it to adore the Father *in spirit and in truth ?* It is, first, to adore, honor and serve God, not in the spirit of Judaism, nor of the Old Law, which was full of exterior ceremony and paid little attention to the worship of the heart, but in that of Christianity and the New Law, which, using few exterior rites, inspires souls to offer to God all sorts of interior service. Secondly, *in spirit*, that is, adoring, praising, blessing and serving God, according to the movements and inspirations of the Holy Ghost, and loving God in Him, who is the love of the Father and the Son, in the most pure and perfect manner. Moreover, we should adore and glorify God on the model and with the motives of our Lord, who is the Increated and Incarnate Truth, and as He adored and glorified God while He lived here below among men.

CHAPTER VI.

SIXTH GENERAL PRINCIPLE OF THE SPIRITUAL LIFE.

The exercise of faith in all things.—Faith is an inestimable gift.

THE sixth general principle of the spiritual life is to ground ourselves solidly in faith, and to do all our actions by its movements. We ought, during this life, to act by faith, and in all things to follow its guidance, because God has willed to save us, neither by reason, nor by science, but by faith. "We are justified by faith," says St. Paul to the Romans: we must believe that faith acquires our justification; and again, justice before God takes its source in faith. In the first Epistle the same saint wrote to the Corinthians: we find these words: "I will destroy the wisdom of the wise and the prudence of the prudent. Where is the wise? Where is the scribe? Where is the disputer of this world? Hath not God made foolish the wisdom of this world? For, seeing that, in the wisdom of God, the world by wisdom knew not God, it hath pleased God by the foolishness of our preaching to save them that believe."

And, certainly, God in this does man a signal favor. Hence the saints by common accord call faith the gift of God. St. Paul, writing to the Galatians, says: "Give thanks that you are saved by faith, and this not of yourselves, because it is the gift of God." By this gift God has rendered us participators of divine things, and of His own knowledge of them, which naturally surpasses our comprehension. But, to put this in a clear light, we must remember the designs our Lord had in coming into this world, which were : to free us from our miseries, to cleanse us of our stains, to heal our wounds, to elevate us to a state supernatural and divine, to unite us to God by grace in this life, and by glory in the next. But our nature, corrupted by sin, could not perceive its inherent darkness and vices, powerful obstacles to this eminent state ; to raise us to it, our mind must first have been cleansed from its corruptions, and then, acquiring requisite purity, operate in a high and sublime manner. To be disposed for union with God, the soul must go out of its own baseness, and receive from above a being all divine ; for the means ought to be proportioned to the end, and the last dispositions should be of the same order as the first.

There are in our soul four things to be remarked : its essence, and its three faculties with their operations, which are *to hear*, *to will* and *to be able*. Now, these qualities should be reformed and ennobled in us, as iron is changed in the furnace, in order to be capable of promoting our union with God. Grace and the Holy Ghost do the first work in this mystery, when the soul gives them entrance. Then they ennoble the soul, they perfect its being in an admirable manner, they clothe it with shining qualities, and render it a new creature, as St. Paul calls it. In Christ, the soul becomes a new creature, because grace is a communication of the divine nature which makes us like gods, according to these words of David : "I have said you are gods and children of the Most High ;" and of St. Peter : "That you may become participators in the divine nature." (Second Epistle of St. Peter, i, 4.)

The will ought to despoil itself of its mere natural manner of living, because it is for that purpose that God has given it part of His charity wherewith He loves all things, according to what St. Paul says : " The charity of God is poured into our hearts by the Holy Ghost, who is given to us ;" God being charity, as the beloved disciple teaches us : " He who dwelleth in charity abideth in God, and God in him." But, as man, of himself, is only imbecility and impotence, he must, in order to acquire union with God, renounce his natural powers, confess his poverty and weakness, and through hope unite his weakness to God's omnipotence, in order that, absolutely diffiding in his own strength, and confiding entirely in God, he may say from the abyss of his own nothingness, like the apostle : "I can do all things in Him that strengthens me."

Subtle and clear-sighted as our mind may be, it could never, by its own unaided efforts, attain to the knowledge of supernatural things, because they necessarily surpass its capacity. Man must be diffident as to his natural powers of hearing and knowing them, and be enlightened by a superior light, which is commensurate with these things. Our understanding, says St. Thomas, is extremely weak in spiritual things. When it wishes to raise its eyes to the first Being, it is like a little field-mouse which opens its eyes for the first time to the sun : the sight of the first is not unlike that of the second, though God be cognizable, and the sun visible. One of the friends of Job said to him : "Behold, the greatness of God infinitely surpasses the capacity of man, and all our elevations are infinitely below the eminence of His perfections, and the heights of His mysteries." After him, David says: "Thy knowledge is wonderful to me. I know not how to seek it, it is too high for me."

"The things of God," says St. Chrysostom, "are so much elevated above the human mind that a man cannot show his folly more plainly than by thinking he can attain to them by his own power, and discover by the light of reason what can be perceived only by the light of faith. It is ridiculous to strive to penetrate what is above our capacity, for, in doing so, all our discourses and all our reasoning are like the webs of spiders." Explaining these words of the Corinthians, "The sensual man cannot perceive the things of the Spirit of God," he says that, so far from understanding things spiritual, he even looks on them as extravagant imaginations. The reason of this is, that he examines them with a terrestrial mind, or by the rules of human reason; while they ought to be considered and judged by the light of faith, and with a mind illuminated from on high. The most piercing corporal vision cannot see the things of heaven, nor even many of the things of earth. Optical illusions can be practised on the keenest eye. If we consider the things of God by mere natural light, we shall not only not see them as they are, we shall even rank among follies that which is replenished with the most profound wisdom. And hence the apostle tells us that the mysteries of religion are far above our comprehension, and that they must be examined by faith, rather than by reason. "All the knowledge we can have of a thing," says St. Thomas, "is founded upon its substance, for, according to the teaching of Aristotle, the foundation of demonstration is to know the essence of a thing and its origin; afterward it will be easy to discover all its properties and peculiarities. If a man knows well the essence of a stone, or of the triangle, he can easily discover the rest. But the essence of God is infinitely above our natural capacities; and it is not wonderful that, if being ignorant of His essence, His mysteries and designs should be unknown to us, unless He reveal them."

The torch that discovers these sublime things is faith, and faith is nothing but a supernatural light, a ray of the divine Face, a participation in the divine knowledge, a flowing out of God upon man. Faith raises a man far above himself; it draws him from the land of error to the region of truth; it makes him view things by a light far different from that of the senses; it teaches him to esteem and to condemn, to love and to hate, in a manner otherwise than nature teaches. In this, God does man an inestimable favor. Our understanding is our ruling faculty, because it directs the will, so that in it is found the root of all our good or evil. But, on the other hand, it is far from being clear-sighted in the things of salvation, or even in the merit of other things; for it deceives us strongly every day, causing us to despise what we ought to esteem, and esteem what we ought to despise, mistaking light for darkness and darkness for light, as the prophet Isaias remarks. God designs to protect us from these errors, and to prevent the misfortunes that would otherwise result from our ignorance, and, by a favor which surpasses our comprehension, renders us participators in some measure of the knowledge He has of Himself.

Therefore, whatever we know of His Divinity, of the Unity of His Essence, of the Trinity of Persons, of the excellence of His perfections, the mysteries of the Incarnation, the Redemption, the Resurrection, and the Holy Eucharist; the judgments we form of the vanity of the honors of this life, of the dangers of riches and pleasures, of the profit we may derive from poverty, contempt and suffering,—we know all this by faith; we judge of these mysteries as God judges of them, only that God sees them clearly in the splendors of His inaccessible light, while we know them obscurely, but yet with the same knowledge.

Nevertheless, this knowledge is not identical in species, if I may so speak, because in God it is a substance and God Himself, while in us it is simply accidental. But it is the same: first, because the object is the same; and second, because its source is the same; for our knowledge is derived from the exterior word of God, which is only the expression of His interior word and His knowledge; and thirdly, it is the same, because it participates in some of His attributes,—in His truth, which is but the conformity of the knowledge with the object; and the certainty with which the mind seizes this known object, which certainty is stronger in proportion as the motive which formed it is more powerful.

The knowledge of the disciple is the knowledge of the master; for, as the mind of the scholar is as an empty vase into which the teacher pours a portion of his own knowledge, so the knowledge of the things of faith which is possessed by man, who is the disciple of God, as St. Thomas calls him, is the knowledge of God communicated to him, and therefore the same knowledge as that which God has of them.

Hence St. Paul calls faith the *knowledge and the wisdom of God*, because it is a ray of the divine light. And St. Peter calls it the *light of God*, saying: "He has called you out of darkness into His admirable light." Light truly admirable, because of the Sun of justice from which it emanates, and because of the wonderful things it discloses. Of this, Isaias speaks when he says: "The Gentiles shall walk in Thy light, and kings in the brightness of Thy rising." But this light God communicates, not as a man instructs his disciple, by words, by looks, by speaking in his ear or placing his writing before his eyes, but in the interior, speaking even in the depths of the soul, and giving His light as a torch to the understanding, which it continually illumines.

§ 1. *Divine qualities of faith.*

Since faith is a ray of the wisdom of God and a participation in His knowledge, we must conclude that it possesses His certitude, His infallibility, and the other glorious qualities which make it surpass all other knowledge that is, or can be, acquired in this life. It ennobles our minds, of which it is the richest and most precious ornament, and it beautifies our souls more than all other kinds of science. If, as Aristotle affirms, an imperfect and slight notion of superior and spiritual substances gives the mind more content and delight than a clear knowledge of inferior and material things; if it is true that we love to discourse of the heavens and know something of them, even in a doubtful way, we may conclude, with St. Thomas, that a slight knowledge of high and divine things, and, consequently, faith, conduces powerfully to the perfection of our mind.

If the imperfect knowledge of a high thing is so desirable, how much more the perfect knowledge, and, consequently, faith, which is a very perfect knowledge of the Divinity and of high things, and which consequently confers on the soul an inconceivable dignity! I call it a very perfect knowledge, because it is absolutely certain, being founded on the first truth, and an emanation of the wisdom of God, and a communication of His own knowledge. "Faith," says St. Denis, "is to the faithful man a firm foundation which establishes him in truth, and enables him to see things as they really are." "There is," says St. John Climacus, "a constancy of mind regarding the knowledge it conveys which nothing can shake." St. Bernard, writing to Pope Innocent against Abelard, who wished to consider faith as a simple opinion, says with vehemence: "In the first lines of his extravagant theology he defines faith to be an opinion. He proposes as doubtful that which of all things is the most certain. But; thanks to God! faith is not an opinion, as this dreamer teaches; nor is it a deduction from our vain thoughts: it is a certainty, not an estimation."

I have called faith a very perfect knowledge, because it renders a man most wise, teaches him the most profound secrets, the most beautiful and sublime mysteries, the most useful and necessary things in this world. St. Paul writes, as follows, to the Corinthians: "We speak wisdom among the perfect; yet not the wisdom of the world, neither of the princes of this world, that comes to nought. But we speak the wisdom of God in a mystery, which is hidden, which God ordained before the world, unto our glory."

How many nights of profound contemplation and days of

subtle disputation did it not cost Plato to reason out the immortality of the soul ; and yet, as St. Chrysostom remarks, he died without being able to persuade one of his auditors of the truth of this assertion. Faith, on the contrary, has taught the immortality of the soul to the world by the ministry of unknown and unlettered fishermen, who announced it, though the act cost them their lives ; it makes philosophers of villagers, teaching them the immortality of the soul and the resurrection of the body, to contemn the things of this world, and to desire those of the next.

Explaining these words of St. Paul, "Christ Jesus, who of God is made unto us in wisdom," the same St. Chrysostom says : "Who then, my brethren, is wiser than you who have not the science of Plato, but that of Jesus Christ, and who even have Jesus Himself for your wisdom? The apostle speaks in this manner of the profound treasures you possess. We are more learned than the disciples of Plato, since the Holy Ghost is our Master."

You tell me that faith is an obscure knowledge, and that this obscurity tarnishes its lustre. I answer, that faith is certainly obscure, it knows not things in themselves, it sees not with its own eyes, but with the eyes of others ; but I say, also, that it is voluntary, and that, consequently, it brings God great glory and man great merit, which it could not do if it were not enveloped in clouds. Were there clear evidence, there would be no liberty. I must believe that fire burns, because I see it, while it is in my power to believe or not to believe something told me, because, not realizing it, I am not constrained to believe it ; and if I do believe it, I do so because I wish to believe it. Hence St. Augustine says : "If thou *sawest* the mysteries of religion, thou couldst not *believe* them ; but, believing without seeing, thou shalt be recompensed by one day seeing clearly." St. Paul says that the faith of Abraham was reputed justice in him. If it was meritorious, it certainly was voluntary; for merit always takes its root in liberty.

If faith is obscure, there is, nevertheless, light enough in its obscurity to conduct us well, and hinder us from wandering and falling. St. Denis, speaking of mystical theology, gives it these splendid eulogies, which we may justly apply to faith. He calls it a brilliant obscurity which shows us divine things, and which in sombre darkness makes them shine very brightly, and discovers mysteries which can neither be touched nor seen, by replenishing the understanding of those whose eyes cannot gaze upon them. Faith is an obscurity, because it does not discover things clearly, but shows them in a veiled manner. Yet, because of God's infinitely clear knowledge of things, and the revelation which He has made of them, upon which faith is grounded, it is a very bright obscurity. It is from this revelation that faith derives its certainty,—a certainty incomparably greater than that which can be proved by all the demonstrations, experiences and reasonings of creatures. What appears folly to men is better than all their wisdom, says St. Paul; and St. Denis remarks that all human knowledge is only ignorance, compared to the knowledge of the angels. The wisdom of God, which, in our sense, is faith, is supremely elevated above all reason; before it the wisdom of men is lost, and their prudence noxious, and yet this wisdom is the cause of their understanding and their reason.

After all, if faith is an obscure knowledge, it is so only in our mind; in the mind of God it is infinitely clear, and that is enough for us. Besides, this obscurity will lessen by degrees, and faith will become vision in a happier life. Hence St. Thomas teaches that faith will be eternal as regards knowledge, and temporal as regards its obscurity, and that in heaven it shall unveil the covered countenance and open the eyes which on earth it held closed.

§ 2.—*Why God obliges us to believe.*

Faith, we repeat, is a very precious gift of God, and a very great grace. God, having resolved to save us by faith, not by science, has revealed as objects of our faith two sorts of things. The first we could arrive at by our own application, as, that there must be a Creator, which is self-evident; the second we could not attain by our own lights, as, the Trinity of Persons in a unity of essence. St. Thomas does not give the reasons why we ought to believe things which surpass our comprehension, but Lessius, a pious modern author, throws great light on this subject.

First: God wishes first, that, subjecting the understanding to faith, as St. Paul says, we should offer it a holocaust to God; and by acknowledging the littleness of our own mind and the greatness of His wisdom, we should honor Him in a sublime manner. Secondly, to ennoble and perfect our mind; because, if God proposed only what did not exceed its capacity, it would languish in its baseness, and be unable to dispose itself for the clear vision of God. Faith holds the rank between natural science and the Beatific Vision. Thirdly, our beatitude, which God has prepared, being immeasurably superior to our nature, it is suitable that the things which conduct to it should partake of its elevation.

I add, for a fourth cause, the doctrine of St. Thomas, which is, that an imperfect thing perfects itself only by the action of a perfect cause, which cause does not act at one blow, but by little and little, and, at first, somewhat roughly, but later on with more delicacy, polishing its work more and more, till it gives the final stroke of consummate perfection.* Thus we see that the disciple must first believe what his master says, and this belief is the channel by which he receives his doctrine; and though this manner of receiving it be imperfect, yet it disposes him, later on, to gather it in its plenitude and perfection, which happens when he does not simply *believe* the doctrine of his master, but *knows* it. Thus his docility conducts him to knowledge. We must here below believe supernatural things in an obscure manner, that is, by faith, that we may dispose ourselves to see them as they are in a future life, for credulity produces evidence, according to these words of David : "As we have heard, so we have seen, in the city of the Lord of Hosts, in the city of our God : God hath founded it forever."

Now, to come to the reasons for which the wisdom and goodness of God exact of us that we believe things which we could not understand of ourselves, St. Thomas remarks that it is to obviate three great inconveniences which would otherwise follow, and in an affair of such paramount importance as is our spiritual good, to give us an easy means and a secure way, namely, faith. The first inconvenience is, that, if God had not taught us those things concerning Himself which we can by our own reason discover, sublime as they are, and necessary as they must be, few would have intellect and leisure enough to seek them ; because the preservation of human society requires that the greater number be employed in manual works, such as, tilling the earth and working at trades, and these people would be excluded from a knowledge of them. Those who have leisure, but are unlettered, who are too delicate to apply the mind closely, or who have no taste for speculative studies, would also be condemned to this most pernicious ignorance.

The second inconvience is, that even those who are most liberally gifted by nature, and who join, to their talent, diligence and industry, could acquire this knowledge only after a long time ; for these truths are profound and above the senses, and many other sciences would be necessary to prepare the mind for their reception. Besides, youth, being subject to the fury of the passions, is not capable of the consideration of these high things ; so that few could attain to them were reason and science the only aids, and consequently the greater munber would remain plunged in darkness, deprived of the knowledge which could render them virtuous, and prepare them for eternal beatitude.

The third inconvenience is, that our mind, however capacious, is nevertheless very narrow, and its views always feeble, because of its imprisonment in matter, and its union with the senses; hence, left to itself, it might easily mingle darkness with its lights, and falsehood with its truths. This happened to the ancient philosophers, whose minds were cast in nature's best mould; for, despite all their subtlety and investigation, some were atheists, others could not agree in matters regarding the providence of God, the immortality of the soul, the transmigration of souls, their Tartarus and their Elysium, and other things, concerning which the wisest of these great minds came to very erroneous conclusions.

It is well known, says St. Prosper, that the philosophers of Greece and Rome took immense pains to investigate these things, and yet, with all their labors and contentions, they succeeded only in embarrassing their minds in a thousand perplexities, and losing themselves in the labyrinth of their thoughts. They obscured the thing more than they enlightened it; because, in the search for truth, they would have no other guides than themselves. St. Augustine, who was St. Prosper's master, had said before him: "The wise Athenians assembled in crowds in the Portico, in the Academy, in the Gymnasium and in the public gardens, and each warmly strove to maintain his own opinions and overthrow those of others. Hence truth and falsehood were combated with equal ardor, so that no city ever deserved so well the mysterious name of Babylon, which signifies confusion."

St. Chrysostom elegantly remarks, on this subject, that the Greeks, with all their science, were only children. Among themselves, one had previously said: "The Greeks are always children ; there are no ancients among them." Children do not care to hear about useful things, they prefer to romp and amuse themselves ; so the Greeks passed their time in disputes that generally came to nothing. And as when we instruct children in something necessary for them to know, instead of listening attentively, they often laugh at it, so the Greeks behaved when they were spoken to about salvation ; and even when they enunciated truths, they mingled them with errors, and corrupted them by their mockeries and blasphemies.

Since, then, men so wise were, nevertheless, so weak in what concerns divine things, even such as were not beyond their capacity, God shows us great mercy, and gives a great proof of His desire to save us, in giving us, by faith, an infallible means of arriving at this sublime knowledge. This means is short and easy : it is simply to believe what He tells us by His Church ; it is done as soon as we wish to do it. This means is also secure, because faith is founded on the knowledge of God Himself, and the exterior manifestation He makes to us of this knowledge. Thus all may promptly and easily learn divine things, without fear of illusion, and experience the effect of these words which St. Paul addressed to the Ephesians : "One Lord, one faith, one baptism. That henceforth we be no more children, tossed to and fro, and carried about by every wind of doctrine, by the wickedness of men who lie in wait to deceive. That henceforth you walk, not as the Gentiles walk, in the vanity of their mind."

§ 3.—*Another prerogative of faith.*

The second reason which obliges us to act by the movement of faith is, that, having the honor to be Christians, we bear the name, not of reasonable men, of philosophers, of *savans*, but of the *faithful ;* because faith is our rule, not only in what we ought to believe, but also in the things we ought to do, and, in a word, the universal principle of our conduct. It is the light, the eye, which guides the understanding and all the powers of the soul and body. "Lord," said David, "Thy word is a lamp to my feet." The word of God, as St. Ambrose remarks, is the motive of our faith, and this word is the light which burns in the lamp of faith. In virtue of this supernatural quality, the faithful man nourishes himself by faith only. "Faith is the substance of things to be hoped for," says St. Paul; the substance, and not the accident, the principal, and not the accessory. It is the aliment which nourishes the faithful, according to the same apostle, who says: "The just man lives by faith." Hence the Holy Scriptures call the law the bread of life and understanding, the waters of heavenly wisdom, divine milk, delicious food, sweeter than honey. St. Macarius observes that it is peculiar to Christians to use no other food and drink than truth. Now, in this life truth belongs not properly to reason, nor to philosophy, nor to all natural sciences combined, but only to faith. "As new-born babes," says the Prince of the Apostles, "desire the rational milk without guile, that you may grow unto salvation."

The third reason is derived from the excellencies of faith. It would take an immense volume merely to touch on these very lightly. Faith is one of the theological virtues, and, consequently, raised above all moral virtues, because it refers directly to God. It is the first of these virtues, for, the apostle says, " He that cometh to God must believe that He is:" no one seeks an imaginary person. It is the base of its companions, hope and charity; for, as St. Bernard asks, " How can we hope for what we do not believe in, or how can we love it?" "Christ," says the apostle, "dwells by faith in your hearts. For God hath shined in our hearts to give the light of the knowledge of the glory of God, in the face of Christ Jesus."

Faith is the principle of our salvation. "It is," says the

holy Council of Trent, "the commencement of man's salvation, the root of his justification, without which he cannot please God, or be ranked among His children." "Faith," says St. Augustine, "is the source of all our advantages, and the origin of our salvation. If we will not walk in the darkness of faith, we shall never arrive at the light of glory, and we shall never see what we refuse to believe." St. Chrysostom calls it the mother and the source of all the favors which God does us. St. Eucherius says it is the entrance into life, the pilot of salvation; and that whoever leaves it to follow the guidance of his erring mind, and desires to open the treasures of the knowledge of God's mysteries with the key of science, is like one who builds a house without a foundation, or strives to enter a building by the roof, or traverses dangerous places at night without a torch. Our Lord has given us faith as a flambeau to indicate the road to Him, in order that, seeking Him, we may believe Him, and find Him through this belief.

4. Faith is the root of all virtues, as St. Augustine takes notice. and, like a good root, it turns into fruit the rain with which it is moistened. It is the measure of all virtues; for your hope and charity, your patience, meekness and all other virtues, will be in proportion to the liveliness of your faith, as, in a tree, the trunk and branches will bear proportion to the root. Hence St. Chrysostom calls it the highest point of all virtues, because it enables all respectively to attain perfection. And St. Augustine says that the reason why the ship in which our Lord slept was in danger from the tempest was, because faith slept in the hearts of her crew. Jesus Christ watches not in him whose faith is sleeping; therefore, if the vessel of thy heart is agitated, if thy virtues are in danger of shipwreck, awake Jesus Christ and thy faith, and the storm shall cease.

5. Faith in this high sense signifies, in the Holy Scripture, not only the particular virtue of faith, but also hope, charity

and all the gifts and graces of God, because it is the cause of them all. "We pray always for you," writes St. Paul to the Thessalonians, "that our God would make you worthy of His vocation and fulfil all the good pleasure of His goodness, and the work of faith in power;" that is, the patience and constancy and all other virtues which you require. Our Lord, giving to Magdalen the full pardon of all her sins, in consideration of her love, said to her: "Many sins are forgiven thee because thou hast loved much;" and a little after, He added: "Go in peace, thy faith hath saved thee." As bread, in the Scripture, signifies all sorts of nourishment, because it is the foundation of them all, so we ordinarily say, this tree nourished me, meaning its fruits, and this physician healed me, meaning his medicines and regimen.

6. The sixth prerogative of faith is explained by these words of St. Peter, recorded by St. Luke in the Acts: "God purifies the hearts of the Gentiles by faith." Faith purifies the heart in an excellent manner, because it purifies the understanding and the will. It purifies the understanding of ignorance and error, and enlightens it with a true knowledge of God. It removes its fallacies, satisfies its doubts, strengthens its weakness, and enables it to understand things in a manner incomparably above nature. Hence the holy Fathers often call faith the eye of the heart. Faith is the eye of the soul, says St. Cyril, which enables it to perceive sublime things. And St. Augustine says: "Faith has certainly eyes greater, more lively, more piercing, than those of nature. And these eyes have this singularly estimable quality, that they have never deceived any one, or caused a person to make one false step."

Faith, in the second place, cleanses the will from vicious affections and all other disorders. It makes it love and esteem things according to the will of God. But only actual faith can do this; for we see Christians, who, satisfied with the habitual faith they received in baptism, entertain erroneous opinions concerning riches and poverty, honors and contempt, prosperity and afflictions ; who love the first, and fly the second, with as much ardor as if they were pagans. Go to Turkey and to other infidel countries, and see what passes in them ; consider the ancient monarchies of the Assyrians, Persians, Greeks and Romans, and examine if the ambition, the vanity, the sensuality, the avarice of these people, have been much greater than those of a large majority of Christians. This is what Salvian, the holy and zealous Bishop of Marseilles, so bitterly and so eloquently bewailed.

Verily one would think that the greater number of Christians were victims of some enchantment, like those who, by magic, see what is only a nest for owls as if it were a grand palace. The spirit of illusion blinds them, and causes them to look on phantoms as realities. Faith dissipates these charms, and enables us to see things as they really are. The medium through which we look at objects makes us see them differently : if we look through a green glass, everything seems green ; if through a yellow glass, everything is yellow. Thus the sight may be deceived. Faith alone shows things as they are ; it is the only medium which cannot deceive, the only infallible means of knowing the truth in this life. St. Augustine relates that the Manichean heretics, great enemies to faith, promised, in pompous and magnificent terms, those who embraced their doctrine, "to conduct them to God, and deliver them from all their errors in an admirable and easy manner, and make all things, even the most sublime, evident to their reason." The same saint relates that the pagans did not wish to hear of faith because of the captivity of the understanding to which it obliges ; and that Porphyrus, one of the most celebrated among them, held that God could be known only by philosophy ; and that, if, through idleness or want of capacity, we did not study philosophy, we should never be able to contemplate the first principle and sovereign spirit, whom he calls the father of all spirits.

The same holy doctor says in another place : "All the true peace and union we can have with our Creator come to us from our Lord, the Mediator, by whom we are purified and reconciled with Him from whom we were unfortunately separated by death in sin ; for, as the proud spirit has made the proud, rebellious man die, so the humble Jesus Christ has rendered life to the humble, submissive man ; and as the demon precipitated himself by attempting to elevate himself, and endeavors to make man, through a similar pride, a participator in his ruin, so Jesus Christ, having humbled Himself by the infamy of His death, was raised to glory by His resurrection, in which we, through faith, participate." Then he speaks of certain inventions, charms and diabolical sciences which the Gentiles used in order to purify and elevate souls, and which they called *Teletal*, that is to say, means of perfection, as if these occult arts could raise a soul to union with God ; and he thus concludes : "Souls could not purify themselves of their vices, and reconcile themselves with God by sacrilegious phantoms and the impious rites of magic, for the devil cannot bring souls to God ; but he inspires affections in them which are the more impious, as they are the more full of his pride." All these affections cannot purify a soul or enable it to fly upward, but they augment the weight of its vices to press it downward. Certainly, the wicked expiations of the Gentiles can sully the heart of man, but not purify it ; they can make the soul more vicious, but they cannot perfect it ; they can project the soul from God, but not attract it. To faith alone the glory of these advantages is due. Hence we ought to conceive a great love for this virtue and a very high esteem of it, and apply earnestly to its practice.

§ 4.—*The practice of faith.*

The first thing I have to say regarding the practice of faith is, that we ought to exercise ourselves continually in it. We are Christians, the *Faithful*, in all times and places, and whatever we do, we cannot divest ourselves of this august quality, since its imprint is indelible; so, in all our works, we ought to act by faith which makes us Christians, who are called the faithful. A second motive which excites us to this continual exercise of faith is, that we are incessantly surrounded by the objects of faith; such as, in the supernatural order, the mysteries of the Blessed Trinity, the Incarnation, the Resurrection, the Eucharist and others, which are the proper matter of faith,—natural things which God has inserted in the Holy Scriptures, and which consequently we must believe; things taught us on His part as means of salvation and perfection: health, sickness, adversity and prosperity, and all other things which God sends us. David, speaking of God, says: " The word of the Lord is right, and all His works are faithful." We ought to do all our works in faith and by its movement, that they may, in truth and fidelity, correspond to the works of God.

Faith must be used on all occasions, for it is the sole infallible rule which we can apply to all events. Without it, we should be shrouded in darkness, as we well know; for, every day we are tempted to make little esteem of what God prizes, and admire what He despises. In this we deceive ourselves: our judgments can be equitable only as far as they accord with His, which are the sole rule and measure of all good judgments, and of all the true and sound opinions which creatures can form. Therefore, as we walk among honors and opprobrium, health and sickness, pleasures and pains, we must view them all by the light of faith, else we can make no fair estimate of them. A man does not purchase cloth in a dark shop, without bringing it to the light to examine its texture : in like manner, we must not judge of anything by our own obscure powers, but carry all things out into the clear light of faith. It is then necessary that we should always and everywhere bear this torch in hand, and hold it close to all occurrences as they happen, that we may see them as God sees them.

This lamp will discover to us the beauty of things truly beautiful, and the ugliness of things really deformed. It will take the mask from many an apparent deformity, and show under it true grace and loveliness. Now, as faith is absolutely necessary to accomplish this, so it is entirely sufficient. We need no other torch to illumine our ways, no other word to assure us, no miracles to persuade us, no visions angelic or divine to instruct us, no logic or demonstrations to convince us, no experience to teach us. Faith alone suffices. The apostles converted the world by faith ; and our Lord Himself did not teach His doctrine by choice words and pompous eloquence, or by arguments derived from philosophy, but He grounded it on the faith with which He willed that it should be received and practised. Hence He exacted simple faith of all with whom He treated concerning salvation. He answered them by passages of Scripture, and, when He cured their diseases, He referred their cure to their faith.

Faith preserves us from being vanquished by our enemies, and even enables us to tread them under foot. Moreover, it disposes us excellently to the practice of hope, charity, humility, patience, and all other virtues. When a servant during the night hesitates to open the door for his master, it is because he does not know who is knocking, whether his master or an enemy ; for, if he knew that it was his master, he would open immediately. In like manner, once we really believe, the rest will come easy to us. Faith, says St. Augustine, is the helmet of a Christian ; it is his cuirass, his shield, his coat of mail, which covers him from head to foot. There is nothing more terrible to the devil than faith, remarks St. Cyril of Jerusalem: "For this is the victory that overcometh the world, our faith." This renders us invulnerable to all the attacks of the enemy, and irreprehensible in our lives. "The weapons of our warfare," says St. Paul to the Corinthians, "are not carnal, but mighty to God, unto the pulling down of fortifications and the destroying of counsels, and every height that exalteth itself against the knowledge of God, and bringing into captivity every understanding into the obedience of Christ." "To bind the kings with fetters and the nobles with iron manacles," as David says; and, as St. Thomas explains, to render princes and wise men captives to Jesus Christ and His disciples.

Faith is so powerful and so secure of victory, that St. John calls it *the victory that overcometh the world*, to show that it alone can vanquish the world and all our adversaries. For this reason St. Gregory remarks that God communicates to the soul of which He wishes to become the special protector, a firm faith; whence St. Peter, after telling us that the devil goes about like a roaring lion seeking whom he may devour, presently adds: "Whom resist ye, strong in faith;" for thus he cannot possibly injure us, but must cover himself with confusion.

Therefore, the great maxim of a Christian and the true secret of success in the important affair of salvation is, to make faith his guide in all things, to use it for armor on all occasions, for offensive weapons and for defensive, for flying vice and practising virtue. He should view every occurrence by the light of this beautiful lamp. The proper manner of acting for the faithful is to act everywhere by faith. Hence St. Paul tells us that the just man lives by faith; as we say of an artisan that he lives by his trade, because his trade gains him subsistence. Let us now see more in detail how we ought to exercise faith in all things; how we ought to use this beautiful lamp, and handle these arms.

§ 5.—*The practice of faith more in detail.*

The habit of faith, without its acts, is not sufficient to enable a Christian to live by faith. Yet many deceive themselves on this point; for, after having received faith in baptism, "they retain truth captive in their souls unjustly:" as St. Paul says of the Gentiles, who allowed the knowledge of God to remain sterile in their hearts. In effect, things are rendered perfect, not by the habit, but by frequent acts, to which the habit tends as to its perfection and end, as the tree to its fruit. Experience proves this; for we know that Christians, despite all their habitual faith, run after the things of this world, and plunge themselves into the depths of vice, with as much facility as if they had never received faith. The habit of faith is not therefore sufficient to keep a man from sin and impel him to practise virtue, since it does not always hinder him from leading a disorderly life, and living more like a pagan than a Christian.

Wherefore, when it is said that Christians have not faith, this is not to be understood of habitual faith,—which, when once received, can be lost only by heresy or infidelity,—but of actual faith. And truly, whoever has only habitual faith is as if he had no faith, for it is to him merely a sword in the scabbard, which he does not draw out for his defence. If a man who is attacked by an enemy knows not how to use his sword, or will not use it, it is clear that he might as well have no sword. Having only habitual faith, we allow ourselves to be enchanted by the false goods of this world: we weep over losses which are advantageous to us; we complain of that for which we ought to bless God, and we rejoice when we have true cause of sorrow. But actual faith prevents these errors, for it shows us things as they really are; it makes us see that poverty, contempt, and all other things which men call evils, are means of salvation and instruments of perfection, and that in this life, correctly speaking, there is no evil but sin. It is then to this actual faith we must chiefly apply ourselves.

To vivify and exercise our faith, we have to do three things. The first is to know what faith teaches touching the object in question. The second is to produce an interior act of faith in the infallible truth of the things taught. And the third is to act in entire conformity to the teachings of faith in this particular.

For example, concerning the end of our creation, faith teaches us, in the first place, that it consists in loving and serving God; to unite ourselves to Him by grace in this life, that we may prepare ourselves to be united to Him in glory in the next; that, in this union, consist our perfection and beatitude, and that, without it, we shall always be miserable; that all things in this world, sin excepted, are steps of a ladder that reaches to God. In the second place, we should make many lively acts of faith in these truths; and in the third, use our best efforts to act in conformity with our faith.

If we propose to ourselves the presence of God, we must first know what faith teaches on this subject, then make an act of lively faith in it, and afterward regulate all our thoughts, words and actions, in short, our whole lives, by this rule.

If we consider the riches and grandeurs of this world, we must see first what our Lord has said in the Gospel on this subject, and receive His words as an oracle; then, conforming our sentiments and judgments to His, despise these transitory things as slippery steps which often lead to perdition. We may exercise our faith in a similar manner on all the other truths which religion teaches.

I say further, that, to render our faith vivid and energetic, we must not examine things by the obscurity of the passions, nor by the moonlight of reason, but by the brilliant sheen of faith, which alone can show them as they are. We ought to act in this manner, particularly as regards riches, honors, pleasures, and things which we naturally desire, and which are capable of leading us to sin; and even with reference to things purely spiritual, which of themselves make less impression on our minds as the channels by which God sends special graces to our souls, such as certain fundamental truths of religion— the sacraments and other great mysteries; also the daily graces we receive, the ordinary actions in which we are engaged, and which we are in danger of performing by mere routine. Concerning these things, I will make three very important observations, of which you must take particular notice.

1. As our mind and imagination are naturally in danger of being carried away by things present and agreeable, we ought to carefully use the light of faith in considering these things. Faith must be the mistress, and subject the understanding and the will to its unerring laws, otherwise imagination and reason will supersede faith, in doing which they are extremely dexterous and agile; and faith, finding the understanding preoccupied and the will persuaded, can do but little to rectify our errors of judgment and practice. Therefore it is essential that faith assume the lead in all things, that it direct the mental faculties before they have time to take their own peculiar views. Abraham believed God, says Moses, and it was reputed unto him justice. On these words St. Ambrose remarks: "It was reputed justice, because he demanded not of God the reason of His commands, but believed promptly. It is proper that faith precede reason, and that we do not exact of God, our Lord, as we do of men, the reason of what He tells us."

2. We ought not, in difficult and dangerous conjunctures, to listen to what human understanding and natural science suggest, for all our ability and knowledge are infinitely beneath the knowledge and spirit of God, from which the truths of faith emanate. Otherwise, we should resemble a

child who would contest a certain proposition of Aristotle, or a demonstration of Euclid, because he could not understand it. We do the same when, by our reasonings and discourses, we undertake to combat what faith teaches us; or, rather, we do far worse: for a man who disputes against God is immeasurably more foolish and ridiculous than a child who rails against Aristotle and Euclid.

3. We ought not to trouble ourselves much even with what natural sciences and wise men allege, to confirm the truths of faith; for we should hold in such high esteem the source whence these oracles flow, as to make little account of what the greatest minds discover in their confirmation. If an ignorant villager should draw comparison from his flocks to justify the doctrine of a consummate physician, would not every one laugh at him, and his companions despise him? We cannot form ideas sufficiently high to be of much service in illustrating these sublime things; and besides, by simple faith, our mind is touched with greater respect for them, and our will better disposed to practise the virtues they inculcate. But we will conclude this subject by speaking of the exercise of faith still more in detail.

§ 6. *Practice of faith still more in detail.*

We must often produce lively acts of faith in the following truths, for these truths will procure us, if we firmly believe them, inestimable blessings; and, moreover, we ought always to have some text of Scripture which may serve as a basis to our exercise. The first of these truths is the being of God and our own nothingness. This is the source of true humility, and the most efficacious means of exciting us to love and serve God, and of detaching us from creatures. We must believe that God alone exists by Himself, that we are, of ourselves, simply nothing in soul and body, in grace and glory, and that, before our creation, as David says, "our substance was as nothing before God." We must believe that God has a being so perfect, a beauty so ravishing, a goodness so excessive, a wisdom so profound, a power so strong, that those attributes are all infinite; and that, in comparison to His, all other beauty, actual or possible, is only ugliness, all other goodness malice, all other power weakness, all other wisdom ignorance, and all other perfection only deformity. "Behold," says Isaias, "the Gentiles are as a drop of a bucket, and are counted as the smallest grain of a balance: behold, the islands are as a little dust. All nations are before Him as if they had not any being at all, and are counted to Him as vanity and nothing."

On this foundation we can build an admirable edifice and produce a quantity of acts of virtue, as of hope, charity, adorations and praises of God, and disesteem of creatures, as well as detachment from them.

The second of these truths is that which concerns the presence of God, which we should strive never to forget; because, without remembrance of it, we should certainly commit many faults. "The eyes of the Lord," says Solomon, "are in all places, on the good as well as the wicked." It is necessary often to recall this truth, to retain ourselves within the bounds of duty, to hinder us from doing or saying anything wrong, to animate ourselves to good works; and from time to time, we should say with the prophet: "The Lord liveth in whose sight I stand."

The third truth concerns the divine and infinitely adorable person of our Lord. We must believe that He is our Saviour, our Redeemer, our All; that, by means of Him, we shall assuredly be saved; that without Him we should certainly be lost; and that, consequently, we should attach ourselves inseparably to Him by all possible means. "Neither is there salvation in any other name," said St. Peter; "for there is no other name under heaven given to men whereby we must be saved."

The fourth truth concerns our mental and vocal prayers, and all our pious exercises, which we must perform as in the presence of God, with great faith in His goodness, mercy, liberality and fidelity; and prepare for these exercises, that we may make them with respect, attention, affection and profit. Otherwise, irreverence, distraction and negligence will render exercises which should be so profitable, useless or even injurious. Hence St. John Climacus calls faith the wing of prayer; without it prayer could not soar to heaven.

The fifth truth concerns the providence of God, which governs the world in general, and each of us in particular. We must believe this firmly, for God alone presides in all that happens to us, physically or mentally, as regards honor, wealth and everything else. He governs the universe, conducts the changes in states, empires and families, with goodness, love and wisdom, permitting nothing to happen that can injure us, and doing all for His own glory and our good. "I am the Lord," says He by Isaias, "and there is no other. I form light and I create darkness. I make peace and I create evil. I, the Lord, do all things." Long before, He had said by Moses: "I kill and I make alive, I wound and I heal." "There is no evil in the city," says the prophet Amos, "but the Lord hath done it."

We must often produce lively acts of faith in these truths, with the greatest possible fervor. They will produce in us wonderful effects, they will teach us to receive, with patience and great spiritual profit, all the inconveniences of this life, to convert thorns into roses, to preserve peace of mind in the midst of tempests, and, finally, to submit to all the orders of God, in which submission consists our perfection.

There are in the spiritual life two excellent kinds of blindness, which we must practise with great care. The first concerns all that God has said : and this refers to faith. The second, which depends on the first, regards all that God does: and this is His providence. By these sorts of blindness we receive all that God says and does, without examination, without murmur, without desiring to dive into His councils, but with profound respect. He is the Sovereign Wisdom, the Essential Truth, the Infinite Goodness: this is enough for us. He cannot say what is not true, He cannot do what is not good. And, certainly, God is a reason incomparably better and more capable of satisfying man, than all the reasons which men or even angels could give.

These blindnesses are darkness, and yet light : darkness, since they close the eyes to human reasoning; light, since they are illumined by the light of the Sovereign Truth, God Himself, who conducts those that are thus blessedly blind, in the way of their salvation, and shows them a thousand things that are hidden from others. He says, by the mouth of Isaias : "I shall lead the blind by paths which they know not. I shall change their darkness to light. I shall plane for them the rough ways. I have given them my word, and I shall not abandon them."

St. Luke relates, in the Acts of the Apostles, that St. Paul having said to our Lord in the first moment of his conversion, "Lord, what wilt Thou have me to do?" he lost his sight· and remained blind for three days, and during his blindness heard ineffable secrets, and saw ravishing wonders, and received immense treasures of grace. This is a correct image of the blindness we treat of,—a blindness which necessarily follows the submission we render to the words and ordinances of God, after we have said to Him with St. Paul, "Lord, what wilt Thou have me to do?" Behold me ready to believe all that Thou shalt say, and to accomplish all Thou shalt ordain,— a blindness, in fine, which is always followed by great lights and abundant graces.

§ 7.—*Conclusion of what has been said in the preceding paragraphs.*

In this manner, then, we must practise faith, and perform acts of it, especially on the subjects which have been given. But we seldom do this, and hence flow most of our misfortunes. It is difficult, said St. Cyril of Jerusalem, to find a man truly faithful, one who governs himself entirely by faith; but such a man is greatly elevated above others, even though they wear crowns, and wield sceptres, and are skilled in all human sciences.

By the frequent exercise of faith, the faithful man acquires great light, excellent knowledge, and immense facility for understanding the Scriptures. As faith is a participation in the science of the Lord, this participation increases in proportion as faith grows in the soul. Faith becomes so firm that, though all wise men should strive to prove the contrary by a thousand arguments, they would have no effect on the soul; for it is established in truth, like the house built on a rock, which no floods nor tempests could injure. Thus we advance, as St. Paul says, from weak faith to strong faith; for heroic virtues are the recompense of virtues even commonly well exercised. Whoever practises faith carefully in the ordinary manner will soon receive a very high degree of it.

This exercise enables the just man to work out his salvation, not only with security, but also peacefully, without troubling or embarrassing the mind. It fills him with singular joy, according to the words of St. Peter: "Though you see him not, you believe, and believing, shall rejoice with joy unspeakable and glorified." The faithful man is perfectly obedient to the Church as a child to a parent, and receives with submission and respect whatever she ordains, even though it be not ordered as a point of faith; so that he always prefers the judgment of the Church to his own and to the judgment of other tribunals.

This exercise inspires him with esteem and veneration for all her ceremonies, even the smallest, and disposes his mind in an excellent manner as regards all that concerns faith.

Finally, the frequent exercise of faith shields a person from all evils, renders him invincible to his enemies, animates him to the practice of good works, acquires him immense merit, and teaches him to profit by every occurrence. For, as Solomon says, the faithful man turns all things to his profit, but the unfaithful man derives no good from anything. To this latter we may apply these words of the apostle to the Corinthians, "Your faith is vain and useless to you:" it will only serve for your condemnation, and render you more miserable.

Let us, then, use all possible diligence to acquire a lively and ever-active faith, that we may view all things, not in their natural colors but by the light in which faith presents them. Let us live in faith, as fishes live in the sea; and let us think, speak and act by its impulse, that it may be said of each of us, as of St. Gregory of Nyssa, that "faith was his country, his house, his riches." Let us cultivate it most carefully, by frequent acts, as being the principle of all our good: like the gardener whose greatest pains are not bestowed on the branches of his trees, but on the roots, for he knows that branches, leaves, and fruits depend on the root.

Let us refer to faith all our natural lights, since things less perfect ought always to be referred to such as are more perfect. Thus, the vegetative life tends to the sensitive, the sensitive to the reasonable, and the life of grace to the light of glory. We should frequently beseech God to augment in us this precious gift, saying with the apostles: *Lord, increase our faith.*

Faith is the first duty which justice obliges us to render to God, for we are bound by our creation, redemption and adoption, to give ourselves entirely to God; and we can do this only through faith. Christianity is established on the basis of humility, consequently faith ought to hold the first rank in our souls; for faith is the true humility of our mind and judgment, since it is the perfect submission of them to God.

Hence let us hear and follow this counsel of St. Paul: "Be vigilant, stand firm in faith. Continue in faith, grounded and settled immovable. In all things showing good fidelity, that you may adorn the doctrine of God, our Saviour, in all things."

CHAPTER VII.

SEVENTH GENERAL PRINCIPLE OF THE SPIRITUAL LIFE.

Continual prayer.

ONE of the greatest maxims of Christianity, and one of the duties which our Lord most earnestly recommended by Himself, and by His ministers, is, to pray to God continually. "We must always pray and not faint," says He in St. Luke; that is, we must pray as unceasingly as our strength will permit. He attests that our salvation is the one thing necessary, and warns us to "watch and pray at all times." St. Paul, writing to the Thessalonians, tells them to "pray without ceasing." And to Timothy he says: "I desire that men pray in all places." Again, he tells the Ephesians to "be constant in prayer and continual supplications, made in the spirit and with invincible perseverance." The Prince of the Apostles, in his first Epistle, admonishes us to "be prudent and to watch in prayer." And long before him, the preacher had given this advice: "Be not hindered from praying always."

By these passages we see that the exercise of continual prayer is highly recommended, and that we should esteem it as most necessary. But how can we practise it? How can we observe it so as to suffer no interruption on account of the necessities of our body and the instability of our mind? How are we to explain and understand this precept?

Some understand it, not of each Christian in particular, but of the whole Church in general, in some part of which, prayer is always being offered up to God. This interpretation is correct, but it is nevertheless too limited, for our Lord certainly meant more. Hence these words should be taken as regarding each person in particular. Now, how is this to be done?

1. St. Basil, Venerable Bede, and the Gloss, agree that whoever employs himself in good works without ceasing, prays to God incessantly; because a good work is a prayer, not of the mouth or mind, but of hand and effect. He prays always who does good always, and a man never ceases to pray, if he never cease to do good.

2. St. Augustine says that he prays continually who wishes continually to pray, who desires to have strength of body and soul to pray without intermission. In the next place, Venerable Bede, Pope Nicolas and others, take the word *always* in a moral sense as it is taken among men, that is to say, at stated times. Thus we say of a canon or a religious who never fails to be present at divine service, that he assists always at choir. David said to Miphiboseth, the son of his beloved friend, Jonathan: "You shall eat always at my table," meaning at the ordinary hours every day. Others apply to this the parable of the widow, who, by her importunities, extorted from the unjust judge what she desired. "For," say they, "the Holy Ghost has taught us by this woman that we ought to pray with unshaken perseverance, without ceasing till God grants what we desire." Finally, the word *always* signifies very often: as we say of a gambler, that he plays always, or of a man who loves study, that he studies continually; which does not mean that either plays or studies without intermission, but only that he makes it his chief occupation, and prefers it to all others. So when we say *pray always*, we mean pray as often as you can, as often as the weakness of nature will permit, and love prayer exceedingly. Let us now see the reasons which oblige us to continual prayer, and which should persuade us to practise it.

One reason should suffice, if we desire to render to our Lord the deference we owe Him. He has often recommended prayer, and recommended it with the most pressing earnestness. But, besides this reason, I shall notice two others, namely : the utility and the necessity.

As to utility, I say that prayer procures us advantages and treasures, the value of which surpasses all our words and thoughts. It is a mine whence we draw immense spiritual riches ; it is a canal through which the mercies and graces of God flow upon us ; it is a fertile field in which the reaper finds a full harvest ; it is a defensive armor able to vanquish all our enemies ; it is a well-tempered sword given us from heaven, as the golden sword which the prophet Jeremias gave to the valiant Judas Machabeus, with these words : "Take this holy sword which God presents you to destroy the adversaries of my people Israel." Who can recount the wonderful victories which this sword has gained,—how it destroyed thousands of Sennacherib's army, how it defied a million of men led by Zara, King of Ethiopia, and gained the memorable victory of Josue over Amalec ; for the Israelites succeeded while Moses held his hands elevated in prayer, and, when he lowered them, the enemy prevailed ?

Prayer is most profitable : it merited Jacob the benediction of the angels, and delivered him from the anger of Esau ; it rescued Jonas when the whale swallowed him, and it delivered Susanna from death. It was prayer that restored to life the son of the Sunamite woman, and saved Daniel from the lions, and the three children from the fiery furnace. I refer other wonders which prayer has wrought to its necessity, which I regard as the strongest and most important reason for making continual prayer.

§ 1.—*Necessity of prayer.*

To understand well the necessity of prayer, we should know that it is a constant opinion in our holy religion,—an opinion which has even passed into an article of faith against the Palagian heretics,—that the grace of God is absolutely indispensable to enable us to resist temptations, to conquer our passions, to practise virtue, to perform good works, and to obtain final perseverance. As birds cannot fly without wings, as quadrupeds cannot walk without feet, so man, without the grace of God given through the merits of Christ, can do nothing toward his salvation. "Without me," says Jesus Christ, "you can do nothing," as regards your salvation and beatitude : for, if you could save yourself, I should not be your Saviour and Redeemer. Now to come to our subject :—

Prayer is necessary to obtain of God His grace and assistance, which, if we do not ask, we shall not receive. St. Augustine says . "No one can truly desire his salvation, unless God give him this desire, and no one can work out his salvation, if God does not assist him ; and no one can obtain of God this assistance, unless he ask it. It is true that God confers certain gifts which we have not asked, as the commencement of faith and the first grace ; but there are others which He does not give without prayer, as a final perseverance and a happy death."

The reason of this is that God wishes to keep us humble, grateful and dependent on Him ; to the end that we may know that of ourselves we are poor and unable to resist the allurements of vice and practise virtue, and that it is He alone who can aid us to live holily and die happily. With this before our eyes, we shall beg His graces, and, having received them, we must acknowledge that we owe to Him our virtues, our good works, and our salvation : and so far from being vain glorious of these things, we should refer to Him alone all the praise and glory of our good actions. This is why God wishes.

us to pray. But, nevertheless, this ought not to be understood only of His ordinary guidance : for, being absolute Master, He gives His goods when and how He pleases, and to whom He pleases.

This doctrine is so true, that even things which should happen, because He has resolved on or promised them, are not accomplished without prayer, which is, as it were, the last disposition necessary to effect them. This the Angelic Doctor acknowledges, when he affirms that prayer is the principal means which the providence of God uses to execute His designs ; and on this subject he quotes St. Gregory the Great, who says : "Things which are not asked of God cannot be obtained, and those which the saints obtain, they obtain by prayer : for God predestined the elect to eternal glory in such a manner that they must acquire it by their labor, rendering themselves worthy, by their petitions, of receiving in His own time what He has resolved from eternity to give them."

This holy doctor proves what he advances by the memorable example of Abraham, to whom God promised several times, and even with an oath, that He would multiply his posterity above the stars of heaven, and that through Isaac this promise would be fulfilled. And yet Isaac had a sterile wife. How can this promise agree with sterility ? What God determined, is accomplished only by prayer. Wherefore Moses says: "Isaac prayed to the Lord for his wife, Rebecca; and God heard him, and rendered her fruitful."

In like manner, the holy patriarchs and prophets by their prayers and vows obtained of God the Incarnation of His Son, whom He had promised. Daniel, though the Messias had been often promised before his time, asked His coming with extraordinary eagerness and with daily prayers. Hence, when the Archangel Gabriel appeared to him, he said : "O Daniel ! I am now come forth to teach thee ; and I am come to show it to thee, because thou art a man of desires." This knowledge of the time of the Incarnation is given thee because of thy ardent desires and continual supplications.

When St. Peter was cast into prison,—though, according to the prediction of our Lord, he was destined to govern the Church for a long time, and to die old,—St. Luke relates that prayer was made for him incessantly by all the faithful. In like manner, according to St. Austin, it was the prayer of St. Stephen that caused the conversion of St. Paul, whom the Lord had predestined to become a vessel of election, and a torch to enlighten the Gentiles with His knowledge. Our Lord Himself obtained by prayer the heritage of the Gentiles which was due to Him, and which He had acquired : hence His Father says to Him by the mouth of David : "Ask of me, and I will give Thee the inheritance of the Gentiles, and the uttermost parts of the earth for Thy possession." Behold how necessary prayer is for our salvation, and even for the accomplishment of the things which God has already resolved on !

But, as theologians remark, a thing may be necessary in two ways : firstly, in quality of means ; secondly, as a thing commanded. A thing is necessary in quality of means when we know that a particular end cannot be achieved without it. The second necessity is not so rigorous, because the thing which it demands is necessary only by reason of the command, which does not oblige in all cases ; such for example, as the fast of Lent and the hearing of Mass on certain days, which are necessary for salvation only as things commanded ; yet the obligation ceases in sickness.

Now, if you ask whether prayer is necessary as a means or as a thing commanded, I answer : first, that it is of precept ; whence it happens that, when the obligation of the command presses us, as in grave temptations, in dangers that imperil our salvation, if we do not have recourse to God and pray Him to assist us in these emergencies, we do wrong, because we fail in the observance of a law given us by God. Secondly, prayer is necessary in quality of means, because, without it, according to the ordinary ways of God's providence, we cannot be saved. St. Chrysostom says that it is impossible to live in the practice of virtue without prayer. Indeed the Holy Scriptures would not recommend it so often, and with such pressing instance, if it were not extremely necessary ; they do not inculcate in this manner counsels, or even commandments, which may be more easily passed over.

God, in His holy providence, wishes that the second cause concur with Him as far as possible. Now, the least coöperation of man toward his own salvation, after he has received from God the first impulse, is to implore His assistance. The least a beggar can do is to ask what he wants ; and we are generally of opinion that a thing is not worth much, if it be not worth the asking. Assuredly, having such great need of grace, which was purchased for us with the blood of Jesus Christ, and which is so precious, it is only just that man should at least beseech God to bestow it on him.

§ 2.—*Conclusion to be drawn from this truth.*

Since prayer is necessary for salvation, both as a means and as a thing commanded, we must conclude :—

First, that we ought to use the greatest care, inasmuch as we desire to be saved and to obey the teachings of our Lord and His apostles, to pray always, and not to become remiss in this holy exercise. Without the particular assistance of God we cannot avoid evil and do good, neither can we hope for final perseverance : it is clear, then, that we ought to ask this assistance ; and since we always have need of it, we ought continually to ask it of our Lord Jesus Christ.

This was the practice of the saints, and we may say of each

of them what the Church says of St. Martin : "Having his eyes and hands always raised toward heaven, his spirit was so intent on prayer that nothing could divert him from it. They sometimes spent whole days and nights in prayer, thus knocking continually at the door of God's mercy. But when their health, their occupations, or the necessities of life, did not permit them to make long prayers, they made frequent aspirations, which they called *ejaculations*, because they are as darts sent forth toward God, His mercy, His justice, His power, His wisdom, or some other of His attributes, according as they exercised the acts of the purgative, the illuminative, or the unitive way ; and *aspirations*, because, as air which is necessary for the life of the body is received by respiration, so, grace, which is necessary for the life of the soul, ought to be continually asked by the heart and the lips, since we have continual need of it : like those people of the Levant who always keep in their mouths a certain salutary herb which they chew. The Fathers of the Desert, as Cassian relates, incessantly repeated this verse of David, which they called a wall of brass and an impenetrable shield against the attacks of the demon : "Incline unto my aid, O God ! O Lord ! make haste to help me !" Cassidorus adds that they said it three times before each action. It is in imitation of them that the Church makes us commence the canonical hours by this versicle. Before Prime it is repeated four times, in order to commence the day happily by an invocation for the grace and assistance of God, thus reiterated. This was also the favorite aspiration of St. Catharine of Sienna.

St. Jerome informs us that the monks of Egypt made frequent use of this other verse : "Who will give me the wings of a dove, that I may flee away and be at rest?" The holy Abbot Lucius having asked some religious who visited him, whether they ever performed manual labor, they answered : "No ; we occupy ourselves, according to the counsel of the apostle, in continual prayer." "But do you not eat and sleep?" asked the saint. The good religious having answered in the affirmative, the abbot said: "Then, you do not pray while you are eating and sleeping. Well, now, I will tell you what I do. I have stated times for prayer, afterward I work at basket-making; and while my hands are occupied, my heart and my tongue pronounce incessantly these words of David: 'Have mercy on me, O Lord! according to Thy great mercy, and according to the multitude of Thy tender mercies blot out all my iniquities.' The price of my baskets I give to the poor; and these alms impetrate graces for me while I eat and while I sleep, and thus supply what is wanting to make my prayer continual, which otherwise I should not be able to do."

Denis the Carthusian says that some were inspired to use this petition of the thirtieth psalm: "Make Thy face to shine upon Thy servant: save me in Thy mercy." He adds that others habitually used other verses, and that he himself had chosen these words of the fiftieth psalm: "Create a clean heart in me, O God! and renew a right spirit within me." It is thus that we should use one or several of these verses, according to our affection or necessity. St. Athanasius relates that the devils, being asked what verse in the whole Scriptures they feared most, replied: "That with which the sixty-seventh psalm commences: 'Let God arise, and let His enemies be scattered; and let them that hate Him flee before His face.'" This, they added, compelled them to fly.

Thus the saints practised continual prayer with such assiduity and constancy that nothing in the world could withdraw them from it. During his captivity among idolaters, Daniel prayed regularly three times a day, and he would rather be cast into the lion's den than interrupt this holy practice. And indeed, since prayer is necessary for salvation, we ought not to fail in it for any reason whatever. No person, whether pope, or king, or superior of any degree, has authority to order us to refrain entirely from eating, for eating is absolutely necessary for the preservation of life. In like manner, no occupation should hinder us from praying—for this exercise we must always reserve some time ; because it is by prayer that our spiritual life is preserved, that we satisfy the divine justice, and pay all our debts.

The second thing which proves our extreme necessity of prayer, is the miserable state of those who do not pray. Without doubt, they must necessarily be void of virtues and replenished with vices, unable to offer vigorous resistance to the attacks of the enemy, and every hour running the risk of damnation. You cannot live without food and air ; in the same way, without prayer you cannot live well, and must ultimately lose your soul. We find that persons who do not pray, or who pray but seldom, consent without resistance to all the inclinations of the senses, to all the appetites of concupiscence, and to all the temptations of the enemy ; they remain long in their crimes, and, after they have repented, fall away ; they often commit horrible sins, and scarcely know what it is to practise virtue. The cause of all these disorders is that they do not ask of God His efficacious graces, and God, according to His ordinary ways, will not give them, unless they are asked. St. John Chrysostom says : "When I see any person who does not love prayer, I hold for certain that he has nothing intrinsically noble or good in his soul." This is so true that even the most pious, when they omit prayer, soon experience loss. What David said of himself in this particular applies to all : "My days are vanished like smoke : and my bones are grown dry like fuel for the fire. I am smitten as grass and my heart is withered, because I forgot to eat my bread."

I place, among those who do not pray, those who pray badly : they run nearly the same risks. As persons who eat unwholesome food, or breathe noxious air, cannot be healthy or live long, so those who pray ill, injure their spiritual life, and risk their eternal salvation. This is why the devil strives to withdraw us from prayer, or at least to make us pray negligently. If we inquire into this matter, we shall find that, of all the actions of piety which virtuous persons perform, not one is ordinarily done with more imperfection than is prayer. St. Gregory relates, in his Life of St. Bennet, that one of the religious of the saint absented himself unnecessarily from prayer to occupy himself with useless things, and, though frequently reproved, fell daily into the same fault. One day, the holy Abbot perceived beside this monk a devil, in the shape of a hideous Moor, who pulled him by the habit to make him retire from this holy exercise. Next day, finding the same brother wandering about the monastery at the hour of prayer, the saint gave him a stroke of a rod which chased the demon away, and delivered him entirely from this temptation ; and henceforth he was always present with the others at prayer.

We read, in the Life of St. Bernard, that a learned professor called Stephen of Vitry, having taken the habit at Clairvaux, lost courage after a few months and left the monastery, while many of the youths whom he had instructed faithfully persevered. And this man afterward acknowledged that the cause of his leaving was, that, being with the other novices at prayer, a little Moor withdrew him from their company, and made him abandon prayer. Behold the snares by which the devil strives to withdraw religious from prayer, knowing well that prayer is necessary for our perseverance and salvation !

Speaking of the necessity of continual prayer, St. Diadochus has a remarkable passage : " He who desires to keep a pure heart ought to inflame himself always by the remembrance of our Lord and by prayer, for he must not fancy that those who desire to purify their souls can do so, if they neglect prayer. They must strive to pray incessantly, even outside their oratories. If he who purifies gold lets the fire out, the gold retains its impurities, and becomes as hard as it was before. Just so, he who sometimes remembers God and sometimes forgets Him, loses by this forgetfulness what he had gained by prayer and recollection. Those who are inflamed with a true love of virtue have this property, that they consume all that is earthly in their hearts by the remembrance of God and by prayer, in order that their souls, purified from all stains, may acquire that degree of perfection which God wills they should attain."

§ 3.—*The power of prayer.*

God, having appointed prayer as a necessary means of salvation, has given it a force so powerful, that whatever we ask in prayer is infallibly granted. Doubtless this is a source of much consolation to us in our many miseries. The Angelic Doctor teaches that prayer has three properties, and produces three effects. The first is, to merit new treasures of spiritual riches, an increase of grace, of charity, the gifts of the Holy Ghost, and all infused virtues. The second is, to nourish and fortify our soul. The third is, to obtain what we desire and ask. Prayer produces the first effect, not of itself, but because of sanctifying grace, which gives this quality and perfection to all the good actions which a just man does. The second property, prayer has of itself; for it furnishes good thoughts and pious affections, which are the proper aliment of the soul. The third effect it also has of itself; for, as Suarez remarks very wisely, prayer of its own nature has this power, because it is prayer, for prayer naturally refers to this end, to move the person to whom it is addressed to grant the thing desired, not because it has been merited or purchased, but precisely because it is prayed for : the prayer being an act of humility toward the person addressed, of acknowledgment of his power, of confidence in his goodness and liberality. In fact, if we did not believe that he is powerful and liberal enough to bestow the favor, we should not ask it of him. Hence prayer is of itself capable of obtaining what it asks, for God is good, liberal, rich and powerful, not contractedly so, like men, but without any limits, and in an infinite manner. Besides, he has given His word. And this circumstance confers on prayer a force still greater than it possesses of its own nature ; for, according to the teaching of St. Thomas, prayer has of itself only a power of *fitness* or propriety, which leaves to the person addressed the liberty of giving or not giving, and not an infallible power which certainly obtains what is asked. It has not that strong force which imposes the necessity of giving, without the power of refusing. But the divine promise gives it this quality ; so that, since God has given His word, prayer is omnipotent to obtain what we ask. Our petitions cannot be refused, for He has said : "Ask, and you shall receive ; seek, and you shall find ; knock, and it shall be opened to you. For every one that asketh receiveth, whoever seeketh findeth, and the door is opened to him that knocketh. Amen, amen, I say to you : If you ask the Father anything in my name, it shall be given you."

God having pledged His word, He will not make it void ; for, according to the apostle, "He continueth faithful, He cannot deny Himself." Our Lord, in order to prove this truth, gives two admirable parables : the first is of a poor widow, who, by continual importunity, obtained justice of an unjust judge ; the other is of a man who, going to the house of his friend at midnight to obtain some loaves which he wanted, received more than he asked ; because his pressing instances wearied and annoyed his friend, who therefore arose to give him the bread, that he might rid himself of his importunity.

It is, however, necessary to remark that the promise which renders prayer impetratory for all, is not absolute, but conditional. If certain conditions do not accompany it, God is not obliged to keep His promises; but, if it has these conditions, He gives whatever is asked: His word is pledged to that. These conditions and clauses complied with, the promise, ceasing to be conditional, becomes absolute.

§ 4.—*The conditions necessary to render prayer efficacious.*

In order to be efficacious, prayer, as theologians with St. Thomas teach, requires four conditions. It must be made in the name of our Lord, for the person who makes it, with perseverance and with piety. The first condition our Lord teaches in these words: "If you ask the Father anything in my name." In my name,—that is to say, if you ask anything useful or necessary to your salvation, not what is useless or prejudicial. As St. Augustine remarks, we do not ask in the name of the Saviour what might be hurtful to our salvation. When our Lord refuses something that would be injurious to salvation, continues the same father, he exercises the office of Saviour; as a physician exercises his office, when he refuses to his patient what would hinder or retard recovery. SS. Chrysostom and Theophylact understand, by these words, that prayer ought to be made through the merits of the life and death of Jesus Christ; for the Father can refuse nothing to His Son's merits. Now, since He died for His Father's glory and man's salvation, He has merited that whatever man should ask in consideration of this death, should be granted; so that what is a grace in their regard, is justice in regard of our Saviour. At least we may say that, since He has transferred His rights to us, so to speak, the grant of our requests is justly due to us.

A more modern author, Ribera, is of opinion that these words, *in my name*, signify, *for my sake, on my part;* so that, when we ask anything of God, we ask it, not on our own part, but on the part of His Son, who prays in and by us; that it is properly to him it is given, and not to us; as when a king asks some favor of the pope through his ambassador. Thus when the brothers of Joseph feared that he would avenge on them the cruel treatment he had endured at their hands, they told him that Jacob, their father, had before his death desired them to ask in his name, and for love of him, pardon of the injuries they had inflicted on him many years before. The second condition of prayer is, that the suppliant pray for himself. This is the thought of St. Thomas and St. Augustine. Nevertheless, as the words of our Saviour, *All that you shall ask in prayer*, are universal, and not determined or attached to some particular persons or things, others take them in a more extended sense, and think that prayer made, no matter for whom, provided it have the other qualities, will always be available and produce its effect.

The third condition is perseverance, that is to say, that prayer be continued till what is asked be granted. 1. God sometimes grants a petition very soon. "Thou shalt call," says Isaias, "and the Lord shall hear: thou shalt cry, and He shall say: Here I am." At times, He even prevents our prayers, and is satisfied with our desires. Thus David says: "Thou hast given him his heart's desire;" and again: "Thou hast heard the desire of the poor;" and: "Thy ear is open to the disposition of their hearts." 2. But God often seems not to hear us, and defers granting our petition. In this case, we must be careful not to lose courage, but persevere faithfully till our request be complied with.

God defers granting what we ask, either because we are not yet sufficiently prepared to receive it, or because what we ask would not be useful just now, but will be so, later on;

or even, to make us exercise faith and hope more perfectly than we should, if it were immediately granted. God delays, not because He does not hear you, but because He desires you should redouble your ardor and pray with greater earnestness. You knock at His door, and it is not opened, in order that you may knock more loudly. You cry to Him, and He does not reply; not because He has closed His ears against you, but because He wishes to oblige you to cry to Him with greater instance. When we knock at the door of a house, if it be not opened immediately, we knock again and again ; when we call, if not answered at once, we raise our voice, and use greater efforts to make ourselves heard. To these reasons I add another, which St. Nilus gives in these words : "Be careful not to act the master with God, nor be too eager that He should grant immediately what you ask : know that He uses delay, that you may enjoy for a longer time the benefit of prayer, for there is nothing more excellent than to speak to Him, to communicate with His divine Majesty." Besides, we ought to remember that, however God seems to delay, it is always true to say that He hears us soon, for His delays are as nothing when compared to His eternity : and should He not grant our petitions immediately, it can be only for our greater good. We give a thing soon enough when we give it at the moment it proves most useful, and withhold it as long as it would be pernicious.

There remains the fourth condition of prayer, which is piety ; but because this requires a longer notice, we shall speak of it in a separate section.

§ 5.—*Another condition requisite for prayer.*

The fourth condition of prayer is that it be made with piety, that is to say, in the first place, with faith. " If any man want wisdom," says St. James, "let him ask of God, who giveth to all men liberally and upbraideth not, and it shall be given him. But let him ask with faith, nothing wavering. For he that wavereth is like a wave of the sea, which is moved and carried about by the wind. Therefore, let not that man think he shall receive anything of God." We must be animated with a lively faith, firmly believing that God is infinitely good, rich, powerful, liberal, and faithful to His promises; that He entertains for us an extreme love, and watches over us with a providence more than maternal, for we are His children; that He knows how much need we have of His assistance, and He alone can help us; that He will assuredly give us what we ask, if it be conducive to our salvation; that He has pledged His word to this effect, in which He cannot and will not fail. "*All* things whatsoever you shall ask in prayer, believing, you shall obtain," says He in St. Matthew and St. Mark.

God ordinarily exacts this virtue of those who pray to Him for anything. To the blind, who asked Him to open their eyes, He said: "Do you believe that I can do this?" And when they answered in the affirmative, He gave them sight. When the afflicted father prayed for the deliverance of his son who was horribly tormented by the devil, our Lord said to him: "If thou canst believe, all things are possible to him that believeth." The father answering, "I do believe, Lord: help Thou my unbelief," his son was delivered. Our Lord says in another place: "If you have faith, you shall obtain whatever you ask." Theophylact remarks, on this subject, that He has bound faith and prayer together, because faith is the foundation, the sustenance, of prayer, and, as it were, the soul which animates all its parts. For this reason our Lord was accustomed to refer the cures He wrought to the faith of those whom He cured, saying to them individually: "Thy faith hath made thee safe." Hence St. Augustine says: "If faith fails, prayer perishes with it, and is buried under its ruins." "Whoever invokes the name of the Lord shall be saved," says the apostle. But to show us that faith is the fountain whence prayer flows, he adds : "How shall they call on Him whom they have not believed ?"

2. It is necessary that prayer be made with hope, says St. James ; that is, according to the language of Scripture, a strong and vigorous hope, which amounts to a certainty that we shall be heard. This confidence is so requisite that, without it, prayer would not be efficacious ; for, as St. Thomas remarks, prayer derives its power to merit eternal life from the virtue of charity, and its power to obtain what is asked, from the virtue of confidence. Long before him, the Abbot Isaac had said : "He who fails in holy confidence may be certain that his prayer will not be granted." We must then, as St. Paul admonishes us, approach the throne of mercy full of confidence, and with an unshaken hope that God will certainly hear us favorably. The source of hope is the infinite goodness of God, His incomparable liberality, His more than royal munificence, and the inclination He has to bestow favors ; His inviolable fidelity to His promises, His immense riches, which cannot be diminished by His largesses, but are rather augmented, since, in showing mercy, He renders Himself more merciful, and, consequently, more worthy of honor, praise and love. We ought also to ground our hope on the fact that He desires we should pray ; that He has rendered prayer necessary to salvation ; that His Son, our Lord, has taught us the formula of all our petitions ; that, in order to give us courage to pray, He reminds us that if men, wicked as they are, will not give their children a stone for bread, a serpent when they ask for a fish, a scorpion for an egg, still less will God refuse to grant the petitions we address to Him with filial confidence : for He is our true Father, and exercises toward us incessantly the care and love of a

father. He even presses us to ask His graces and favors, and reproaches us when we fail to do so. All this clearly shows that He has an ardent desire to give, and that, infallibly, we shall obtain the thing we ask, if it be good for us.

To increase this confidence still more in all hearts, I will quote a remarkable passage from St. Augustine. Speaking to his flock, he says: "My dear brethren, our Lord is sweet and gracious; the door of His palace is kept open by piety and by mercy, that those who knock may not be sent away. He blames those who, through tepidity or indifference, do not approach to ask His favors; because, as they can ask nothing of Him which He does not possess, they cannot be put to shame by a refusal. His liberality is equal to His riches, and He gives without reproach. His coffers so overflow with wealth that He is, in a manner sad, when no one asks part of His treasures. He is pleased when we extend our hands in earnest supplication toward Him; our eagerness to participate in His riches is most agreeable to Him. Behold how He invites us: 'Hitherto you have not asked anything in my name,' says He. 'Ask and you shall receive. I am the door, knock and it shall be opened to you;' there are no guards to prevent your entrance. My angels are indeed there, but not to keep it closed against you, but to open it; not to frighten you away, but to teach you how to make your petitions. Whenever a poor orphan knocks at the door of God's paternal goodness, immediately the angels make known his arrival, saying: 'Lord, here is a poor child who implores Thy assistance. Be pleased to assist him. Remember Thy prophet has asserted that Thou art the refuge of the poor and the protector of the orphan.' The rich Father of mercies replies: 'Yes, I will take care of him, for I am the Judge of widows and the Father of orphans.' The Lord loves to see Himself surrounded by a great multitude who pray and importune Him. Hence, when no one knocks at His door to demand

His graces, He excites all to pray, saying: 'Ask, and, if you receive not, continue to ask; persevere in knocking.' Depart not till you shall have received an alms, for God will not let the just man perish with hunger at His own door."

3. Prayer should be made in a state of charity, because charity renders the suppliant just, and makes him a child of God, and, consequently, very agreeable in His eyes. All this contributes greatly to render prayer efficacious. But several doctors assert that charity is not absolutely necessary; so that, if a person whose soul is sullied with mortal sin should pray, with the other conditions of which we have already spoken, he would certainly obtain what he asks; because the force of prayer depends, not on the merit or virtue of him who prays, but on the mercy of God and on his promise,—a mercy and a promise not given solely to the just, but to all in general, since He says: "*All* those who ask shall receive." Now He who says *all*, excludes none.

You may perhaps object these words of David, "If I have looked at iniquity in my heart, the Lord will not hear me;" and those of the man born blind: "We know that God doth not hear sinners; but if a man be a server of God and doth His will, him He heareth." But St. Thomas answers that it is true if the sinner, inasmuch as he is a sinner, prays to God, that is, asks Him for something bad, or something good for a bad end, he is not heard; but if he prays for something good regarding his conversion or eternal salvation, he is then heard, because he makes his petition, not as a sinner who wishes to remain in sin, but as a sinner who wishes to abandon sin, and as the commencement of a just man. Let the sinner, then, take courage, and rest assured that, if he petitions God for his salvation, for deliverance from the captivity of the demon, for the eradication of his vices, and for grace to practise virtues, he shall certainly obtain his requests. Now, if the prayer of the sinner is so available before God, what shall we say of the prayer of the just?

4. The spirit of piety requires that prayer be accompanied with attention and respect, that we may remember it is God to whom we speak, that we may be careful what we ask of Him, and that we may evince toward Him the reverence we owe Him. If we be not attentive to what we say; if we treat with God in a wandering, irreverent manner, and with a dissipated mind; in short, if we do not hear ourselves, how can we expect God to hear us? If we, being men, atoms and worms of the earth, forget the infinite Majesty of Him whom we address, how can we expect that He will favorably listen to our prayers? It is clear, then, that attention and respect are absolutely necessary to render prayer efficacious. If a king promised to give a peasant all he should ask, it would be supposed, though it were not mentioned, that the requests of the peasant would be granted, provided he made them with the propriety and reverence due to a personage so great as a king. But if he present his petitions with a careless air, his head turning from side to side, his face expressing only grimaces, it is evident that he deserves to be punished, rather than gain what he asks.

§ 6.—*Of affection and fervor in prayer.*

In the fifth and last place, prayer, in order to be successful, must be made with affection and fervor, and with a true and ardent desire of obtaining what we ask. Hence, in the Holy Scriptures, prayer is compared to incense which cannot ascend and exhale its perfumes, unless it be ignited. When David prays, he does not say he *speaks*, but he *cries out*, to show the immense fervor with which he prays, for a loud cry is made with effort. "Lord," says he, "hear my prayer, and let my cry come unto Thee." And again: "In my affliction I cried out to my God. All the day I cried to Thee, O Lord!

I stretched forth my hands to Thee. I prevented the dawning of the day and cried: I cried out to Thee with all my heart." And so, in many other places, he tells us that he groaned and cried until he became hoarse: "I have labored with crying; my jaws have become hoarse." And this must not be understood solely of physical effort, but chiefly of the affection of mind and heart with which he prays, as we may gather from these words: "From the depths of my heart I have cried to Thee, O Lord! Lord, hear my voice." In this sense St. Paul says to the Romans: "You have not received the spirit of bondage, the spirit of the Old Law, which is a spirit of servile fear; but the spirit of adoption whereby we cry, *Abba, Father.*" Upon this, Cardinal Cajetan remarks that the apostle does not use the term *we say*, but *we cry*, *Abba, Father*, to show the greatness of the affection with which true children address themselves to God. In a subsequent verse, he tells the Romans that the "Holy Ghost Himself asketh for us with unspeakable groanings." If this affection and ardor be wanting to our prayers, they shall have no force, or very little. David says: "The Lord shall hear me when I shall cry to Him;" for if I speak in a low voice, that is to say, if I pray with coldness or tepidity, I shall obtain nothing. "He shall hear me as often as I cry to Him." God Himself said to the prophet Jeremias: "Cry to me, and I shall hear thee." If thou dost not cry, thou shalt not be heard, because my ears are open only to earnest prayer.

If the incense should not burn, it will neither ascend nor give forth its perfumes. Cold has no power to ascend; it is heat that renders things light, and gives them the dispositions necessary to mount upward. Prayer does not ascend to God and spread its odors before His Majesty, if it be not heated by the fire of devotion; cold and tepid prayers remain unheard. At the time of our Lord's passion St. Peter denied Him, and all the other apostles fled, because they had not had recourse to prayer, notwithstanding the warning of our Saviour; or if they prayed, it was with tepidity and drowsiness. It is not enough to pray, if we do not pray fervently. It is not enough for a soldier to have a sword with a blunt edge, he must have a sharp one. The Philistines, victorious over the people of God, allowed the vanquished to use pointless weapons, because they knew these could not inflict injury. In the same way the demon permits us to make as much mental and vocal prayer as we please, provided we make it in a cold, languishing manner, without affection and without fervor, aimless and without point.

It is only those who pray with a good heart and fervently, that are heard, for fervent prayer proceeds from an inflamed heart and an ardent desire, which God prefers to all other dispositions. If a child ask something of his mother with a certain negligence, very often he will not obtain it; but if he ask it with eagerness and with tears, she will not refuse him, unless the granting of his request would be prejudicial; and even though it should, she sometimes accords it, because she cannot bear to see her child weep. David teaches us that "God keeps His eyes fixed on all who invoke Him in truth," and He is well disposed to hear their petitions. What is the meaning of the phrase, *Who invoke Him in truth?* It means, who invoke Him with affection and fervor, not with tepidity and coldness; for he who invokes Him thus, invokes Him not in truth: his negligence shows that he has no real desire to obtain what he asks, that his prayers are mere words, and that he cares little whether they be heard or not, since, if he did, he would certainly make them with greater fervor.

Therefore, let us strive to animate all our prayers with an ardent affection; let them be as burning incense, and let us strive that they come from the depths of our heart and soul. Wonderful were the immense fervor and love which animated the prayers of the saints. The disciples prayed so fervently that, according to St. Luke, the house in which they were, trembled. "If thou seest me in this state, wholly transported," said Anna, the mother of Samuel, to Heli, "do not take me for a person who has drunk wine, but I have poured out my soul before the Lord." I have laid all my affections and all my sentiments before Him. We read of St. Francis, that one of his religious saw him one day praying with such ardor, that flames seemed to issue from his mouth and eyes, and he was lifted at least a foot from the ground. John the Deacon assures us on oath, in his Life of Saint Simeon Salus, that, seeing the saint with hands uplifted in prayer, he perceived large sparks issuing from his mouth, and the space surrounding him was like a burning furnace. St. Paphnutius praying in his prison during the night, his guards, seeing a great light, were astonished, and going to his cell, found him at prayer, his arms extended toward heaven, appearing like two flaming torches. We could relate hundreds of similar instances. Many, during their prayers, experience such ardor and affection that the body is affected as well as the soul, as the large drops of perspiration which appear on the countenance, and even moisten the garments, amply testify. These always obtain what they ask,—effect follows petition. Such are the models on which we ought to form ourselves to prayer.

Yes, when we pray to God, we must enliven our desires, inflame our hearts, and be fervent and animated. It is commonly said that he who cannot pray, should go to sea to learn; for, as the first tempest arises, when he finds himself in danger of shipwreck and death, he quickly becomes fervent and devout, he will pray to God with singular affection and eagerness. Alas! we navigate a sea far more dangerous,—a sea wherein perils are more numerous and shipwrecks more frequent. In navigating our salvation, we require immense assistance; and this assistance we should seek with the greatest instance, if we realized its importance.

And then, when we ask of God things relating to our salvation, do we really know well what we ask? We demand goods so great and high, that they surpass all our thoughts and words. We pray for His paradise, His glory, His riches, His pleasures, the eternal possession of Himself. Is there anything in the world comparable to these goods? Are not all the empires of the earth as a grain of dust in comparison? We ask for humility, patience, charity, the gifts of the Holy Ghost : now, the smallest participation in any of these is a greater good than the possession of France, of all the empires on earth, and is more valuable than everything rare and beautiful in nature. And shall we ask these immense and precious treasures as if they were of little importance, and almost as if we ceased to care whether our petitions were heard or not?

Certainly, if we were very hungry or thirsty, we should ask a morsel of bread or a glass of water with more importunity than we now use in asking of God the kingdom of heaven and eternal beatitude. Where, then, is our common-sense? What has become of our judgment? And whence comes it that so few persons obtain, as the effect of their prayers, the gifts of God? The tepidity and negligence of their prayers prove they are not in a condition to receive His favors. You wish that God should give you the immense treasures that cost the blood of His Son, and you ask them as if they were worth little or nothing. Great favors ought to be asked with great affection ; there should be some proportion between the vehemence of the desire, the ardor of the supplication, and the excellence of the thing desired and supplicated.

To confound ourselves, and at the same time receive instruction, let us cast our eyes on criminals before their judge, when they are in danger of being condemned to death ; and on the sick, when the physician is about to perform some painful operation,—what ardent, eloquent and piteous prayers do they not make, those to escape death, these through fear of pain ! St. Augustine relates of an advocate of Carthage, named Innocent, that the physicians, having made a successful experiment on him, left uncut a fistula which it was necessary to remove, but which they had accidentally overlooked. When the poor man heard that it was determined he should undergo another operation, he was seized with terrible apprehensions, remembering the pain he had suffered in the former ; and those who saw his extreme desolation firmly believed that he would die in the hands of the surgeons. The Bishop of Carthage, another bishop, and all the priests and deacons of the church, visited him and encouraged and consoled him as much as they possibly could. But the day preceding that on which the operation was to be made, he besought them, with abundance of bitter tears, to come next day and assist rather at his death than at his torments. "Before leaving his house," says the saint, "we all prostrated ourselves on the earth, to implore the assistance of heaven. The sick man himself united with us, and cast himself on the ground as one overwhelmed with grief : but who could describe his prayer ? With what emotion, with what transports, with what rivers of tears, with what burning words, with what groans and sighs which made his whole frame tremble, and nearly suffocated him ! For me, I knew not what I said, so greatly was I moved at this sad spectacle. All I could do was to utter in the depths of my heart : Lord, what prayers wilt Thou hear if Thou reject these ? This man can add nothing more unless he expires praying ! We all rose up, and having received the benediction of the bishop, we left the house. Next day, when we returned, the surgeon was preparing to commence the operation, but a closer inspection convinced him that it was unnecessary, for the prayer of faith had saved the sick man !"

Now, if this poor patient asked of God, with such burning ardor, the health of his body and deliverance from temporary pain, how much greater should be our ardor when we pray for victory over our passions, freedom from the torments of hell, the health of our souls and the possession of eternal beatitude! Certainly, as the things relating to our salvation are incomparably greater, we should ask them with greater earnestness and fervor. But, though we prayed only for a crumb of bread or a drop of water, we are so insignificant before God, whose immensity infinitely surpasses our comprehension, that there is no sort of respect, no kind of honor, no species of humiliation and abasement, no sign of submission and adoration, no reverential and suppliant posture, which we ought not to adopt and use.

Let us then present our petitions to God with affection and fervor; let us ever supplicate Him with pressing and importunate eagerness; let us conjure Him by His goodness, His mercy, His promises, His zeal for His own glory, by the love and service of which He is worthy, and by all that could move Him to hear us; let us use force, if we may say so, and do Him violence; let us say to Him with tears, as Jacob did to the angel, "I will not let thee go, except thou bless me." Let us weep and make supplication as Osee did, who prevailed over the angel; let us tell Him we will not leave Him without His benediction; and let us be certain that He will hear us immediately or in a short time, and always immediately, when this is for our greater advantage.

With these conditions, prayer is omnipotent to obtain everything, because God has pledged His word. But without these conditions, God is not held by His promise. Hence the secret of prayer is to make it, as far as possible, with these conditions. We daily ask many things of God, and yet obtain nothing; we ask humility, patience, charity and other virtues, and yet continue proud, impatient, choleric, and envious. Whence comes this misfortune? Does not God desire to bestow His favors and to save us? Doubtless it is, according to

St. James, because we do not ask these things as we ought: "You ask and you do not receive, because you ask amiss." A well-tempered sword can perform great exploits, but it requires a good arm to direct its movements. Prayer, says St. Chrysostom, is the key of God's treasures; with it you can open His coffers and take what you please. But remember that a key will not work unless it be fitted to the lock, and moved in the right direction; otherwise, the treasures you covet cannot be placed within your reach. It is the same with prayer, considered in reference to the riches of God: if you use it rightly, they are yours; if not, though you hold in your hand the means of enriching yourself, you shall always remain in poverty and misery.

CHAPTER VIII.

EIGHTH GENERAL PRINCIPLE OF THE SPIRITUAL LIFE.—PEACE OF THE SOUL.

"SEEK for peace," said the Royal Prophet, "and pursue it diligently." If asked what is the best disposition in the spiritual life to make great progress and acquire perfection,—whether it be to walk in light or in darkness, to have much sensible fervor or little, to be healthy or sick, to be rich or poor, in honor or in opprobrium, I answer, that it is to keep the heart and soul in unalterable peace in all these states and dispositions. On this subject we will consider, first, what peace and its advantages are; next, in what we should practise it; and, thirdly, how we ought to acquire it.

1. Peace, says St. Austin, is serenity of mind, tranquillity of soul, simplicity of heart, and the bond of love. It is the arrangement of things similar and dissimilar, equal and unequal, in such a manner that each holds exactly the rank it ought to have. It is the tranquillity of order. "Peace," says St. Thomas, "consists in this: that all the passions which can excite a man are in repose, so that he is never unduly moved or agitated, but always calm and tranquil." Where everything is in order, in its natural place, there is peace; on the contrary, where there is disorder, there also is trouble. "Things, when not in their respective places, are in continual trouble," says St. Augustine, "but, when they take their proper rank, they immediately find peace. Peace of body is the just temperament of all its component parts; peace of the sensitive

soul is the satiety of its appetites; peace of the reasonable soul is the mutual agreement of its faculties and their operations; and the peace of man consists in the obedience he renders to the will of his Creator.

We should have a high esteem for peace, and practise it with special care. The first exercise to be undertaken in the spiritual life is, according to the saying of the masters of this great and sublime science, that of interior peace and the repose of the soul. This repose, this peace, is an inexhaustible source of good. St. Augustine remarks that peace is not only a great good, but the source of all other goods, and there is no good which should be desired more earnestly. On the contrary, no evil is more hurtful than discord. The sovereign happiness of a kingdom consists, according to the opinion of all sensible persons, in maintaining peace and concord among its subjects: this done, each applies, without inquietude, to his own functions. But the greatest misfortune that can befall a country is civil war: then all is strife. The father is armed against his son, and the son against his father; and citizens, who should live as brothers, are intent only on slaying one another. Hence all wise politicians consider the preservation or restoration of peace as the highest point of their science, and their own most glorious mission.

The two greatest goods to be procured in this life are the grace of God and peace of the soul; the two greatest evils to be feared are sin and trouble. St. Peter begins his Epistle by wishing the faithful *grace and peace*. St. Paul commences all of his in the same manner, and in this sense he says to the Romans: "The prudence of the spirit consists in grace, which is the life of the soul, and in peace."

The demon employs all his artifices to deprive the soul of grace and peace. His first step is to rob us of the grace of God, which is the life of the soul and the pledge of salvation; and when he cannot do this, he strives to destroy our peace, knowing well that, when peace is lost, grace is easily forfeited : for the soul, when divested of peace, is already in the disposition to sin, and is near a fall. The man who has lost his peace cannot do anything well, because trouble, by the clouds and obscurity with which it replenishes the mind, hinders him from acting properly : just as one cannot walk steadily at night, or work well in the dark. Peace is the shortest and most secure road to perfection. When one desires to reach perfection, the first thing he must do is to keep a pacific vigilance over himself interiorly and exteriorly, and to preserve great tranquillity in all circumstances. He may be certain that this path will speedily and easily lead him to high perfection, for peace is an excellent disposition to virtue, and prepares the soul for divine graces and communications. "The Lord will replenish His people with virtues," says David, "the Lord will bless His people in peace ;" and St. Basil, writing on this passage, calls peace the most perfect of the benedictions of God. St. Climacus says that tranquillity of soul is ornamented with virtues, as the firmament is adorned with stars ; and he calls peace the heaven of the soul. The tranquil soul easily becomes learned, says the philosopher. And the Holy Ghost teaches, in Ecclesiasticus, that wisdom is easily acquired when the soul is in repose. The peaceful soul is a lively image of the infinitely calm nature of the Divinity, which is never troubled, but always remains in repose. In bodies which turn upon an axis, one point is invariably held to be firm and immovable. God is the immovable point of the centre round which all creatures revolve : the nearer you approach Him, the more tranquil shall you become ; and the farther you recede from Him, the greater will be your agitation. " His dwelling is made in peace," said David ; whence we must conclude that the demon has *his* dwelling in discord and confusion. "The tranquil soul is the throne of God," says St. Climacus ; "but the soul which is in confusion is the seat of the devil." If the peaceable soul is the dwelling of God, it follows that God abandons the soul which abandons peace ; or, at least, that trouble deprives her of the sentiment of His presence, and hinders His operations in her.

The tranquil soul is in the true state to practise virtue and work with perfection. St. Augustine judiciously observes that the Jewish Sabbath, which w's chiefly spent in prayer, and on which servile works were prohibited, is a figure of the peace of the soul. The Scriptures remark that sinners are always agitated and troubled. "O my God !" says David, "make them like a wheel, and as stubble before the wind." And in the same thought, Isaias adds : "The impious are like a raging sea, which is never at rest." Cain, as Moses relates, spent his life restless and wandering ; and this, St. Jerome understands rather of the troubles and agitations of his poor soul, which had no stability, no repose, than of his frequent changes of dwelling to shelter his body.

I say more : peace is not only the road to perfection, but perfection is found in peace. The perfection of the soul consists in the mutual agreement of all its powers, as that of the body consists in health, which is only the peace of its humors and members. Perfection is in peace, says St. Augustine ; hence the children of God who are most accomplished and perfect, are called by the name *pacific*. "The climax of wisdom," says St. Ambrose, "is to preserve an inviolable tranquillity." "Yes," says St. Augustine, "the man who attains to this has acquired consummate perfection." Those wise men who acquired this glorious quality had, often in the mouth, and always in the heart, the praises of this delightful tranquillity. St. Denis describes as "excellently virtuous, men who are not divided in themselves, but are one and in peace." Origen remarks that the Scripture qualifies Elcana, father of Samuel,—a name which signifies possession of God ; that is, a man who is not unequal, but always the same.

Seneca has established the felicity of man in constant tranquillity of mind. Aristotle has placed it in the calm of soul which tends to the most noble object. In effect, the place where we shall possess perfect happiness is the heavenly Jerusalem, which signifies vision of peace.

Finally, peace renders a man proper to treat with his neighbor in an agreeable, useful, and efficacious manner. It belongs only to fixed things to give motion to volatile things, and a peaceable mind is capable of pacifying those who are moved and troubled ; as a vessel of oil cast into the sea is said to calm the agitations of the waves. Since, then, peace is so great a treasure, since it conducts to perfection, and even comprehends perfection, let us strive by all possible care to acquire it. "Seek for peace and pursue it." Remember that the children of Israel were commanded to sanctify the Sabbath ; that is, to apply themselves to acquire repose of soul. St. Macarius, in the homily he made on the ancient Sabbath and the new, remarks that Moses, on part of God, commanded the Jews to celebrate the Sabbath by keeping themselves, and even their domestic animals, from all servile work. This, says he, represents the true Sabbath which our Lord gives to souls in the New Law ; and which is no other thing than the peace and sweet tranquillity enjoyed by souls free from inordinate affections to creatures. These are the souls which, properly speaking, possess the Sabbath of God, and celebrate His day with holy and delicious interior repose ; they experience inexplicable contentment and divine delights, in which even the body shares—as the beasts participated in the Jewish Sabbath,—by its sweet and tranquil movements, by its composed and well-ordered appearance. Thus St. Macarius.

Before him, St. Paul, in his Epistle to the Hebrews, treated of the repose of the body on the seventh day, thence called the Sabbath or rest ; and the repose of the promised land, in which was situated the city of Jerusalem. These are the figures of two other kinds of repose promised to Christians. The repose of the body typifies the repose of the heart in interior peace, during the continuance of which man abstains from all servile actions, and employs himself in those which concern the glory, the worship, and the love of God. The repose of the promised land signifies the repose of the blessed in the heavenly Jerusalem. This is the real Sabbath of the people of God : interior repose in this life, and eternal felicity in the next. Let us advance with great strides toward this repose, proceeds the apostle ; let us make haste to possess this sweet peace of soul.

Peace is a gift which, in a peculiar manner, belongs to Christians. "God has called us to peace," says the apostle to the Corinthians ; and our Saviour is called by Isaias the Prince of Peace. He became man to give peace to the world, whence St. Paul calls Him *our peace*. At the time of His birth the whole Roman Empire was in peace ; the angels with songs of jubilee proclaimed peace to men of good will ; a little before His death He left peace to His apostles as His legacy, and after His resurrection He saluted them many times in these terms : Peace be to you. Finally, He ordered them, when entering a house, to bring tidings of salvation to its inmates, to salute them, saying : Peace be to this house. Peace, then, should be the portion and the exercise of all Christians.

Certainly, it belongs to us more properly than it did to the ancient philosophers, who esteemed it so highly. "Though I should be tormented, persecuted and overwhelmed with misery," says Seneca, "I shall not regard myself as unfortunate, because I have gained so much upon myself that whatever happens cannot destroy my peace." Socrates, at the age of seventy, commenced to learn music, because it serves to appease mental inquietude. Epictetus gave the following advice to his disciple : "Abandon all the rest to others, let them do what they please, let them form good syllogisms and reason well ; but let thy study be to preserve the repose of thy mind. Let them learn what they like, but do thou learn to die, to be poor, to bear injuries patiently, and to preserve thy peace." In another place, addressing his disciples in general, he says : "I teach you, you acknowledge me for your master ; my design is to render you tranquil, constant and equable ; that nothing may disturb or embarrass you, that you may be free and happy, and regarding God in everything, great or small. A philosopher [and still more a Christian] should be able to say of himself : 'No exterior thing can disturb me. Calamities, earthquakes, robbers, have no power over me. Everything within me is in perfect repose.'" The pagan philosophers were rich in beautiful words, but we ought to be rich in effect ; they promised a peace of soul which they never tasted : but peace is proper to the Christian, it is a treasure which can be possessed only by the just, by those who are truly virtuous, which the philosophers were not. Let us now see in what consists the practice of peace.

§ I.—*In what we ought to practise peace.*

"In all things I sought rest," says the Sage. The Venerable Girard surnamed the Great, whose life Thomas à Kempis has written, was of opinion that man ought not to allow anything in this world to trouble him. Peace, after the grace of God, is the greatest treasure we can possess here below ; and trouble, after sin, is the greatest misfortune that can befall us. But this life is greatly subject to trouble, because of many daily accidents, and the force of exterior objects which strike our senses, make an impression on our minds, and, by reason of the vivacity of the passions, easily carry us away. Hence Job had cause to say : Man's life on earth is a warfare. We shall now speak of the practice of peace more in detail, and first in our particular actions.

1. We ought to preserve peace of soul and be master of ourselves when we act alone. For this end, we must be careful never to commence an action while moved or disturbed ; for, if we did, we should fail in peace at the very beginning of the thing. On the contrary, we should bring to all our employments a tranquil spirit, that we may commence them in the light of peace, not in the obscurity of inquietude. Few men, says Seneca, conduct their affairs with judgment. The greater number are carried away by impetuosity, and blinded by the waves of passion. To avoid these inconveniences, peace is necessary.

2. We should, before each action, recollect ourselves a little, that we may dispose ourselves to do it well. Those who play on the lute or violin, tune the instrument before playing, and do not commence their performance till they have properly adjusted it : we ought, in our daily conduct, to imitate the example given us in this respect by good musicians.

3. We must not be precipitate in our actions. Everything has its own time, says Solomon, in Ecclesiastes ; and, in another part of the same book, he says : "The wise man has judgment to discern in what time each action should be done : all affairs have their movements and their conjunctures." Our Lord often said : "My time is not yet come." His time He neither hastened nor retarded ; but awaited peaceably, in perfect resignation to His Father's will.

4. We must never prescribe to ourselves a certain time in which to accomplish an action, in such a manner that it must be done by a certain day and hour, at any price ; for, by acting thus, we should endanger our peace of mind, if it happened that circumstances did not admit of our doing the thing, or doing it well, in the specified time. Besides, who can assure us that some unforeseen event will not prevent or retard the

execution of our design? Let us resolve to give to all our business the necessary time and attention, but make no other limits. We must not allow anything whatever to rob us of peace. Finally, let us do things quietly, avoiding eagerness and impetuosity. We must take our time, work carefully and leisurely; diligently indeed, but not therefore precipitately. "One does a thing quickly enough when he does it well," said Cato. "Too much haste has injured many, even good men," says Tacitus; "a little delay in things we are inclined to expedite too much, is always salutary." Dogs are born blind, because, as Galen remarks, they seem to be produced before the time nature requires to perfect their organization. It is an ancient proverb that those who work too fast are often the slowest, because they make so many mistakes that they sometimes are obliged to do their work twice. Those who dress too hurriedly can hardly dress without some disorder or negligence, as St. Augustine observes. It belongs only to the heavens to move very fast, and at the same time make no mistake. Those who gather fruit before it is ripe, gather what is no good to them, and deprive themselves of the hope of ripe fruit, which they could have had if they only had a little patience. So, those who are too precipitate in their affairs often ruin them, instead of conducting them prosperously.

Let us, then, in our actions, avoid eagerness and precipitation, which are the great enemies of peace, and the destruction of true devotion. God produced all His works without losing an atom of His repose; He is our model. If we work as He did, we shall work well; if we work otherwise, we shall work ill.

It is easy to guide a ship over a tranquil sea; but very difficult, if not impossible, to steer her safely through a tempest. It is not so much the doing of a thing, as the doing it well that is the point. Our mind we should apply entirely to the business in hand, and, if distractions come, we should put them away gently, or take no notice of them ; like a good servant who, being sent on some business by his master, passes through the streets without minding the children that are playing there, or answering them if they call after him, but goes direct where his business brings him, and thinks only of transacting his master's affairs.

With our neighbor.

When we transact business with our neighbor, we are very liable, unless we take great care, to lose the precious treasure of mental tranquillity. To avoid so great an inconvenience, we must remember what has been already said, and also what will now be advanced.

1. It is no small matter to treat well with our fellow-creatures. Inconstancy, weakness, ignorance, the passions and self-love, are so strong in us all that, if it is easy to begin an affair with a man, it is very difficult to conduct it to a good end. Our Lord, during His life on earth, advanced very little the salvation of the Jews, notwithstanding all His miracles, His preaching, His industry and His labors. God Himself, who continually showers His gifts and graces on Christians and heathens, finds very few to accomplish His designs. Is there a peasant or an artisan whose orders in his own family are so often transgressed, as are the orders of God in His own world?

2. Never undertake too many things, nor things too great; even if they be good, their number or their weight will overwhelm you. Before undertaking a thing, consider, as the saying is, whether you are able to lift it, and be sure to adjust it to your own strength. A porter considers whether he can carry a burden, before he lifts it on his back ; before loading a horse, it is necessary to know how much he is able to carry. We ought to do the same with regard to the burden of the spiritual life. To know how to restrain ourselves

within the proper limits, and thus go sweetly and calmly through life, is great wisdom. Seneca says: "The salutary advice of Democritus is very useful to teach us to preserve peace of mind:" in public and in private let us undertake only what we are able to accomplish well. He who embarrasses himself with a multiplicity of affairs, cannot spend the day happily; either through his own fault or the fault of those he treats with, or even through accident, something will happen to annoy him, or put him in bad humor. Those who walk in the most frequented streets of Rome must necessarily be crushed and elbowed, make some false steps, and be often stopped—get their clothes, or even their faces, spattered with mud; while those who go through the quiet streets may walk at their ease, without meeting obstructions or inconveniences. It is the same with those who strive to get through too much business. Hence, if we would go peaceably through life, it is not wise to undertake things too numerous or too difficult, but only such as are proportioned to our strength, for it is easy to carry a light burden and change it from one shoulder to another; but, if the load be too heavy, we must, when we grow tired, charge others with part of it, or cast it off entirely, or sink under it. Consequently, to anticipate and prevent these inconveniences, we must always beforehand consider well what we undertake, and measure our own strength, and the strength of those who labor with us."

If those with whom we work or transact business be impatient, apt to take umbrage, rude, importunate or disagreeable, we must be still more careful to keep ourselves tranquil, remembering that we are on a very slippery bank; and as he who carries a lighted torch in the midst of straw, or in the vicinity of gunpowder, must use great circumspection to hinder a conflagration or explosion, so we must take all sorts of precautions when we deal with ill-disposed persons. Even with well-disposed persons, we must use great address; and in order not to disturb their peace or ours, balance ourselves with a just temperament, and tread as carefully as do those who walk on a rope extended over a precipice.

If some one comes to hinder or distract you in your occupations, be not troubled, preserve your interior and exterior calm ; consider that if this person prevents or interrupts one action, he gives you an opportunity of doing another, a very excellent one,—an act of patience ; of which St. James says : "Patience hath a perfect work." We must remember that, in Christianity to act, is not more noble than to suffer. It is suffering that has saved us ; and suffering includes an heroic action, that is to say, victory over self.

Man need never be idle, unless he wishes to be so. When hindered from executing his designs, he need not trouble himself, for he can, at all times and in all places, find excellent occupation in making interior acts of faith, hope, love, adoration and thanksgiving toward God. No one can prevent him from thus employing himself. When we act with those of our own house, we must be particularly guarded, that we may not give them occasion of impatience, nor sadden them, nor complain of trifling matters that occur every day ; for, as these persons, to a certain extent, depend on us for their happiness, and with whom we naturally feel inclined to take greater liberty, we are apt to be less reserved than we ought to be in our intercourse with them.

In our desires, even such as are good.

To maintain our souls in peace, we must take particular care to govern our desires, for there is no more fertile source of interior mutiny than ill-regulated desires to acquire some good, or to be delivered from some evil. Such desires are scourges which wound us, thorns which pierce us, worms which gnaw our souls. Hence, if we wish to enjoy true peace, we must be careful to indulge no irregular desires, saying to God with the Sage: "Lord, my true Father, take from me all desires capable of troubling me;" or with David: "Lord, deliver me not to the sinner through my desire." St. Augustine, explaining this passage, remarks that each one, by his desires, opens the door of his heart, and gives entrance to the demon, who is here understood by the "sinner," and who is the author of inquietude, confusion, and trouble.

If you have any desires, moderate them in such a manner that they will not hold you captive. By this you will gain an important victory over yourself. Be not carried away by the promptitude of your spirit; let the impetuosity of the first movement pass, decide on nothing, do nothing while it lasts; wait for the second movement, and act by its impulse: for, as we were like plants and beasts before we became men,—that is, as we performed the actions of the vegetative and sensitive life, before we performed those of the reasonable life,—so our first movements are commonly movements of passion. The second are produced by reason and discernment, and hence the ancient adage: "Second thoughts are wiser than first thoughts."

If you feel pressed with any desire in a manner that disturbs your peace, do nothing till your agitation has entirely subsided. If it involve something that cannot be deferred, do it, but take care to hold a tight rein with this unruly horse, that is, with this inordinate desire, that it may not run away with you; moderate it as much as possible; perform the action, not because you desire it, but because your duty obliges you to do it. To cool your inordinate ardor, remember that God is looking at you; hold yourself in His divine presence, and tell Him that it is for His sake alone you act—not to content your will or satisfy your desire, but to please Him and accomplish His will.

What I say is to be understood even of the good desires which refer to the holiest things. In effect, when these desires cease to be moderate, they cease to be good ; they are no longer means of salvation, but rather impediments to it : for there ought to be some proportion between the means and the end, some relation between the road and the term. We read of St. Louis Gonzaga that he banished from his mind not only all desires and affections for things indifferent, but even for holy things, when they gave him any superfluous anxiety, or seemed likely to disturb his peace of mind. And hence he always enjoyed profound tranquillity of heart and soul.

We include here even zeal for the salvation of souls. Though this be the most excellent, and, as St. Denis affirms, the most divine of all things, yet it must be regulated. To procure the salvation of a neighbor is to participate in the office of saviour ; hence we ought to exercise our zeal in the spirit of Jesus, which is a spirit of peace and charity, not a spirit of passion and trouble. Let us never forget the example which God and our good angels give us : they desire, they solicit incessantly, the salvation of those for whom you work, and that with far more solicitude and ardor than you, and yet they are never embarrassed or disquieted. Your own perfection ought to be dearer to you than that of others. To advance theirs, you must not retard your own. God has established this order in the love we should entertain for ourselves and for our neighbor. And truly it would be great folly to injure our own souls in assisting the souls of others. What will it profit you to gain the whole world if you lose your own soul ? What will you give in exchange for your soul ?

It is related of the learned and pious John of Avila that, having been solicited by several, because of the great repute in which his life and doctrine were held throughout all Spain, to remove to the city where the king held court, he would never do it, though he might have saved more souls there than elsewhere ; and the reason of his refusal was, that he wished to employ himself for the salvation of souls in a manner that would not be perilous to his own perfection : and this he could hardly do in the midst of the noise and intrigues of a court. So he practised himself the counsel he was accustomed to give to such of his disciples as were preachers: "Not more children than milk ; not more business than strength."

In our losses.

When we lose anything regarding this life, as parents, goods, honor, reputation, friends, health, and such like, we must strive to possess ourselves in peace, remembering that trouble and inquietude cannot restore what we have lost ; on the contrary, they would rob us of a thing still dearer and more precious, namely, our interior peace. We must consider that God recalls what He had only lent us, and that what He judges fit to take away is no longer useful to us. Hence we must not grieve to excess, but think chiefly of turning our loss to our profit, and our temporal calamity to the increase of our eternal felicity. When a merchant returning from India is in danger of shipwreck, he saves as much of his treasure as he can ; but, if he cannot save any, he strives at least to save his life. Let us do the same in our losses ; let us save our souls whatever happens, and preserve our interior peace, and thus we may turn all our misfortunes to the profit of our eternal salvation.

In our imperfections and sins.

We must constantly endeavor to preserve interior tranquillity, not allowing anything, even our imperfections or vices, to disturb our serenity.

1. We should never be troubled or discouraged by our defects or relapses, saying that it is always the same with us ;

that, after all the remedies we used, we are still sick; that, instead of making progress, we fall away; that we never can come to the end of our passions and vices. We ought not to speak in this manner, for words and sentiments of this nature, far from curing an evil, change it from bad to worse. If troubles and dejection of mind could operate a change of heart, or contribute ever so little toward it, then I should advise you to continue them; but, instead of that, they harden the heart, freeze the ardor of the will, deprive us of courage, and rob us of the power of desiring to amend; they cast us into a certain despair of being able to do better. Now, all this being incontestable, every sensible man will banish and condemn them.

Disturbance of mind never improved any one. "Man troubles himself in vain," says David; his inquietudes only injure him. Trouble obscures his reason, corrupts his judgment, casts him interiorly and exteriorly into disorder, destroying all the harmony of his nature. Now, in such a state, how can man be at all capable of receiving the lights and inspirations of God? We must necessarily conclude that whatever robs one of interior peace cannot come from God, but must come from the devil, who is the author of division—or from corrupt nature. Hence, when we commit a fault, we must not lose our peace, but turn interiorly to God; humbling ourselves profoundly before His mercy, confessing our sin to Him, and avowing that we should fall into worse without His aid; acknowledging sincerely before Him our great inclination to evil, and our inability in all that is good. Afterward, conceiving a true sorrow, let us ask pardon of Him as a child of his father, with a firm purpose not to commit the fault again. We must in future watch carefully that we may not relapse into it, without wasting our time examining whether we fully explained it in confession, or had true contrition for it, or wondering whether God has forgiven it or not: these and similar disquieting reflections serve only to torture the poor mind. This is how we ought to behave after every fault, and always in the same order, with the same confidence in God, and the same interior repose, the last time as well as the first. All that God asks of a sinner is, to be sorry for his sin, to confess it to the priest at the tribunal of penance, if it be a mortal sin, to make satisfaction, and to resolve to amend. He demands nothing more; but we must do what He requires.

Whenever we fail, we ought to go to God with the same confidence with which a child who has fallen in the mud rises up and runs to his father or mother. See how the poor little one cries, and holds up his soiled hands, which his mother cleans, all the while consoling and appeasing him. It is thus God comports Himself toward souls that are truly penitent, and run to Him with confidence.

Of scruples.

A word on scruples. Generally, they are a source of much pain to the soul, and a great obstacle to interior peace.

1. I say, then, that a scruple is a malady of the soul by which one imagines there is sin where there is none, and deduces this from ill-founded suspicions and deceitful reasoning.

2. Scruples injure the soul very much, and greatly hinder advancement in perfection. The etymology of the word shows this; for *scrupus*, of which *scrupulus* is the diminutive, signifies a little pebble in the shoe of a traveller which pains him, and retards his progress. Scrupulosity causes great weariness and dejection, filling the soul with darkness, making one imagine things that are not, while it hides things that are; it is a source of pain and anguish, and greatly impedes the operations of grace in the soul. God's operation requires a calm, peaceable soul; and as He will not have libertinism or dissipation, so neither does He want vain fears

and constraint, for, says the apostle, where the spirit of God is, there is a holy liberty. Scrupulosity is a cloud which eclipses the rays of the sun of justice; a blast of wind which dissipates the breathings of the Holy Spirit; a venom which poisons the heart, gnaws the soul, dries up all unction, attenuates the mind, if we may so speak, and reduces it to a state, of which a body containing only skin and bone is a fit emblem or illustration.

3. This disease may be cured easily and speedily, if the patient will only receive and act on the counsels of a capable director. But, otherwise, scrupulosity is incurable.

4. The scrupulous person does not easily sin mortally in the matter of his scruple, for I suppose that, in the depth of his heart, he does not wish to offend God; and as the scrupulous ordinarily have too great a fear of God to purpose deliberately to offend Him, if they had a clear knowledge of sin, and as they have not sufficient light to make a just discernment, they are hardly capable of committing grievous sins. Besides, in simple obedience to a good director, they cannot err. If any inconvenience occur, the fault lies with him; and the humble submission of the scrupulous will shield them from all blame. Let them, therefore, receive with humility the advice he gives them, freely submitting to his judgment, despising their doubts and fears as vain phantoms which should be capable of scaring only children. If the scrupulosity be of a nature at all curable, this course of treatment will infallibly cure it. But, without obedience to one's director, scrupulosity cannot be cured.

Conclusion.

Behold, then, how we ought to preserve our tranquillity under all circumstances. Our principal study should be to maintain our hearts in peace; and if anything occur to move us ever so little, we must calm our emotion and appease our trouble. "The just man shall never be moved," says the Sage. Nothing can disturb him; come what may, he will always preserve the repose of his soul and the joy of his heart, whatever else he may lose.

It is strange that peace, being so sweet and useful, and trouble so bitter and painful, there are, nevertheless, persons who are enemies to peace, and friends to disturbance. If there be no one to torment them, they torment themselves; they are so very ingenious in annoying themselves with superfluous cares, false imaginations, vain, useless desires, and incessant intrigues, that they resemble certain kinds of fish which cannot live except in troubled waters. These are the men of whom David says: "The way of peace they have not known." Job says, "The pleasures of unruly minds are worms;" and St. Gregory adds, in explanation of this passage: "The pleasures of a disorderly mind are worms, that is to say, to be eaten by worms; so that its food and delight seem to consist in incessant agitation and trouble." Elsewhere the same Job says: "They ate grass, and root of junipers was their food. They counted it delightful to be under briers." Such was the last Duke of Burgundy, Charles the Bold, who consumed his days in continual troubles, and who said in his last moments that he never had any repose in life—miserable and unfortunate that he was. In these turbulent people, storms and agitations are not solely an effect of their nature, but also a chastisement from God, who punishes unquiet souls, according to this saying of the Royal Prophet: "I have sworn to them in my wrath that they shall not enter my repose." They mistake peace for war, and war for peace, as the Book of Wisdom remarks: "Whereas they live in a great war of ignorance, they call the greatest evils with which our life can be troubled, peace."

Let us guard against this terrible suffering as much as possible, and use our best endeavors to acquire peace of soul, and enjoy repose of heart. The God whom we serve is a God of peace, and certainly there is no reason why we should serve Him in commotion. "The wise and prudent man," says the Holy Ghost, "is sweet to his own soul," and keeps it in tranquillity, for peace is necessary to the service of God and the practice of virtue. "My son, do thy works in meekness. Keep thy soul in meekness, and honor it according to its deserts;" for it is very noble, being the image of God and the masterpiece of His hands, destined to enjoy Him forever.

Having shown that peace should be maintained in all the occurrences of this life, we will now consider the means by which to acquire and preserve this most precious treasure, interior peace.

§ 2.—*Means to preserve peace of soul.*

The first means refers to the source of all our conduct, that is to say, our mind, which we must purify of its errors, replacing them by good and true opinions. It is very rare to find a man whose mind is not corrupted by certain extravagances and false notions. Many things disturb us most unreasonably : the mere imagination of a slight evil, which perhaps will never happen, is sufficient to depress us; a shadow, a chimera, makes us start, just as a hideous mask frightens children, or a scarecrow frightens birds. "What happens among beasts," says St. Seneca, "you may remark in men, if you observe them closely. Vain and ridiculous things are sometimes sufficient to cause a panic. Anything red irritates the bull. Asps start at shadows, and bears and lions are easily roused. Whatever is naturally savage is readily moved, and unquiet minds are subject to similar accidents : the mere suspicion or appearance of an untoward thing is sufficient to wound them and destroy their peace.

They judge of things only by the present, by appearances; few unmask things to consider them, and, in forming judgments of them, consider their consequences, their future." One of the first counsels Pythagoras gave in order to attain wisdom was, not to walk in the public roads; that is, as Philo explains, not to follow the vulgar opinions, which, like torrents, overwhelm a great part of the world. "What saddens us," said Epictetus, "is not any particular thing in itself, but the opinion we have formed of it." We ought then strive to rectify our erroneous judgments. The same author remarks, very wisely, that he who is born free can never be a captive, unless he pleases: only himself can imprison his soul, or put his mind in irons; nothing has power to trouble his repose, if he wishes. He must do himself this prejudice, and thus become his own tormentor, his own murderer: this he does by his opinions, judging things to be different from what they really are. When a beautiful and rich object presents itself before us, let us take care not to be carried away by first impressions, but leisurely examine whence it comes, whither it goes, what good it can procure us. We must discuss it freely in all its bearings, because on our opinions depends our liberty or our servitude, our peace or our trouble.

Whoever desires to possess tranquillity should not allow things outside of himself to have much power over him; he ought to seek and find in the depth of his soul, and in God who dwells there, his repose and felicity. This was a maxim with the ancient philosophers, but which they preached better than they practised. "The wise man finds his happiness within him," says Seneca. "I carry my wealth within me," said the master of Zeno, when he saw his city taken and sacked. The wise man can wish only to live well. To live, many things are necessary; but to live well, one thing suffices: a sound, peaceable mind, superior to fortune. "Nature has wisely provided for our wants, by ordaining that they should be few. Every one can possess happiness if he pleases, it is in his own power; exterior things can do but little to increase or diminish our interior contentment. Therefore all our thoughts should tend to this object, all our cares centre in this end, all our desires converge toward this point: to possess peace in our own souls, and to be content with our own goods; the rest we should freely abandon to God. What happiness can approach more nearly to divine felicity than this? Restrain thyself to few things, and let those few be such as depend only on thyself." Thus says Seneca.

When the philosophers affirmed that every man could find his beatitude in his own soul, they said a great deal too much, as St. Austin well observes. It is absolutely necessary that a cause more noble than self should produce this excellent effect. Our happiness we can indeed find within ourselves, but only when God is there. We are naturally mutable and unquiet; our understanding, our will and all our powers are, of themselves, changeable and inclined to disturbance; it is only God who can make us constant, and establish us in true and solid repose.

In the reign of Justinian, the city of Antioch was frequently disturbed and tormented by earthquakes, and the only remedy the inhabitants could find for this misfortune was to write on their doors the following words which had been been revealed to a servant of God : "*Jesus Christ is with us, remain firm.*" All the houses on which this was inscribed were saved, while those destitute of this safeguard were destroyed. For this reason, the emperor ordained that the city should renounce the name of Antioch, which it had taken from its founder, a proud, turbulent man, and assume that of Theopolis, which signifies city of God. In like manner, it is necessary that God come into our heart to deliver it from its troubles and agitations, and dwell in it to establish it in peace forever.

To place ourselves beyond the reach of all inquietude, let

us make our dwelling in the heart of our Lord. There we shall find unalterable serenity, for nothing can enter that sanctuary to injure those who dwell therein.

2. Patience produces peace as its proper effect, its natural fruit. Patience enables us to suffer all transitory calamities with interior tranquillity, showing no sign of emotion by word or deed. Tertullian beautifully paints this virtue in these admirable words: "Patience carries a sweet and gracious countenance, a serene forehead, eyes meekly lowered, and brows never contracted by anger. Its mouth speaks little, and its whole deportment eloquently testifies to a good conscience." "In patience you shall possess your souls," said our Lord. By this virtue you shall become masters of yourselves, and enjoy peace.

"The dominion of the soul is attributed to patience," says St. Gregory, "because patience is the root and guardian of all other virtues. Now, we acquire the perfect dominion of our souls by patience; for it teaches us to command ourselves and to restrain ourselves, to rule and govern our passions." Without it, we should lead a life of chagrin and misery. It is impossible that we shall not have much to suffer from ourselves and others in this life: well, if we fail to acquire patience, we shall always be discontented, and on thorns. It is the part of a wise man to sweeten the evils of life, and, since he has to walk on thorns, to let them prick him as little as possible. The remedy for all annoyances is to bear them patiently, and to accommodate ourselves gently to what cannot be avoided. It is high prudence to make a virtue of necessity, and, when we cannot avoid a thing, to render it, if not useful, as little prejudicial as possible.

3. The third means is humility. Our Lord taught us this, when He said: "Learn of me to be meek and humble of heart, and you shall find rest to your souls." St. John Climacus observes that, as clouds are dissipated by the light

of the sun, so troubles and bitterness are chased from the soul by humility. In another place he personifies pride, and, when he asks its origin, it makes reply : "My father is Ostentation, and my greatest enemy is called Humility."

The mystical doctor, Rusbrocius, on this subject, writes : "True humility possesses this wonderful advantage, that it bestows the precious treasure of peace ; for it banishes all fears of abasement, contempt and affronts. If we examine the cause of our sadness, we shall find it to be some hidden pride, some subtle ambition, some secret self-esteem, and always some deficiency of humility. Now, as a thing can be in repose only in its centre, or at least in the effort to reach its centre, so the man, who is in the centre of his own nothingness, where humility places and retains him, possesses true tranquillity ; outside of this centre, he should be in continual agitation and trouble."

4. The fourth means is, to have few desires, and to moderate even those few. As winds agitate the sea, so desires disturb the peace of the soul. When the tempest ceases, the sea becomes calm. When ardent desires are banished, the heart enjoys peace. This is so true, that even blind persons have perceived it. Tiresias said that the best kind of life is that in which nothing is desired or loved with excess. Chilo, the Lacedæmonian, wrote, in letters of gold, on the temple at Delphi : "We ought not to desire anything with too much ardor."

These four means are very useful to pacify our hearts, and keep our minds in repose. There are many others, but the best and most efficacious of all, the one to which all may be reduced, is conformity of our will to the will of God, perfect submission to all the orders and dispositions of His providence. In fact, our trouble and uneasiness can come only from our resistance to the appointments of God.

"Who can resist God and have peace?" asks Job. On

the contrary, David says: "Those who love Thy law and follow Thy orders shall enjoy profound peace, and nothing shall be able to scandalize them;" because they know that nothing happens but by the will or permission of God, who governs all with infinite wisdom and goodness: consequently they believe that all events may be turned to their profit. "Never do anything unwillingly," says Seneca; "keep your mind in such a state that nothing can happen to you against your will. Do not act in opposition to your inclinations, by force or constraint, but will all things as they occur." Will what God wills, and you will always follow your own will.

On this subject we can say many profitable things, which we will range under three heads: the first, the dispositions which God makes of us, and the ways by which He conducts us to salvation; the second will show how we ought to follow them; and the third, the immense advantages which perfect submission to the divine will confers upon us.

§ 3.—*Of the ways of God with men, and some of the qualities of His ways.*

The Holy Ghost will open this subject for us by the words He said of the patriarch Jacob, and which the Church applies to the just: "Wisdom has conducted the just man by right ways."

These ways are the means and inventions which God employs to turn us from sin, to correct our depraved inclinations, to eradicate our vicious habits, to extinguish the fire of our concupiscence, to incline us to exercise good works, to lead us to the perfection to which we are called, and to operate our salvation. As a traveller reaches his journey's end by roads and ways, so by these means we reach salvation. These ways are different for every one of us. It is true there are common ways, as there are great beaten tracks: such are the commandments of God and His Church for Christians; such are the rules and constitutions for those who embrace a religious life. But, besides these common ways, there are also particular ways,—little by-paths through which God conducts each soul ; and as there are not in the world two persons with faces exactly alike, two characters entirely simlilar, two of the just who have attained precisely the same degree of grace, or will attain in the next the same degree of glory, so God has his own particular way with every soul. Hence the Church says of each of the elect : "There was no one found like this one." It adds extremely to the magnificence of heaven and the beauty of its august and glorious company, that, though all are endowed with admirable and ravishing perfections, yet no two are alike. Hence the Royal Prophet sings that the Queen, that is the Church, is " clothed with golden robes, surrounded with variety." Now, if men are dissimilar in a state of glory, they must be dissimilar in grace, which is glory sketched, and, by consequence, in the means of grace.

Each soul has a particular path by which to go to God. As in a circle all the lines go from the circumference to the centre by different ways, so souls have come from God, their first principle ; of whom an ancient said very well, that He is a circle of which the centre is everywhere, and the circumference nowhere ; and they go to Him, as to their centre, by different routes. One goes to Him by light, another by darkness ; one by poverty, another by riches, one by health, another by sickness ; and he who to-day is dazzled with light, and leaps for joy, may, to-morrow, be obliged to advance in darkness and tread among thorns and briers.

All these ways are good, because they are marked by the goodness, wisdom and power of God. Hence Habacuc describes them as paths to eternal felicity. Solomon called them *ways which conduct to justice*, virtue and perfection ; and his father David styles them *ways of life*, and *right ways;* that is to say, according to the definition mathematicians give of the right line, the shortest roads to salvation, which cannot stray between the two extremities, the term of departure and the term of rest: because they come from God, and they go to God.

Besides the rectitude and goodness which distinguish the ways of God, they have other qualities which are very remarkable, for they are wonderful, hidden, and often apparently contrary to their ends. "God is wonderful in His saints," says holy David. He is not only wonderful in His saints when He has perfected His own work in them, but also when He is accomplishing that work. He is admirable by the forms He gives them, by the traits He impresses on them, and by the instruments with which He fashions them. Speaking of the journey of the Israelites toward the promised land,—a journey which typified that of the predestined toward heaven, the Sage says: "God brought them out of Egypt and led them to Palestine in a wonderful manner, and by strange roads; doing prodigies in heaven, on earth and in the waters, on men and on beasts, to conduct them thither."

But the better to comprehend this, we must mount higher, even to the source. Let us rememeber, then, that the greatest of God's designs is the salvation of man,—of man, not of angels; for, though angels be more noble and perfect, He had decreed to receive incomparably more honor from the human nature than from the angelic. This truth clearly appears in our Lord, whose least action has given more glory to His Father than all the homages which angels could ever render Him. The same may be understood also, in its measure, of our Lady. As, then, the salvation of man is the highest project which God proposes to Himself, in order to execute it, He has selected means the most admirable and excellent, and the best adapted to such an end.

I need not enlarge on the fact that He has, for the salvation of man, created heaven and earth, the sun, the stars, and all things animate and inanimate; that He has given us, for guardians, His angels, the princes of His court. We include all when we say that His only Son became man for this end, that He was born in a poor stable, led a life of suffering and labor for thirty-three years, which He terminated by dying in the most bitter anguish on a cross between two thieves. This is surely a wonderful means which God has chosen for the salvation of man. Add, to all this, the holy sacrament of the altar, in which, for our sakes, and to apply to us the merits of His life and death, He works such immense prodigies, and reverses all the order of nature.

Since, then, the universal means is so wonderful, the particular means, which are dependent on it and follow it, ought to resemble it in some manner. All the elect are fashioned on our Lord, they are images of this grand Prototype, living copies of this Divine Original; for they are elected, as St. Paul often repeats, to be associated with His dispositions, to be incorporated with Him, to share in His grace and His glory. They are, as it were, branches of this tree of life, living on its sap; they are formed on the same rules, cast in the same mould, and conducted by similar paths. This made Him say to the apostles: "I dispose to you, as my Father hath disposed to me, a kingdom." I shall lead you by the same ways that conducted me thither; to reach it, you must adopt similar means. Now, as those assigned me by my Father were so strange, that no created intelligence could divine them, yours ought to bear them, even in this point, some resemblance.

§ 4.—*The ways of God are hidden.*

The ways of God on souls are not only admirable, they are, moreover, hidden and obscure, so that we sometimes cannot discern them. God, as Job remarks, leads man by obscure paths, so that it looks as if the journey to salvation was to be made in the darkness of night. "The bird hath not known the path," says this holy man, "neither hath the eye of the vulture beheld it. Hast thou entered the depths of the sea, and walked in the lowest parts of the deep? Have the gates of death been opened to thee, and hast thou seen the darksome doors? Hast thou considered the breadth of the earth? Tell me if thou knowest all things. Where does light dwell, and where is the place of darkness? That thou mayest bring everything to its own bounds, and understand the paths of the house thereof. Hast thou entered into the storehouses of the snow, or hast thou beheld the treasures of the hail? Which I have prepared for the time of the enemy, against the day of battle and war. By what way is the light spread and heat divided upon the earth? Who gave a course to violent showers, or a way for noisy thunder? Dost thou know the order of the heavens, and canst thou set down the reason thereof on earth?" All this is hidden from thee.

St. Augustine therefore called the vocation of the elect profound and secret, because of the means chosen by God to secure it, as poverty, sickness, contempt, sorrow, afflictions, and all the others which refer to it and compose it. "All the ways of God are mercy and truth," says David. But, as St. Austin explains this verse, "as the ways of God cannot be investigated, and His proceedings are hidden, by consequence, His mercy to deliver and to do good, and His justice to judge and to punish, are hidden also, and cannot be investigated."

The Israelites were conducted to the promised land by paths and solitudes which no person had previously trodden. "They journeyed toward Jerusalem," says the Book of Wisdom, "through wildernesses that were not inhabited, and in desert places they pitched their tents. To conduct them through roads of which they had no knowledge, they received for a guide a burning pillar of fire," during the night, and a cloud during the day. These directed their course, making them turn now to the north, and then toward the south ; now eastward, again westward ; advance, recede or stop, without knowing what they were to do next, "going many times around the mount of Seir," as Moses expresses it. This is a figure of the ways by which the elect are conducted to salvation, and of the dispositions of God in the government of men, which are often an enigma to our minds.

In fact, are we not surrounded by such enigmas as these : Why does God cut down, in the flower of his age, a man who is capable of rendering great service to His Church, while He permits others to live, who are useless or even injurious to society? How is it that, sometimes, a person of talent and capacity cannot succeed in anything, while another, who is his inferior, succeeds in all his undertakings and is applauded on all sides? Whence comes it that a man who has pure intentions of advancing the glory of God, and is resolved to do great things to promote it, is often controlled, hindered and prevented from executing his good designs ; and that, not only by the wicked who compass their own evil ends by the ruin of his good ones, but even by well-meaning men, who, actuated by good motives, imagine that they ought to act in this manner?

But consider what happens frequently regarding the vocation of persons to the religious life. There are many who ardently desire this vocation, and yet never receive it. Others have the vocation, but yet cannot enter religion for want of health or want of means. Some, on the contrary, God constrains to enter it, forcing them, if we may so speak, to take this step. How many ladies of noble birth who, because they have not wealth enough to marry according to their rank, and have too much pride to marry beneath them, determine to become religious, which they would not think of doing if they were richer! How many men have entered religion because they met with reverses and disappointments in the world! "O the depths of the riches of the wisdom and the knowledge of God!" exclaims St. Paul. How incomprehensible are His judgments, and how unsearchable His ways!

To appreciate these mysterious obscurities with which God envelops His conduct, hiding the paths by which he leads us, we must remember that this life is a life of darkness and faith, as the next life is a life of brightness and vision. "We walk by faith and not by sight," says St. Paul. Our salvation is a mystery of faith, not only as regards what we must believe, but also as regards what we must do and suffer. Our interior and exterior afflictions, our sadness, the injuries done us, our maladies, our antipathies, our natural contrarieties with our neighbor; the overthrow of our plans, the oppositions we encounter, and all the other pieces which compose the work of our salvation, are secret, and, like articles of faith, there is much more to be believed concerning them than can be seen.

As the mysteries of the Old Law were figures of those of the New, so the mysteries of the New Law, and the state of grace in which we live, are shadows of those of the state of glory in the future life, in which we hope to live forever. And as the Jews did not comprehended the truth of the mysteries of their law, a truth clearly unfolded in ours, so the mysteries of our law and the economy of our salvation are now hidden with a veil, which shall be drawn back in another life.

"The law," says St. Paul, "having a shadow of the good things to come," was an image of the goods of grace, not the truth and substance of them. "The Church refers the goods of the New Law to those of paradise, and speaking of the greatest of our sacraments and the most adorable of our mysteries, prays in these words: "Grant us, O Lord! the eternal possession of Thy Divinity, of which the temporal participation of Thy precious body and blood is a pledge and a figure.'

"We now see things through a glass and in a dark manner," says St. Paul; "but in heaven we shall see them face to face."

The apostles themselves did not understand the greater part of what our Lord revealed to them. When He walked upon the sea, they took Him for a phantom, and shrieked out for fear, "because their heart was blinded, and they understood not concerning the loaves" which, a little before, He had miraculously multiplied to feed His followers; nevertheless, they might easily have seen that He who wrought one miracle could perform another. When He said to the Jews, "Destroy this temple, and in three days I will raise it up," it was to the apostles an enigma, of which He gave no explanation, and which they understood only after the resurrection, when they saw that His body, which had been destroyed by death, was gloriously resuscitated. Going up to Jerusalem for the last time, and speaking of the passion and the death He should there suffer, His disciples, according to St. Luke, "understood none of these things, and this word was hid from them, and they understood not the things that were said." When St. Peter resisted, and would not suffer our Lord to wash his feet, He said to him: "What I do, thou knowest not now, but thou shalt know hereafter." When His holy Mother expressed the grief which His three days' absence had caused her and St. Joseph, saying, "Son, why hast Thou done so to us? Behold Thy father and I have sought Thee sorrowing!" He answered: "How is it that you sought me? Did you not know that I must be about my Father's business?" And St. Luke remarks that they "understood not the word He spoke unto them." Thus are the ways by which God leads us, obscure or secret.

Among the mysteries of faith, there are some to which we could attain by the sole light of reason: such as the unity of one God, Creator of the universe, the necessity of death, the immortality of the soul. But there are others which, with all our capacity, we could never discover: as the Trinity of Persons in God, the Incarnation, the Blessed Eucharist, and the greater number of revealed truths. So, with regard to the great business of our salvation, many things certainly and visibly tend to it: as the sermons we hear, the good books we read, the holy inspirations we receive, and similar things. But there are also many others which, covertly and in secret, tend to the same end: as reverses, misfortunes, sickness and other accidents, which displease us when they come, but which, later on, we shall find to have been very salutary. Our Lord, in these occurrences, says to each of us as He did to St. Peter: "What I do, thou knowest not now, but thou shalt know hereafter." Be patient; in a little while you shall experience that all things turn to your profit, if you use them as they come, according to my design. God's conduct in our regard may be compared to the course of certain rivers, as the Tigris in Asia and the Niger in Africa, for example, whose waters flow sometimes above-ground, visible to all, and sometimes through hidden canals and subterranean passages.

§ 5. *Why the ways of God are so hidden.*

Why do we not see the paths by which God leads us, or why do we see them so slightly? I answer, first, that it is because we have so little intellect and light. The greater part, even of corporal things which strike our senses, and which are not beyond our capacity, are unknown to us, for who understands all the properties and effects of material things? And this being so, ought we to be astonished if we cannot attain to the knowledge of things spiritual and divine? For, with all our understanding, says the Book of Wisdom, "hardly do we guess aright at things that are upon earth; and with labor do we find the things that are before us. But the things that are in heaven,—who shall search out?"

Verily, if we do not easily know what we see and touch, it would be unreasonable to expect that we could have much knowledge of interior things. It is not so difficult, I admit, to learn that pride reigns in our mind, obstinacy in our judgments, weakness in our will, disorder in our affections, and extravagance in our imaginations; but to remedy these evils, to find a specific for each one of them,—this is no easy matter. It is the same with the maladies of the soul as with those of the body. You can feel the fever which consumes you, the wound which tortures you, but you do not always know how to break the fever or heal the wound ; what medicine you ought to take, and how often you should take it ; whether it would serve you to be bled, and if so, in what part ought a vein to be opened.

2. Though we had much greater minds than we have, we should not be able to penetrate the ways and designs of God ; because they are extremely high, and surpass our comprehension. "Who can understand the ways of God?" asks the wise son of Sirach. And before him, David had said : "Lord, Thou hast proved me and known me : Thou hast known my sitting down and my uprising. Thou hast understood my thoughts afar off, and hast foreseen all my ways. Behold, O Lord ! Thou hast known all things. Thy knowledge is become wonderful to me : it is high, and I cannot reach it." Eliu, the friend of Job, had said before David : "Behold, God is high in His strength, and none is like Him among the lawgivers. Who can search out His ways? Behold, God is great, exceeding our knowledge." Hence the Spouse, speaking of the hair of her Beloved,—that is, according to the interpretation of Theodoret, the thoughts which emanate from His mind,— says : "His locks are as branches of palm-trees, black as a raven." His thoughts are like the palm, which is an emblem

of love, and which is useful for many purposes. As we ascend a palm-tree, its trunk grows softer, the ascent becomes more easy, and on the top we gather excellent fruits. The thoughts of God in our regard, the ways by which He conducts the business of our salvation, proceed from the love He bears us; and though they are often contrary to our desires and painful to our nature, yet they are always very salutary for us. But they are black like the raven, because they are obscure.

3. Though we had sufficient light and capacity to comprehend the dealings of God with our souls, God would, nevertheless, hide them from us, as He hid from the demons things concerning the life and death of our Lord, which they could have learned naturally. God acts in this manner with us, to place us in the happy necessity of practising faith, confidence, humility, submission, love and many other virtues. Now, all this evidently shows that secret and obscure ways are better for us here, than open and clear ways would be.

§ 6.—*The ways of God often seem contrary to their ends.*

As God infinitely surpasses in excellence and perfection all created things; as angels and men, the noblest of His works, are, before Him, only atoms and dust; as all their intellect and wisdom is, in comparison with His, only ignorance and darkness,—so the orders and designs of God must be infinitely more elevated than theirs. As, moreover, the felicity God has prepared for man,—considered either in the operating cause, which is God; or the final cause, which is the eternal possession of Him,—is the most sublime of all things, we must conclude that the ways by which He conducts man to beatitude ought naturally to transcend all our ideas. "My thoughts are not your thoughts," says He by the prophet Isaias, "neither are my ways your ways: as the heavens are elevated above the earth, so are my thoughts exalted above your thoughts, and my ways above yours." In conducting an affair, God does what we would not do, under the circumstances, and leaves undone what we should do. For example, if God and a man love the same person, they comport themselves very differently toward her : the man believes himself obliged to procure, for her, honors, riches and pleasures ; he would never think of treating her harshly, of sending her sickness, of exposing her to persecution and contempt. But God shows His love by sending all these evils, and refusing or retrenching all those goods ; as evidently appears by the manner in which He acted toward His Son, our Lord, toward our Blessed Lady, and all those whom he specially loved.

St. Peter, being scandalized to hear our Lord speak of His sufferings and death, " began to rebuke Him, saying : Lord, be it far from Thee : this shall not be unto Thee." But Jesus reproved Peter, saying that he spoke like a man animated with a human spirit, not with the spirit of God ; thus showing the diversity of the respective sentiments of God and man.

Do we not often see that those whose position gives them much facility for promoting the glory of God and the happiness of men, as the great, will not do so ; and those who desire to promote the honor of God and the good of man, as the just, have neither the authority nor the ability to do so? God often gives graces to persons who, He knows, will abuse them, and denies them to others who would have made a good use of them. These are the rains of which Job speaks, which fall in desert places and on rocks, while neighboring lands that would have profited by them, are parched with thirst. Now, if these things depended on us, it is certain that, following our own light, we should act otherwise ; we should give the power to do good to him that had the will to use it, and graces to those who would turn them to good account. We do not sow wheat on sand, but in a good soil; we do not give our money to a person who, we think, might throw it into the river, but to one who will employ it well. Thus, the ways of God are different from ours. Still more: very often the ways of God seem contrary to the ends to which they refer: heat is not more opposed to cold, or dryness to humidity, than the ways of God are opposed, in appearance at least, to the ends He has in view. He promised a numerous posterity to Abraham, through his son Isaac, and then commanded him to kill this son. Now, if He wishes to multiply the race of Abraham through Isaac, why does He command the slaughter of Isaac? And if He intended that Isaac should be offered in sacrifice, why did he make such a promise? Afterward, God gives Isaac a sterile wife. What bond can her sterility have with the promised fecundity, or the fecundity with the sterility? God sent Gideon against an immense number of Madianites, Amalekites and other peoples, to defeat them; nevertheless, He desires him to disband all his men except three hundred, and these have for arms only empty pitchers, with lighted lamps and trumpets. Our Lord gives sight to a man born blind: but how? By putting clay on his eyes,—a proceeding which would suffice to blind him, if his sight were ever so good.

But let us, in proof of this, examine at greater length the history of Joseph and that of David. God had resolved to elevate Joseph above his brethren, and, though he was nearly the last in age, to make him the first in dignity, so that the rest should bow down before him; as was foreshown him in two dreams which he had, and which he related to his father and brothers: the first, of his sheaf, before which the sheaves of his brothers bent; the other, of the sun and moon and eleven stars that adored him. God, then, has formed this design; but let us now see the means He uses to accomplish it.

At first, He permits the brothers to conceive so great a hatred for Joseph, that they never speak a kind word to him. Later on, in consequence of this hatred, they resolve to put him to death. However, not wishing to imbrue their hands in his blood, they cast him into a deep pit, and leave him there to die of hunger. They are not moved by the sweet name of brother, by his beauty and innocence, by his prayers and tears, or by the consideration of their father whom the loss of this dear son would render inconsolable. Rescued from the pit, he was sold to some merchants, and by them to Potiphar, an officer of Pharaoh's household. Potiphar, deceived by his wife, cast him into prison, and thus recompensed the signal services he had rendered him, and the heroic chastity he had practised. There he dwelt, according to Philo, thirteen years, and, according to others, three, in anguish and misery, for he was scourged, outraged and ill-treated. Speaking of this illustrious innocent, David says: "They humbled his feet in fetters, the iron pierced his soul, until the word of the Lord came. And the king released him, and made him ruler of all his possessions."

Now, how did God elevate Joseph? By what degrees did he mount to the glory destined for him? By the envy and hatred of his brethren, by slavery and imprisonment, by false accusations, chains, and all sorts of evils. Afterward, the favor of the king, the plenty and famine of Egypt, the necessities of Jacob and his other sons, were secret ways by which the design of God was carried into effect. And God might well say to Joseph what He afterward said to another by his prophet Ezechiel: "You shall know that I have not done without cause all that I have done in these events."

Let us now speak of David: God designed to make him king in place of Saul. Let us consider the means by which He put the crown on his head. Contrarieties in abundance occurred in the fortune of this famous shepherd. First, as to time: he is anointed, and with the unction receives the right to the kingdom, in the twentieth year of his age and the eighteenth of the reign of Saul. He must wait, nevertheless, till the death of this prince to enjoy the throne, but, even after this, Isboseth, son of Saul, disputes it with him for seven years and a half. Secondly, as to obstacles: how great were those which he encountered, and from which he suffered! Saul, gnawed by envy, employed all his power and all the inventions of his malice and fury to destroy him. He persecutes him incessantly, and seeks him everywhere. Having heard that he was sick in his house, he sent officers to seize him, saying, "Bring him to me in the bed that I may kill him." Three times he cast at David the javelin he usually held in his hand, "thinking to nail him to the wall." He sent him to fight with the Philistines, hoping that he might be slain. He constrained him by violent pursuits to hide himself in caves, and rocks, and inaccessible places, says the sacred text; to seek protection of strange princes, as the King of Gath and the King of Moab. In fact, the fury of Saul went so far that he ordered to be massacred in his presence eighty-five priests, of whom Abimelech was the chief; and, after that, caused all the inhabitants of their city, even children and beasts, to be slain, because Abimelech had innocently allowed David to pass through Nobe, the city of the priests, and did not arrest him. One day, while at table, he darted his javelin at his own son Jonathan, because Jonathan loved David and took his part. See through what afflictions David had to pass before he enjoyed what God had solemnly promised him!

But in the ways of God there is nothing more extraordinary than the means He adopted to save the human race; that is to say, the death of His Son, who died nailed to a cross. This has always appeared so strange, so extravagant, and so contrary to reason, that, according to St. Paul, the Greeks held it to be pure folly; and the Jews, who possessed the knowledge of the true God, who were instructed by His prophets and governed by His laws, esteemed it a scandal and a blasphemy to think or to say that Christ was the Son of God.

St. John Chrysostom, explaining these words of St. Paul, "We preach Christ crucified : to the Jews indeed a stumbling block, and to the Gentiles foolishness," says : "When we solicit the Jews to believe, they answer : 'Cast out devils, raise the dead, work other miracles, and we shall believe.' And what do we reply, but that He in whom they should believe, was crucified !" This, far from attracting those who do not wish to come, would naturally drive away those who are eager to join us. If we ask the Greeks to embrace our faith, they demand logic and eloquence, they desire riches, honors and pleasures ; and we despise these things, and preach only the cross, in which they see but poverty, contempt and sorrow,— the cross which was first announced by unknown, ignorant fishermen, the refuse of the world. Since, then, we do not give what is asked of us, and even give what is diametrically opposed to it, and, nevertheless, subject souls to Christ by this means, it is clear that God leads us to salvation by ways that seem contrary to it.

Thus, the immense riches of heaven are promised to voluntary poverty, glory and greatness to opprobrium and abasement ; pleasures and delights in paradise are exchanged for sufferings of body and mind ; and the clear vision of all mysteries is the recompense which awaits the obscure knowledge which faith gives us here below. Thus, by darkness we go to light, by misery we reach happiness, by sickness we acquire health, and by temporal death we attain to life eternal.

§ 7.—*The ways of God are often contrary to our desires.*

Not only are the ways of God often apparently contrary to their ends, but they are, still more often, contrary to our desires, to our enterprises, to our honor, and to our convenience. They compel us to do what we would avoid, and avoid what we would gladly do. We daily meet with divers obstacles to our designs. They proceed from times, places, accidents, business which comes inopportunely; from persons, and not unfrequently from sources, whence we should not expect them. Sometimes the merest trifles impede us, as flies and gnats tormented Pharaoh, whose pride God wished to tame, not by lions or elephants, but by these weak insects.

I could relate many examples on this subject, but I shall content myself with that of St. Bernard, which is very illustrious. This holy man, being inspired by God to preach the Crusade, and commissioned by the pope to the same effect, went through kingdoms, provinces and cities, exciting every one to this holy enterprise, with such zeal and success, that the Emperor Conrad III, the King of France, and other princes, with an immense multitude of men, formed an army of Germans, Franks, Italians and natives of all parts of Europe, to proceed to the Holy Land, and in this Crusade to increase the conquests which the Christians had made in the preceding ones. The design was holy, the war just, the zeal laudable, but the success was not commensurate: for, through the perfidy of the Greeks, the army perished almost entirely in Syria. The emperor was constrained to return to Germany, and King Louis to France, without having gained any conquest, but not without suffering serious loss.

The blame of this misfortune fell entirely on St. Bernard, for he had been the prime mover of the enterprise. His sanctity and miracles were forgotten, he was regarded as a deceiver, a hard-hearted man who had sent multitudes of persons, ecclesiastical and secular, of every rank and condition, to be butchered in a foreign land. Writing to Pope Eugenius, the saint himself says : "We announced peace, and there was no peace; we promised rest, and behold only trouble! Did we then act rashly, and of our own will? Did we not follow your commands, or rather those of God, in following yours? All the world knows that the judgments of God are true ; but the late event is so profound an abyss that we may well call those blessed who do not take scandal at it. But how shall human presumption dare to blame what it cannot understand? Let us call to mind the acts of Providence in times past, that we may obtain some light on this matter. Moses, when he brought the Israelites out of Egypt, promised them a better land ; for, if he had not, they would not have followed him. He brought them out, but he failed to bring them to the land he promised them ; and yet we certainly cannot charge this grievous event to the temerity of their leader. He acted by the command of God, who foresaw everything, and confirmed his words by a miracle." St. Bernard adds that, as the sins of the tribes of Israel caused them to perish, so those of the Crusaders, who imitated them in their sin, were the cause of their misfortune. He next recalls what happened to these tribes of Israel, who, though they fought by the command of God, were twice beaten by the tribe of Benjamin. "Now, how, I pray you," adds he, "would the Crusaders have treated me, if I had prevailed on them to return a second time to the battle ; and if, after a second defeat, I had said to them, 'Go back a third time'?" And yet this was actually the case with the Israelites ; and it was not till the third time that they obtained the victory.

Certainly, when the saint reflected on all the circumstances of this Crusade, he seemed to have some reason to say to God, as Jeremias the prophet did : "Thou hast deceived me, O Lord! and I am deceived. Thou hast been stronger than I, and Thou hast prevailed. I am become a laughing-stock all day: all scoff at me." But St. Bernard never doubted the truth of his divine mission; he knew that God never deceives in reality, though he does not always execute His promises according to the interpretation which men give them.

§ 8.—*Why the ways of God are thus contrary.*

Why are the ways of God contrary to their ends, at least in appearance, and why are they really contrary to our will and inclinations? For this, I shall give two reasons.

1. The first regards God. Being infinitely wise, and having indicated our ends, He alone knows the means most proper to reach them. Hence, if He conducts us by ways which are apparently opposed to their ends, we ought to hold for certain that these ways are the best for us.

God being infinitely powerful, all means are good in His hands, and there is nothing so weak or insignificant that He cannot turn it to account when He pleases. In His hands, everything can become a means of salvation. Water, which, naturally, is useful only to wash away physical uncleanness, He uses in baptism, to cleanse away the stains of the soul; fire, which naturally burns, refreshed the children in the furnace of Babylon. Through poverty He confers riches, through sickness health, and through infamy glory. This is not the case with men, or with most of natural causes, for it is necessary that there should always be some proportion between the means they use, and the end they propose. If we want to write, we must take a pen; if we want to learn, we must study. But when God employs His absolute power over His creatures, when He moves these arms which all nature must obey without resistance, bitter and deadly things become sweet and salutary, because He, in whose hands they are, is infinitely good, wise and strong. In our hands, without the aid of God, the sweetest things become poisonous. So, then, the contrariety of the ways of God is such only in our eyes and to our minds—to God all things are proper for the accomplishment of His will : a good medicine may be bitter to the taste of a sick man, but to health it is very useful.

2. The second reason is drawn from ourselves. There is no greater obstacle to the designs of God and our own happiness, than we ourselves. God, to lead us to true felicity, designs to take us, as it were, from under our own control, to annihilate us, to break our unruly will, and destroy our false judgments, the two great sources of all our evils. Now, He executes all this very adroitly and efficaciously by these contrary ways.

Certainly, since we cannot be content by the possession of ourselves, but only by the possession of God, it is absolutely necessary to go out of ourselves, that we may be replenished with God. The best means of quitting self, and becoming united with God, are to die to our corrupt nature, to purify it, to go out of it, and, in this manner, empty our souls of self, that they may be filled with God.

§ 9.—*Conclusion.*

To sum up in a few words all that has been already said, we must remark and retain that the ways by which God conducts us to salvation are various ; that they are adjusted to the respective conditions of all persons, and the designs He has on each ; that they are admirable because of their principle and their end, because of their dependence on the wonderful means He adopted to save the human race, namely, the incarnation, life and death of His Son ; that they are hidden, because in this life we walk in the obscurity of faith, of which they are secrets and mysteries ; that they are often contrary to our inclinations, and that this is best for us, because they purify us more and make us die to self, thereby rendering us more worthy of the possession of God by grace now, and by glory in the life to come.

These ways are from God, both as a whole and in each of their parts, in their substance and in their accidents, in their circumstances of time, place and persons, yea, in their most trivial details. The waters of the Tigris, whether aboveground or in subterranean canals, have but one source. All the parts of a watch are fashioned by the same maker, so that there is no part which he has not arranged, to which he has not applied his mind, and which is not the effect of his science. It is the same in the matter of our salvation. There is nothing which refers to it, whether loss or gain, honor or contempt, joy or sadness, pleasures or afflictions, health or sickness, life or death, which is not directed and sent from God as means to attain it.

From this we must conclude that all these means are good, holy and divine, that they are ways of perfection, paths of life, and short and secure roads to heaven. All come from God. He has given to each the power to become a means of salvation and an instrument of our sanctification; for, His goodness can have only good ends, His wisdom cannot err, and nothing is impossible to His power. "All His ways are beautiful," says Solomon, "all His designs are adapted to their purpose. The Lord by wisdom hath founded the earth; He hath established the heavens by prudence."

All these truths being certain, every person should, in consequence, make great account of his state in life, and esteem highly his employment, his condition, his rank, and all that God has sent him. The body he has, be it weakly or robust; the soul, the memory, the will; the accidents, pleasant or unpleasant, that occur; riches, poverty, glory, infamy and the like,—he ought to take all as the path by which God designs to conduct him to eternal beatitude; and he ought to follow it conformably to this word which God said by Isaias : "This is the way, walk ye in it : and go not aside, either to the right hand or to the left."

Be careful to take your own road, and not that of another : your own road will lead you to salvation ; another's would lead you to a precipice. The path of your neighbor is good for him, but it would be bad for you : for him it is a road to virtue and sanctity ; for you it would be a road to vice and imperfection. Let each, then, follow his own road which God has marked out for him, and not mind the paths of others. Let him follow it faithfully and constantly, let him make a good use of everything God sends him, for all things are sent for his salvation. But to do this, two thing are necessary.

1. Being ignorant and feeble, we ought not to desire to choose our own ways and means of salvation and perfection, but leave to the Divine Providence, who is infinitely good, wise and powerful, the liberty to choose them for us. As God has ordained the means by which man comes out of himself as his first principle, it belongs to Him, also, to constitute those by which man may return to Him as to his last end.

2. Man ought to give himself wholly to God in the way He has destined, and by good use of the means which He furnishes, as if he had no other way, no other means : and, in fact, he has not. He ought to be, so to say, without relish for the ways of God with others, and the means He gives them, and apply himself solely to God's dispositions of himself. By this unity of application to the way God has traced for him, he commences that perfect alliance of the soul with God which conducts to unity of spirit with Him. But he must bind himself to God in the way which God prescribes, and not in any other way, however good ; for he must avoid the secret engagement which self-love negotiates between the soul and God and His graces, taking all things as means and

using them only as such, relinquishing them and adopting them when and how God pleases.

We ought to receive all the dispositions of God regarding us with esteem, honor and reverence: they are holy and divine things. We ought to view them with eyes of respect, and touch them with religious hands, as we do sacred vessels; accepting them with absolute submission and entire abandonment, as selected for us by an infinite Wisdom, as mysteries of faith, celestial secrets and works which surpass our comprehension.

In effect, it would be preposterous that God, being incomparably more wise than all men and angels, immeasurably more elevated above the highest cherubim than they are above the meanest insects,—God, who is essentially wisdom itself, He who made this grand universe, who governs it with an order so admirable, and who has arranged it with a symmetry so perfect; of whom Moses says that all His ways are judgments,—that God being the infallible rule which adjusts all, it would be extravagant, we repeat, that, when He wills to dispose and ordain something for your salvation, you should presume, with your narrow intellect and profound ignorance, to improve, to condemn, or to desire in any way to alter what He has selected for you.

The secret of this important practice consists in making few reflections on the actions of creatures whatever they may be, but raising ourselves above them to the consideration, the esteem and the approbation of Divine Providence who rules all, and by His operations, and those of His creatures, tends always to His ends, the glory of God and our salvation. In all the events of life, we ought to regard with a simple eye the action and the intention of this adorable Providence, without reflecting on or remarking the conduct of his creatures, whom we ought to consider only as His instruments.

All this we ought to do, and yet we neglect it, and often

do the contrary. As a dog bites the stone which has wounded him, not the arm which propelled it, so we stop at the creature, without thinking of God whose instrument he is. The reason why there are so few wise people among us, is because there are very few who, according to the definition Aristotle gives of a wise man, consider things in their sources; very few who regard them in God, their first cause, and judge of them by His rules. Most persons see things only in their secondary causes, and form their judgments accordingly.

God said by Isaias a very remarkable thing: "The King of Assyria is the rod and staff of my anger. I will send him to a deceitful nation, and I will give him a charge against the people of my wrath to take away the spoils and to lay hold on the prey, and to tread them down like the mire of the streets. But he shall not take it so, and his heart shall not think it." Now, the Assyrians, in the chastisements they inflicted on the Jews, did not look upon themselves as instruments of God's justice, nor did the Jews regard them as executors of God's will; in a similar manner, we receive all that happens us, in a purely natural way, and not as coming from God. If any one should displease us, we refer his conduct to his ignorance, or his malice, or his envy, or some other source of a secondary nature, and from this mode of acting come all our troubles; while we ought to refer all occurrences whatever to the clear and pure source of the providence of God, who works for our salvation. This would remedy all our evils, and we should hereby find calm in the midst of every tempest. Let us, then, mount up to God, who sends or permits all things for our good; and enlightened by reason, or rather by faith, believe that whatever is done by His creatures, with the single exception of sin, is done originally by the hand of God.

When the surgeon bleeds us, scarifies our wounds, or cuts off a member, we are not angry with him on account of the pain he causes us, for we think only of the design he has to cure us. We are not displeased with the lancet or the caustic, because we do not consider them as instruments of our pains, but of our health,—instruments which could not pain us, or even touch us, if the surgeon did not apply them: it is by his application that they act on us, that they pain one part and not another, penetrating only where he thinks fit to direct them. It is in this manner we ought to comport ourselves in the ways of God. But let us now see the fruits this practice confers on us.

It is certain that whoever walks faithfully in the ways of God walks in the ways of his salvation, and makes great progress in perfection. A step, however short, if made in the way, advances toward the term, more than a thousand steps made out of the way. "The way I have destined for you," says God by Isaias, "is a holy way which shall lead you to sanctity. There shall not pass by any sinful man, because those who travel by it shall be purified. It shall be a straight way, so that fools cannot err therein; and a secure way, where neither the lion nor any other evil beast can enter."

The Book of Wisdom tells us that Jacob, following the guidance of God, "saw the kingdom of God and received from Him the knowledge of holy things, being made honorable in his works, and in the accomplishment of his labors, and kept safe from his enemies and defended from seducers." Now, this is to be understood, not only of Jacob, but also of all those who permit themselves to be guided by God.

The same book, recounting the wonders which happened to the children of Israel in their journey from Egypt to the promised land, which is a figure of our journey from earth to heaven, says: "God conducted them in a wonderful way, and gave them a covert by day, and the light of the stars by night. And brought them through the Red Sea, but their enemies were drowned in the sea."

But the principal advantage to be derived from perfect submission to the ways of God is peace of heart. It is in this sense that we have particularly spoken of it ; for peace, as has been already said, is the effect of our submission, as trouble is the necessary consequence of our resistance. "Acquiesce in God and have peace," said Eliphaz to Job, for who ever resisted Him, and did not find pain and inquietude? He had already said : "Thou shalt be hidden from the scourge of the tongue : and thou shalt not fear calamity when it cometh. In destruction and famine thou shalt laugh, and thou shalt not fear the beasts of the earth. But thou shalt have a covenant with the storms of the land, and the beasts of the earth shall be at peace with thee. And thou shalt know that thy tabernacle is in peace, and visiting thy beauty, thou shalt not sin." Thus shall peace render thee like the sun, which all the clouds and all the tempests cannot rob of its brilliancy and splendor. "Learn, O Israel !" says the prophet Baruch, "that, if thou hadst walked in the way of God, thou hadst surely dwelt in peace forever. Learn where is wisdom, where is peace ;" learn the true source of thy felicity and repose. It is because thou hast not understood this, because thou hast not followed the will of God, because thou wert not satisfied with the dispositions He made of thee, that thou art sad, unhappy and wretched. Whence come all these evils? asks the prophet Jeremias. " Hath not this been done to thee because thou hast forsaken the Lord thy God at that time when He led thee by the way? And now what hast thou to do in the way of Egypt but to drink of the troubled waters ?"

"All the ways of God with us," as Solomon observes, all the dispositions which He makes of our body and soul, our wealth, our honor, our all, are pacific to such an extent, that they bear the name of "*pacific.*" All His ways are ways of peace, because they are excellent means of peace. "His ways are beautiful, and all his paths are peace. Wisdom is a tree of life to them that lay hold of her, and he that shall retain peace is blessed."

If any one finds these ways painful, and murmurs at poverty, sickness, or any other adversity which God sends him, let him not attribute the cause of his pain to the thing sent, but to his own mind. If a man who has a wounded limb, when travelling on foot through a beautiful meadow, feels it painful to walk, he does not attribute the pain he feels to the path by which he goes and which is very beautiful and agreeable, but to the infirmity of his limb : in a similar way, we must not, when sad and tormented by something God sends us, refer our chagrin to the orders of God, which are always wise and salutary, but to our unhealthy state of mind, to the feet of our soul which are dislocated, and out of their natural state ; that is, to our disorderly affections which can be tranquil and content only by the submission which they render to God, in cheerfully obeying all His orders, and submitting with joy to whatever dispositions He shall make of them.

For these reasons, let us resign ourselves entirely to what God ordains for us ; let us suck the juice of salvation from everything He sends us ; let us not turn to poisons the remedies of our health ; let us not impede the working of the key with which Providence opens to us the door of happiness ; let us not permit that to render us miserable which ought to confer on us the precious gift of peace; and, in fine, let us apply ourselves incessantly to make a good use of everything that happens to us.

The practice of peace.

The practice of peace consists in three points, with a short notice of which we shall conclude this subject.

1. As peace and repose of soul are, as has been already said, the best disposition and the most desirable state in

which the soul can be in order to advance in perfection, and, after the grace of God, the greatest good we can possess in this life; and as the devil strives all day long to ravish us of this treasure, we must make it a particular daily exercise. For this purpose, we ought to take great care to let nothing whatever trouble our peace of mind; and, if we see there is anything likely to disturb us, watch diligently to put it in order, and to prevent this bad effect, ever striving to ground ourselves daily more and more in a state of solid and inviolable tranquillity of soul.

2. The second point is to bind and unite ourselves intimately to the peace of God which resides within us, honoring, loving, adoring and imitating it as far as is possible for us. "God is in the midst of her," says David; "He is in her heart, she shall not be moved."

It is in this union that the soul finds true peace, and acquires perfect firmness. Thus the sacred Spouse says: "I am a wall, and my breasts are a tower. I am become in His presence as one finding peace." Since she has united herself to God, she has become firm as a rampart, and her breasts, that is to say, the most tender and feeble part of her, have become strong as a tower. But this is not astonishing; for, as that which rests on an insecure basis, is necessarily insecure, so that which is attached to an immovable cause, that which rests on God, must be free from agitation or insecurity.

We should also fix our eyes unceasingly on the tranquillity, the sweetness, the serenity and the mildness of our Saviour, who says of Himself: "Learn of me, who am meek and humble of heart." We ought to learn this lesson of Him, we ought to labor to resemble Him in this point; His mildness, gentleness and humility should animate all our conduct.

3. Since our peace consists in the conformity of our will to the will of our God, and since whatever is done in this world, sin alone excepted, is done by His orders, we must will every-

thing as it happens, receiving all occurrences with a spirit of submission, of respect and of love. For this end, it is very advisable to make often sweet and amorous acts of acquiescence of our will in the will of God as regards all passing events, concerning ourselves and others, saying with our Lord: "Yea, Father, for so it hath seemed good in Thy sight." Let us imitate the holy man, Gregory Lopez, who repeated a thousand and a thousand times daily: "Let Thy will be done on earth as it is in heaven. Let it be done, O Jesus! and I shall be content."

Such is the exercise of the wise and just who desire to acquire, preserve and increase the rich and inestimable treasure of peace of heart and repose of mind, the better to honor and serve God,—God the Father, who is the God of peace ; God the Son, who is the Prince of peace ; and God the Holy Ghost, who gives peace as one of His principal fruits : to whom be glory, honor, praise, benediction, adoration and love from all creatures, now and for evermore. Amen.

THE END.

www.ingramcontent.com/pod-product-compliance
Lightning Source LLC
Chambersburg PA
CBHW032043220426
43664CB00008B/839